Brainerd Kellogg, Alonzo Reed

A Work on English Grammar and Composition

Brainerd Kellogg, Alonzo Reed

A Work on English Grammar and Composition

ISBN/EAN: 9783337779436

Printed in Europe, USA, Canada, Australia, Japan

Cover: Foto ©Thomas Meinert / pixelio.de

More available books at **www.hansebooks.com**

HIGHER LESSONS IN ENGLISH.

A WORK

ON

ENGLISH GRAMMAR

AND

COMPOSITION.

IN WHICH THE SCIENCE OF THE LANGUAGE IS MADE TRIBUTARY
TO THE ART OF EXPRESSION.

A COURSE

OF PRACTICAL LESSONS CAREFULLY GRADED, AND ADAPTED TO EVERY
DAY USE IN THE SCHOOL-ROOM.

BY

ALONZO REED, A.M.,

FORMERLY INSTRUCTOR IN ENGLISH GRAMMAR IN THE POLYTECHNIC INSTITUTE,
BROOKLYN,

AND

BRAINERD KELLOGG, LL.D.,

PROFESSOR OF THE ENGLISH LANGUAGE AND LITERATURE IN THE
POLYTECHNIC INSTITUTE, BROOKLYN.

REVISED.

NEW YORK:
EFFINGHAM MAYNARD & CO., PUBLISHERS,
Successors to Clark & Maynard,
771 BROADWAY AND 67 & 69 NINTH ST.
1892.

Preface.

It is generally conceded that a scientific and practical knowledge of one's vernacular is the first essential of an education, yet the position, in our common school curriculum, of grammar, the only study that aims directly to lay a foundation for such knowledge, has been of late desperately assailed.

Some of those who advocate the banishment of grammar from schools are men of high literary culture, whose knowledge of general grammar has been obtained from a study of the classical languages, and whose facility in the use of language has come from being born and bred in the purest literary atmosphere. Such naturally could not see the advantage, to those differently educated and surrounded, of a scientific standard by which to regulate forms of expression.

Others, who without scholarly acquirements have themselves achieved a certain measure of literary success, fail to see why the genius of young writers should be hampered by the restrictions of grammarians.

The regretful recollection of months and years spent in mechanical parsing or in the tiresome and unfruitful memorizing of iron-clad rules and unapplied principles has moved many more to decry the study of English grammar.

Another less thoughtful but more demonstrative class have joined in the hue and cry mainly because it is popular to denounce the old and hail the new.

The majority, however, of thoughtful, practical teachers have never doubted the utility of the study of English grammar. Many, it is true, finding their text-books burdened with non-essential matter and deficient in practical work, have dropped them, or else have themselves assumed the labor of daily revision.

To meet the pressing demands of such educators this series of Lessons in English has been prepared.

From our own extended experience and from the nature of things, we are convinced that the oral instruction, the composition writing, and the studies in literature that are offered as substitutes for the study of grammar, invaluable as they are in themselves, fall far short of their greatest possible good, are more or less loose and erratic, unless based upon the science of language, upon those principles that underlie the structure of the English sentence; and that, on the other hand, the study of technical grammar, divorced, as it too generally has been, from practical language work, although not without value as a mental discipline, is hardly deserving of a place in the common school.

The aim of this work is to make the Science of the Language, of which all the essentials are thoroughly presented, tributary to the Art of Expression. Every principle learned by the pupil is fixed in his memory and, above all, in his *practice* by varied and exhaustive drill in composition. He is constantly required to compose sentences, to arrange and rearrange their parts, to contract, expand, punctuate, and criticise them—the analysis furnishing him materials for the synthesis, and the synthesis supplementing the analysis. Even if the study of grammar were only to lodge in the memory the forms and principles of the language, we contend that this could be done effectively only by work in composition—this, and this only, can make them permanent possessions.

We begin with the sentence, because the sentence is the unit of discourse, because words can be classified only from their function in the sentence, and because the pupil should, from the outset, see that what determines the words in the sentence and the sentence itself is the thought. Rules for Punctuation are given where they are needed, since the marks are as much a part of the sentence as are the words themselves—the sentence is not written till it is punctuated.

The large space allotted to the sentence is necessary, because (1) the offices and relations of words are many and diverse, and they must be mastered by analysis and synthesis before the inflections can be understood ; (2) because Arrangement must be studied, and the relations of clauses in the complex and the compound sentence must be understood in order to secure variety, force, and clearness of expression ; and (3) because, in reading, the pupil cannot express the subordination of the dependent clause to the independent and the co-ordination of independent clauses, till he can detect the relation of these elements at a glance.

In the supplementary Lessons on Composition the pupil is thoroughly drilled in the use of the marks of Punctuation, is made familiar with the cardinal virtues of Style, and is led on to the grouping of sentences into Paragraphs and of Paragraphs into Themes, to the construction of Frameworks for Themes, and to Letter-Writing.

Many years of experience in teaching grammar, both with and without Diagrams, have convinced us of their great utility. But, while believing that no teacher or pupil, once familiar with them, will willingly dispense with their aid, we wish to say that they form no *vital* part of the work. They could be omitted without break.

The sentences given for analysis are largely quotations, but they will not always be recognized. To suit them to the purpose in hand, many of them had to be changed ; and, when changed, they could not be marked as quoted. We, therefore, have given authors' names only in particular Lessons headed " Miscellaneous Exercises in Review."

We have preferred to make no departures from the ordinary classification and nomenclature, unless, as it seemed to us, some practical good would accrue to the pupil.

We wish to add that, while shunning no difficulties that lay in our path, we have not turned out of our path to encounter any. This book was not written to air crotchets or to resolve grammatical puzzles, but for every-day use in the school-room.

"Higher Lessons in English," while in press, was criticised by the distinguished philologist, Prof. Francis A. March of Lafayette College, Easton, Pa., and to him we are indebted for many most valuable suggestions.

Suggestions to the Teacher.

Though professing to be a complete grammar, this work is not intended for *beginners*. In preparing it, we have supposed the pupil to be already thoroughly familiar with "Graded Lessons in English" or its equivalent. Guard, then, against introducing "Higher Lessons" too early into the course of study.

Those who desire a brief course in technical grammar are referred to that outlined in the "General Reviews," pp. 147, 186, 219, 220, 228, 229, 264, 265.

Publishers' Note.

The unprecedented success attending "Higher Lessons in English" during its few years of publication has necessitated new electrotype plates. The publishers have taken this opportunity to enlarge the type and to open the page. The authors have also carefully revised their work, and have made some valuable additions and improvements.

Teachers, however, will find no difficulty in using the two editions in the same class. The *Lesson Numbers* have not been changed.

ALPHABETIC INDEX.

	PAGES.
Abbreviations	30, 31
Absolute Phrase	76, 86, 127, 141
Adjective, The	34, 35
" Classes	158-159
" Clauses	105-108
" " Composition	109-111
" Composition	36-38
" Construction	159-163
" Modification—Comparison	220-227
Adjective or Adverb?	61
Adverb, The	38-39
" Classes	164-166
" Clauses	111-118
" " Composition	118-122
" Composition	40
" Construction	166-169
" Modification — Comparison	220-227
Alphabet, The	19
Analysis	21
Analysis—Additional Selections	148, 269-276
Antecedent	152
Apostrophe, Rules	69, 192, 208-213, 282
Arrangement	93-102, 109, 120, 128

	PAGES
Articles	159-161
As	61, 63, 113, 115, 151, 175, 177
Both... and	49
Bad or badly?	63, 64
Brackets, Rule	282
But	132, 134, 170, 175, 184
Capital Letters, Rules	22, 27-29, 51, 131, 277
Clauses, Kinds	105, 111, 123, 132, 133, 139
Colon, Rules	280
Comma, Rules	44, 50, 67, 68, 77, 87, 109, 118, 119, 127, 128, 135, 136, 277, 278
Complements	57
" Attribute	58-61, 74, 80, 125, 126
" Modified	57
" Object	57, 76, 80, 125
" Objective	62, 63, 74, 82
Conjunction, The	47-49, 174
" Classes	174-176
Connected Terms, Composition	50-53
Connectives	175-180
" Construction	180-182
Consonants	18-20
Contraction	102-104, 120-122, 129, 189

Alphabetic Index.

	PAGES.
Copula	58, 59
Dash, Rules	87, 88, 135, 281
Diagram, The	22
Each other, One another	67, 215
Exclamation Point, Rule	51, 277
Factitive Object	62, 74, 82
For—introductory	81, 243, 244
Grammar, English	16
Hand in hand	55
Hyphen, Rules	282
In or *into* ?	172
If	117, 118, 175, 176, 177
Independent Words and Phrases	85-87
Infinitives	78-83
" Composition	84, 85
" Expansion	141, 142
" without *to*	85
"*Intended to have called*"	257
Interjection, The	47, 48
Interrogation Point	89, 277
Irregular Verbs	236-240
Is being built	247, 248
It	82, 126, 128
It is *me*, etc	217
Language, Natural and Word	15, 16
Lest	175, 176, 177
Letters, Sounds of	18-20
Letter-Writing	306-314
Many a	76, 112
Miscellaneous Errors	157, 163, 168, 169, 182, 183, 218
Miscellaneous Exercises in Review	55, 90-92, 142-144
Mine, thine, etc	214
Modifications of Parts of Speech	187
Modifier, A	35
Noun, The	25, 26
Noun, Classes	149, 150
" Clauses	123-127
" " Composition	127-131
" Declension	213
Nouns as Modifiers	65-70
Nouns and Pronouns, Case	203, 205-213
Nouns and Pronouns, Gender	197-202
Nouns and Pronouns, Number	188-196
Nouns and Pronouns, Person	202-204
Oh, O	51
Object, The	57, 164, 165
Only	90, 167
Paragraph, The	294-300
Parenthesis, Marks of	88, 135, 282
Parsing	34, 56, 207, 208, 224, 252, 253
Participles	72-76, 248
" Composition	77, 78
" Expansion	141
Period, Rules	22, 27, 277
Phrases	41-43, 49, 52, 127
" Composition	44-46
Possessive Forms	69, 208-213
Predicate, The	17, 21, 47, 48, 58, 59
" Compound	47-49
" Modified or Logical	38
Preposition, The	42, 43, 169, 170

	PAGES.		PAGES.
Preposition Construction..	170-173	Subject or Complement?...	60
Pronoun, The..........	25, 26, 151	Subjunctive Mode.......	235, 243,
" Case-Forms—Construction...	65, 216-218		246, 255, 256

Pronoun, The.........25, 26, 151
" Case-Forms—Construction...65, 216–218
" Classes........149–152
" Construction...153–158
" Declension.....214–216
" Person, Number, and Gender—Construction..200–202, 260–263
Questions, Direct and Indirect............ 131
Quotations, Direct and Indirect............ 131
Quotation Marks, Rule...130, 131, 282
Review, Capital Letters and Punctuation..... 53, 44, 92, 283, 284
Review, General—Schemes....147, 186, 219, 220, 228, 229, 264, 265
Review Questions...24, 41, 56, 71, 104, 144–146, 185, 186, 265–268
Semicolon, Rules....135, 136, 279
Sentence, The..........16, 17, 20
Sentences, Classes.. .. 88, 89, 133
" Complex......105–132
" Compound....132–138
Since.............112, 175, 177
Spelling, Rules.......... 222
Style, Qualities.......... 284 294
Subject, The....17, 21, 47, 48, 75, 80, 124
" Compound........ 47–49
" Modified or Logical 35

Subject or Complement?... 60
Subjunctive Mode.......235, 243, 246, 255, 256
Than...................113, 114
That...................114, 117, 124, 155, 175, 176, 178, 184
The...*the*..............113, 114
There..................86, 87
Composition-Writing.....301–305
Thought, A 16, 17
To with the Infinitive..79, 243, 244
Verb, The..... .... 32, 33
" Classes............163–165
" Conjugation.......236–249
" Mode and Tense... 234–235
" Mode and Tense Forms—Analysis.249, 250
" Tense Forms—Meaning............. 250–252
" Mode and Tense Forms -—Construction 254-259
" Number and Person. 234, 235
" Number and Person —Construction .. 260, 263
" Voice.............. 229–233
Vowels................. 18–20
Was lost sight of........ 233
What.........107, 108, 151, 183
When......108, 112, 175, 176, 178
Where 108, 113, 175, 176, 178
While..............112, 175, 179
Will and *would*, *shall* and *should* 258, 259
Yes and *No*............. 165

Classfied Index.

(The numbers refer to pages.)

Part I.—The Sentence and Classes of Words............ 15–148
Part II.—Parts of Speech Subdivided.................. 149–186
Part III.—Modifications of the Parts of Speech.......... 187–268
Part IV.—Composition—Supplementary................... 277–314

Letters.

Sounds of Letters, 18–20. Classes of Letters, 18–20. Capital Letters, 22, 27–29, 51, 131, 277. Rules for Spelling, 222.

The Noun.

The Noun, 25, 26. Classes, 149, 150. Modifications, 187, 188.—Number, 188–196; Gender, 197–202; Person, 202–204; Case, 203, 205, 206, 208–210. Declension, 213. **Construction of Possessive Forms—Cautions,** 69, 210–213.

SEE ALSO "SCHEME," PAGE 219.

The Pronoun.

The Pronoun, 25, 26. Classes, 149–152. Modifications (same as for the noun). Declension, 214–216. Construction of Pronouns—Cautions.—Use of the different Pronouns, 153–157; Number, Gender, and Person—Agreement, 196, 200–202, 261–263; Case Forms, 65, 216–218.

SEE ALSO "SCHEME," PAGE 220.

The Adjective.

The Adjective, 34, 35. Classes, 158, 159. Comparison, 220–224. Construction of Adjectives—Cautions.—Position, Choice, Use, 36, 37, 63, 64, 159–163; Degree Forms and Number Forms, 225–227.

SEE ALSO "SCHEME," PAGE 228.

The Verb.

The Verb, 32, 33. Participles, 72-78. Infinitives, 78-85. Classes, 163-165. Modifications.—Voice, 229-233 ; Mode, Tense, Number, and Person, 233-235. Irregular Verbs, 237-240. Conjugation, 236, 241-249. Compound Forms—Analysis, 249, 250. Tense Forms—Meaning, 250-252. **Construction of Verbs—Cautions.**—Mode and Tense Forms, 254-259 ; Number and Person Forms—Agreement, 26, 33, 260-263.

SEE ALSO "SCHEME," PAGE 264.

The Adverb.

The Adverb, 38, 39. Classes, 164-166. Comparison, 223, 224. **Construction of Adverbs—Cautions.**—Choice, Position, Use, 40, 166-169 ; Degree Forms, 225-227.

The Conjunction.

The Conjunction, 47-49. Classes, 174-176. Uses of Different Connectives, 177-180. **Construction of Connectives—Cautions**, 180-183.

The Preposition.

The Preposition, 41-43, 169-171. **Construction of Prepositions—Cautions,** 172, 173.

The Interjection, 47, 48, 51.
Parsing, 34, 56, 207, 208, 224, 252, 253.
Summary of Rules of Syntax, 315, 316.

Punctuation.

Period, 22, 27, (*Summary*) 277. Interrogation Point, 89, 131, (*Summary*) 277. Exclamation Point, 51, 89, (*Summary*) 277. Comma, 44, 50, 51, 67, 68, 77, 87, 88, 109, 118, 119, 127, 128, 131, 135, 136, (*Summary*) 277, 278. Semicolon, 135, 136, (*Summary*) 279, 280. Colon, 131, (*Summary*) 280. Dash, 87, 88, 135, (*Summary*) 281. Marks of Parenthesis, 88, 135, (*Summary*) 282. Brackets, 282. Quotation Marks, 130, 131, 282. Apostrophe, 69, 192, 208-213, (*Summary*) 282. Hyphen, 282.

The Sentence.

The Sentence, 16, 17, 20.

Subject,—17, 21 ; Compound Subj., 47, 48 ; Subj. Phrase, 75, 80 ; Subj. Clause, 123, 124.

Predicate,—17, 21, 58, 59 ; Compound Pred., 47, 48.

Object Complement,—57, 58 ; Object Phrase, 76, 80 ; Object Clause, 125.

Attribute Complement,—58-61 ; Attribute Phrase, 74, 80 ; Attribute Clause, 125, 126.

Objective Complement,—62, 63 ; Objective Comp. Phrase, 74, 82, 83.

Adjective Modifiers.—Adjectives, 34, 35 ; Nouns, 65-67 ; Phrases, 41-43, 73, 79. Clauses, 105-108, 126.

Adverb Modifiers.—Adverbs, 38, 39 ; Nouns, 69-71 ; Phrases, 41-43, 79, 80; Clauses, 111-118.

Connectives.—Conjunctions, 47, 48, 116-118, 124, 132-135, 174-182; Relative Pronouns, 105-108, 151, 175 ; Conjunctive Adverbs, 108, 112-115, 175, 176.

Independent Parts, 85-87.

Classes of Sentences and Clauses, 88-90, 133.

Composition.—Adjectives, 36-38 ; Adverbs, 40 ; Prep. Phrases, 44-46 ; Connected Terms, 50-53 ; Complements, 63-65 ; Noun Modifiers, 67-69 ; Participles, 77-78 ; Infinitives, 84, 85 ; Independent Parts, 87, 88 ; Arrangement, 36, 37, 40, 45, 93-102, 109, 120, 128; Contraction, 102-104, 120-122, 129, 130, 136, 137 ; Expansion, 109-111, 141, 142.

SEE ALSO " SCHEME," PAGE 147.

Supplementary Composition.

Capital Letters and Punctuation, 277-284 ; Style, 284-294 ; The Paragraph, 294-300 ; Analysis of the Theme, 297-302.

How to Write a Composition, 302-304.

Letter-Writing, 306-314.

LESSON 1.

A TALK ON LANGUAGE.

We wish to talk with you to-day about a language that we never learned from a grammar or a book of any kind. Nor was it ever taught us by parent or by teacher. We came by it naturally and use it without thinking of it.

It is a universal language, and so needs no interpreter. People of all lands and of all degrees of culture use it; even the brute animals in some measure understand it.

This Natural language is the language of cries, laughter, and tones; the language of the eyes, the nose, the mouth, the whole face; the language of gestures and postures.

The child's cry tells of its wants; its sob, of grief; its scream, of pain; its laugh, of delight. The boy raises his eyebrows in surprise and his nose in disgust, leans forward in expectation, draws back in fear, makes a fist in anger, and calls or drives away his dog simply by the *tone* in which he speaks.

But feelings and desires are not the only things we wish to communicate. Early in life we begin to acquire knowledge and learn to think, and then we feel the need of a better language.

Suppose, for instance, you have formed an idea of a day; could you express this by a tone, a look, or a gesture?

If you wish to tell me the fact that *yesterday was cloudy*, or that *the days are shorter in winter than in summer*, you would find it wholly impossible to do this by means of Natural language.

To communicate, then, your *thoughts*, or even the mental pictures we have called *ideas*, you need a language more nearly perfect.

This language is made up of *words*.

These words you *learn* from your mothers, and so Word language is your *mother-tongue*. You learn them, also, from your friends and teachers, your playmates and companions, and you learn them by reading; for words, as you know, may be written as well as spoken.

This Word language we may, from its superiority, call **Language Proper**.

Natural language, as was said, precedes this Word language, but gives way as Word language comes in and takes its place; yet Natural language may be used, and always should be, to assist and strengthen Word language. In earnest conversation we enforce what we say in words, by the tone in which we utter them, by the varying expression of the face, and by the movements of the different parts of the body.

The look or the gesture may even dart ahead of the word, or it may contradict it, and so convict the speaker of ignorance or deception.

The happy union of the two kinds of language is the charm of all good reading and speaking. The teacher of elocution is ever trying to *recall* the pupil to the tones, the facial expression, and the action, so natural to him in childhood and in animated conversation.

DEFINITION.—*Language Proper* **consists of the spoken and written words used to communicate ideas and thoughts.**

DEFINITION.—*English Grammar* **is the science which teaches the forms, uses, and relations of the words of the English language.**

LESSON 2.

A TALK ON THOUGHTS AND SENTENCES.

To express a thought we use more than a single word, and the words arranged to express a thought we call a sentence.

But there was a time when, through lack of words, we compressed our thought into a single word. The child says to his father, *up*, meaning, *Take me up into your lap;* or, *book*, meaning, *This thing in my hand is a book*.

These first words always deal with the things that can be learned by the senses; they express the child's ideas of these things.

We have spoken of *thoughts* and *sentences;* let us see now whether we can find out just what a thought is, and what a sentence is.

As a sentence is a group of words expressing a thought,—the body, of which the thought is the soul,—and so is something that we can hear or see, while a thought is not, let us try to find out what a thought is by looking at a sentence.

In any such sentence as this, *Spiders spin*, something is said, or asserted, about something. Here it is said, or asserted, of the animals, spiders, that they spin.

The sentence, then, consists of two parts,—the name of that of which something is said, and that which is said of it.

The first of these parts we call the **Subject** of the sentence; the second, the **Predicate**.

Now, if the sentence, composed of two parts, expresses the thought, there must be in the thought two parts to be expressed. And there are two; viz., something of which we think, and that which we think about it. In the *thought* expressed by *Spiders spin*, the animals, spiders, are the something of which we think, and their spinning is what we think of them. In the *sentence* expressing this thought, the word *spiders* names that of which we think, and the word *spin* tells what we think about spiders.

Not every group of words is necessarily a sentence, because it may not be the expression of a thought. *Spiders spinning* is not a sentence. There is nothing in this expression to show that we have formed a judgment, *i.e.*, that we have really made up our minds that spiders do spin. The spinning is not *asserted* of the spiders.

Soft feathers, The shining sun are not sentences, and for similar reasons. *Feathers are soft, The sun shines* are sentences. Here the asserting word is supplied, and something is said of something else.

The shines sun is not a sentence; for, though it contains the asserting word *shines*, the arrangement is such that no assertion is made, and so no thought is expressed.

LESSON 3.

A TALK ON SOUNDS AND LETTERS.

We have already told you that in expressing our ideas and thoughts we use two kinds of words, *spoken* words and *written* words.

We learned the *spoken* words first. *Mankind* spoke long before they wrote. Not until people wished to communicate with those at a distance, or had thought out something worth handing down to aftertimes, did they need to write.

But speaking was easy. The air, the lungs, and the organs of the throat and mouth were at hand. The first cry was a suggestion. Sounds and noises were heard on every side, provoking imitation, and the need of speech for the purposes of communication was imperative.

Spoken words are made up of sounds. There are over forty sounds in the English language. The different combinations of these give us all the words of our spoken tongue. That you may clearly understand these sounds, we will tell you something about the human voice.

In talking, the air driven out from your lungs beats against two flat muscles, stretched, like bands, across the top of the windpipe, and causes them to vibrate up and down. This vibration makes sound. Take a thread, put one end between your teeth, hold the other with thumb and finger, draw it tight and strike it, and you will understand how voice is made. The shorter the string, or the tighter it is drawn, the faster will it vibrate, and the *higher* will be the *pitch* of the sound. The more violent the blow, the farther will the string vibrate, and the *louder* will be the sound. Just so with these vocal bands or cords. The varying force with which the breath strikes them, and their different tensions and lengths at different times explain the different degrees of loudness and the varying pitch of the voice.

If the voice thus produced comes out through the mouth held well open, a class of sounds is formed which we call *vowel* sounds.

But if the *voice* is held back or obstructed by the palate, tongue, teeth, or lips, *one* kind of the sounds called *consonant* sounds is made. If the *breath* is driven out *without voice*, and is *held back* by these same parts of the mouth, the *other* kind of *consonant* sounds is formed.

The *written* word is made up of characters, or letters, which represent to the eye these sounds that address the ear.

You are now prepared to understand us when we say that **vowels** are the **letters that stand for the open sounds of the voice,** and that consonants are the letters that stand for the sounds made by the obstructed voice and the obstructed breath.

The alphabet of a language is a complete list of its letters. A perfect alphabet would have one letter for each sound, and only one.

Our alphabet is imperfect in at least these three ways:—

1. Some of the letters are *superfluous;* c stands for the sound of s or of k, as in *city* and *can;* q has the sound of k, as in *quit;* and x that of ks, gz, or z, as in *expel, exist,* and *Xenophon.*

2. *Combinations* of letters sometimes represent *single* sounds; as, th, in *thine,* th in *thin,* ng in *sing,* and sh in *shut.*

3. Some letters stand *each* for *many* sounds. Twenty-three letters represent over forty sounds. Every vowel does more than single duty; e stands for two sounds, as in *mete* and *met;* i for two, as in *pine* and *pin;* o for three, as in *note, not,* and *move;* u for four, as in *tube, tub, full,* and *fur;* a for six, as in *fate, fat, far, fall, fast,* and *fare.*

W is a vowel when it unites with a preceding vowel to represent a vowel sound, and y is a vowel when it has the sound of i, as in *now, by, boy, newly.* W and y are consonants at the beginning of a word or syllable.

The various sounds of the several vowels and even of the same vowel are caused by the different shapes which the mouth assumes. These changes in its cavity produce, also, the two sounds that unite in each of the compounds, *ou, oi, ew,* and in the alphabetic *i* and *o*.

1.	2.	1.	2.
Vocal Consonants.	*Aspirates.*	*Vocal Consonants.*	*Aspirates.*
b	p	r	
d	t	th	th
g	k	(in thine)	(in thin)
	h	v	f
j	ch	w	
l		y	
m		z (in zone)	s
n		z (in azure)	sh

The consonants in column 1 represent the sounds made by the *obstructed voice;* those in column 2, except h (which represents a mere forcible breathing), represent those made by the *obstructed breath*.

The letters are mostly in pairs. Now note that the tongue, teeth, lips, and palate are placed in the same relative position to make the sounds of both letters in any pair. The difference in the sounds of the letters of any pair is simply this: there is *voice* in the sounds of the letters in column 1, and only *whisper* in those of column 2. Give the sound of any letter in column 1, as *b*, *g*, *v*, and the last or vanishing part of it is the sound of the other letter of the pair.

To the Teacher.—Write these letters on the board, as above, and drill the pupils on the sounds till they can see and make these distinctions. Drill them on the vowels also.

In closing this talk with you, we wish to emphasize one point brought before you. Here is a pencil, a *real* thing; we carry in memory a *picture* of the pencil, which we call an *idea;* and there are the *two words* naming this idea, the *spoken* and the *written*. Learn to distinguish clearly these four things.

To the Teacher.—In reviewing these three Lessons, put particular emphasis on Lesson 2.

LESSON 4.

ANALYSIS AND THE DIAGRAM.

To the Teacher.—If the pupils have been through "Graded Lessons" or its equivalent, some of the following Lessons may be passed over rapidly.

DEFINITION.—A *Sentence* is the expression of a thought in words.

Direction.—*Analyze the following sentences:*—

Model.—*Spiders spin.* Why is this a *sentence?* Ans.—Because it expresses a thought. Of what is something thought? Ans.—*Spiders Which word tells what is thought? Ans.—*Spin.

---

* *Spiders*, standing in Roman, names our idea of the real thing; *spin*, used merely as a word, is in Italics. This use of Italics the teacher and the pupil will please note here and elsewhere.

1. Tides ebb.
2. Liquids flow.
3. Steam expands.
4. Carbon burns.
5. Iron melts.
6. Powder explodes.
7. Leaves tremble.
8. Worms crawl.
9. Hares leap.

In these sentences there are, as you have learned, two parts—the *Subject* and the *Predicate*.

DEFINITION.—The *Subject of a Sentence* names that of which something is thought.

DEFINITION.—The *Predicate of a Sentence* tells what is thought.

DEFINITION.—The *Analysis of a Sentence* is the separation of it into its parts.

Direction.—*Analyze these sentences :*—

Model.—*Beavers build.* This is a *sentence*, because it expresses a thought. *Beavers* is the *subject*, because it names that of which something is thought; *build* is the *predicate*, because it tells what is thought.

1. Squirrels climb.
2. Blood circulates.
3. Muscles tire.
4. Heralds proclaim.
5. Apes chatter.
6. Branches wave.
7. Corn ripens.
8. Birds twitter.
9. Hearts throb.

Explanation.—Draw a heavy line and divide it thus :—

———————————|———————————

Let the first part represent the *subject* of a sentence; the second, the *predicate*.

If you write a word over the first part, you will understand that this word is the *subject* of a sentence. If you write a word over the second part, you will understand that this word is the *predicate* of a sentence.

You see, by looking at this expression, that *Love conquers* is a sentence; that *love* is the *subject*, and *conquers* the *predicate*.

These figures, made up of straight lines, we call Diagrams.

DEFINITION.—A *Diagram* is a picture of the offices and relations of the different parts of a sentence.

Direction.—*Analyze and diagram these sentences:*—

1. Frogs croak.
2. Hens sit.
3. Sheep bleat.
4. Cows low.
5. Flies buzz.
6. Sap ascends.
7. Study pays.
8. Buds swell.
9. Books aid.
10. Noise disturbs.
11. Hope strengthens.
12. Cocks crow.

LESSON 5.

COMPOSITION—SUBJECT AND PREDICATE.

To the Teacher.—Let some of the pupils write their sentences on the board while others are reading theirs. Then let the work be *corrected*.

Correct any expression that does not make *good sense*, or that asserts something not strictly true; for the pupil should early be taught to *think accurately*, as well as to write and speak grammatically.

Correct all mistakes in *spelling*, and in the use of *capital letters* and the *period*. Insist on neatness.

CAPITAL LETTER—RULE.—The first word of every sentence must begin with a *capital letter*.

PERIOD—RULE.—A *period* must be placed after every sentence that simply affirms, denies, or commands.

Direction.—*Construct sentences by supplying a* s u b j e c t *to each of the following predicates:*—

Ask yourselves the questions, What tarnishes? Who sailed, conquered, etc.?

1. —— tarnishes.
2. —— capsize.
3. —— radiates.
4. —— sentence.
5. —— careen.
6. —— sailed.
7. —— descends.
8. —— glisten.
9. —— absorb.
10. —— corrode.
11. —— conquered.
12. —— surrendered.
13. —— refines.
14. —— gurgle.
15. —— murmur.

Analysis.

Direction.—*Construct sentences by supplying a predicate to each of the following subjects:*—

Ask yourselves the question, Glycerine does what?

1. Glycerine ——.
2. Yankees ——.
3. Tyrants ——.
4. Pendulums ——.
5. Cæsar ——.
6. Labor ——.
7. Chalk ——.
8. Nature ——.
9. Tempests ——.
10. Seeds ——.
11. Heat ——.
12. Philosophers ——.
13. Bubbles ——.
14. Darkness ——.
15. Wax ——.
16. Reptiles ——.
17. Merchants ——.
18. Meteors ——.
19. Conscience ——.
20. Congress ——.
21. Life ——.
22. Vapors ——.
23. Music ——.
24. Pitch ——.

To the Teacher.—This exercise may profitably be extended by supplying *several* subjects to each predicate, and *several* predicates to each subject.

LESSON 6.

ANALYSIS.

The *predicate* sometimes contains *more than one word*.

Direction.—*Analyze and diagram as in Lesson 4.*

1. Moisture is exhaled.
2. Conclusions are drawn.
3. Industry will enrich.
4. Stars have disappeared.
5. Twilight is falling.
6. Leaves are turning.
7. Sirius has appeared.
8. Constantinople had been captured.
9. Electricity has been harnessed.
10. Tempests have been raging.
11. Nuisances should be abated.
12. Jerusalem was destroyed.
13. Light can be reflected.
14. Rain must have fallen.
15. Planets have been discovered.
16. Palaces shall crumble.
17. Storms may be gathering.
18. Essex might have been saved.
19. Cæsar could have been crowned.
20. Inventors may be encouraged.

Direction.—*Point out the subject and the predicate of each sentence in Lessons* 12 *and* 17.

Look first for the word that asserts, and then, by putting *who* or *what* before this *predicate*, the subject may easily be found.

To the Teacher.—Let this exercise be continued till the pupils can readily point out the subject and the predicate in any simple declarative sentence.

When this can be done promptly, the first and most important step in analysis will have been taken.

LESSON 7.

COMPOSITION—SUBJECT AND PREDICATE.

Direction.—*Make at least ten good sentences out of the words in the three columns following :—*

The helping words in column 2 must be prefixed to words in column 3 to make complete predicates. Analyze your sentences.

1	2	3
Arts	is	progressing.
Allen	was	tested.
Life	are	command.
Theories	will	prolonged.
Science	would	released.
Truth	were	falling.
Shadows	may be	burned.
Moscow	has been	measured.
Raleigh	have been	prevail.
Quantity	should have been	lost.

REVIEW QUESTIONS.

What is language proper? What is English grammar? What is a sentence? What are its two parts? What is the subject of a sentence? The predicate of a sentence? The analysis of a sentence? What is a diagram? What rule has been given for the use of capital letters? For the period? May the predicate contain more than one word? Illustrate.

To the Teacher.—Introduce the class to the Parts of Speech before the close of this recitation. See "Introductory Hints," next page. The matter contained in the "Hints" should *always* be given to the class as a preparation for the next day's work.

LESSON 8.

CLASSES OF WORDS.

Nouns.

Introductory Hints.—We have now reached the point where we must classify the words of our language. But we are appalled by their number. If we must learn all about the forms and uses of a hundred thousand words by studying them one by one, we shall die ignorant of English grammar.

But may we not deal with words as we do with plants? If we had to study and name each leaf and stem and flower, taken singly, we should never master the botany even of our garden-plats.

But God has made things to resemble one another and to differ from one another, and he has given us the power to detect resemblances and differences, so we are enabled to group things that have like qualities.

From certain likenesses in form and structure, we put certain flowers together and call them roses; from other likenesses, we get another class called lilies; from others still, violets.

Just so we classify trees and get the oak, the elm, the maple, etc.

The myriad objects of nature fall into comparatively few classes. Studying each class, we learn all we need to know of every object in it.

From their likenesses, though not in form, we classify *words*. We group them according to their similarities in *use*, or *office*, in the sentence. Sorting them thus, we find that they all fall into eight classes, which we call Parts of Speech.

We find that many words *name* things—are the names of things of which we can think and speak. These we place in one class and call them **Nouns** (Lat. *nomen*, a name, a noun).

Pronouns.

Without the little words which we shall italicize, it would be difficult for one stranger to ask another, "Can *you* tell *me who* is the postmaster at B?" One would not know what name to use instead of *you*, and the other would not recognize the name in the place of *me*, and both would be puzzled to find a substitute for *who*.

I, you, my, me, what, we, it, he, who, him, she, them, and others, are used in place of *nouns,* and are, therefore, called **Pronouns** (Lat. *pro,* for, and *nomen,* a noun), and form the third part of speech.

By means of these handy little words we can represent any or every object in existence. We could hardly speak or write without them now, they so frequently shorten the expression and prevent confusion and repetition.

DEFINITION.—A *Noun* is the name of anything.
DEFINITION.—A *Pronoun* is a word used for a noun.*

The principal office of nouns is to name the things of which we say or assert something in the sentence.

Direction.—*Write, according to the model, the names of things that can burn, grow, melt, love, roar, or revolve.*

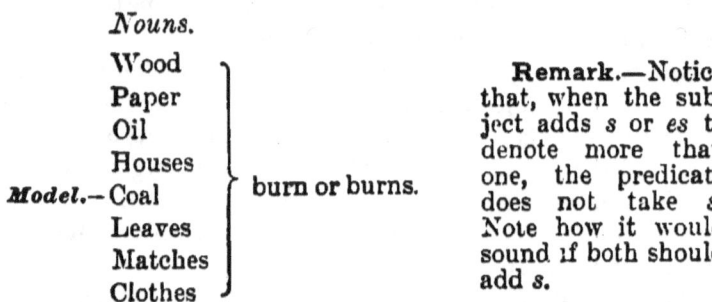

Every subject of a sentence is a *noun, or some word or words used as a noun.* But *not every noun in a sentence is a subject.*

Direction.—*Select and write all the nouns and pronouns, whether subjects or not, in the sentences given in Lesson* 18.
In writing them observe the following rules:—

---

* See 2d foot-note, Lesson 85.

CAPITAL LETTER—RULE.—*Proper, or individual, names and words derived from them* begin with capital letters.

PERIOD and **CAPITAL LETTER—RULE.**—*Abbreviations* generally begin with capital letters and are always followed by the period.

LESSON 9.

CAPITAL LETTERS.

Direction.—*From the following words select and write in one column those names that distinguish individual things from others of the same class, and in another column the words derived from these names :—*

Observe Rule 1, Lesson 8.

ohio, state, chicago, france, bostonian, country, england, boston, milton, river, girl, mary, hudson, william, britain, miltonic, city, englishman, messiah, platonic, american, deity, bible, book, plato, christian, broadway, america, jehovah, christ, british, easter, europe, man, scriptures, god.

Direction.—*Write the names of the days of the week and the months of the year, beginning each with a capital letter; and write the names of the seasons without capital letters.*

Remember that, when a *class name and a distinguishing word combine to make one individual name, each word begins with a capital letter; as, *Jersey City*.

But, when the distinguishing word can, by itself, be regarded as a complete name, the class name begins with a small letter; as, *river Rhine*.

Examples.—Long Island, Good Friday, Mount Vernon, Suspension Bridge, New York city, Harper's Ferry, Cape May, Bunker Hill, Red River, Lake Erie, General Jackson, White Mountains, river Thames, Astor House, steamer Drew, North Pole.

---

* *Dead Sea* is composed of the class name *sea*, which applies to all seas, and the word *Dead*, which distinguishes one sea from all others.

The Sentence and the Parts of Speech.

Direction.—*Write these words, using capital letters when needed :—*

ohio river, professor huxley, president adams, doctor brown, arctic circle, clinton county, westchester county, torrid zone, colonel burr, secretary stanton, lake george, green mountains, white sea, cape cod, delaware bay, atlantic ocean, united states, rhode island.

Remember that, when an individual name is made up of a class name, the word *of,* and a distinguishing word, the class name and the distinguishing word should each begin with a capital letter; as, *Gulf of Mexico.* But, when the distinguishing word can, by itself, be regarded as a complete name, the class name should begin with a small letter; as, *city of London.* *

Direction.—*Write these words, using capital letters when needed :—*

---

* The need of some definite instruction to save the young writer from hesitation and confusion in the use of capitals is evident from the following variety of forms now in use : *City* of New York, *city* of New York, New York *City,* New York *city,* New York *State,* New York *state,* Fourth *Avenue,* Fourth *avenue,* Grand *Street,* Grand *street,* Grand-*st.,* Atlantic *Ocean,* Atlantic *ocean,* Mediterranean *Sea,* Mediterranean *sea,* Kings *County,* Kings *county,* etc.

The usage of newspapers and of text-books on geography would probably favor the writing of the class names in the examples above with initial capitals ; but we find in the most carefully printed books and periodicals a tendency to favor small letters in such cases.

In the superscription of letters, such words as *street, city, county,* etc., begin with capitals.

Usage certainly favors small initials for the following italicized words : *river* Rhine, Catskill *village,* the Ohio and Mississippi *rivers.* If *river* and *village,* in the preceding examples, are not essential parts of the individual names, why should *river, ocean,* and *county,* in Hudson *river,* Pacific *ocean,* Queens *county,* be treated differently ? We often say the *Hudson,* the *Pacific, Queens,* without adding the explanatory class name.

The principle we suggest may be in advance of common usage ; but it is in the line of progress, it tends to uniformity of practice and to an improved appearance of the page. About a century ago every noun began with a capital letter.

The American Cyclopædia takes a position still farther in advance, as illustrated in the following: Red *river,* Black *sea, gulf* of Mexico, Rocky *mountains.* In the Encyclopædia Britannica (Little, Brown, & Co., 9th Ed.) we find Connecticut *river* Madison *county,* etc., quite uniformly ; but not so with *gulf, ocean,* etc.

city of atlanta, isle of man, straits of dover, state of vermont, isthmus of darien, sea of galilee, queen of england, bay of naples, empire of china.

Remember that, when a compound name is made up of two or more distinguishing words, as, Henry Clay, John Stuart Mill, each word begins with a capital letter.

Direction.— *Write these words, using capital letters when needed :—*

great britain, lower california, south carolina, daniel webster, new england, oliver wendell holmes, north america, new orleans, james russell lowell, british america.

Remember that, in writing the titles of books, essays, poems, plays, etc., and the names of the Deity, only the chief words begin with capital letters; as, Decline and Fall of the Roman Empire, Supreme Being, Paradise Lost, the Holy One of Israel.

Direction.— *Write these words, using capital letters when needed :—*

declaration of independence, clarendon's history of the great rebellion, webster's reply to hayne, pilgrim's progress, johnson's lives of the poets, son of man, the most high, dombey and son, tent on the beach, bancroft's history of the united states.

Direction.— *Write these miscellaneous names, using capital letters when needed :—*

erie canal, governor tilden, napoleon bonaparte, cape of good hope, pope's essay on criticism, massachusetts bay, city of boston, continent of america, new testament, goldsmith's she stoops to conquer, milton's hymn on the nativity, indian ocean, cape cod bay, plymouth rock, anderson's history of the united states, mount washington, english channel, the holy spirit, new york central railroad, old world, long island sound, flatbush village.

LESSON 10.

ABBREVIATIONS.

Direction.—*Some words occur frequently, and for convenience are abbreviated in writing. Observing Rule 2, Lesson 8, abbreviate these words by writing the first five letters :—*

Thursday and lieutenant.

These by writing the first four letters :—

Connecticut, captain, Colorado, Kansas, Massachusetts, Michigan, Minnesota, Mississippi, Nebraska, Oregon, professor, president, Tennessee, and Tuesday.

These by writing the first three letters :—

Alabama, answer, Arkansas, California, colonel, Delaware, England, esquire, Friday, general, George, governor, honorable, Illinois, Indiana, major, Monday, Nevada, reverend, Saturday, secretary, Sunday, Texas, Wednesday, Wisconsin, and the names of the months except May, June, and July.

These by writing the first two letters :—

Company, county, credit, example, and idem (the same).

These by writing the first letter :—

East, north, south, and west.

These by writing the first and the last letter :—

Doctor, debtor, Georgia, junior, Kentucky, Louisiana, Maine, Maryland, Master, Mister, numero (number), Pennsylvania, saint, street, Vermont, and Virginia.

These by writing the first letter of each word of the compound with a period after each letter:—

Artium baccalaureus (bachelor of arts), anno Domini (in the year of our Lord), artium magister (master of arts), ante meridiem (before noon), before Christ, collect on delivery, District (of) Columbia, divinitatis doctor (doctor of divinity), member (of) Congress, medicinæ doctor (doctor of medicine), member (of) Parliament, North America, North

Carolina, New Hampshire, New Jersey, New York, postmaster, post meridiem (afternoon), post-office, Rhode Island, South Carolina, and United States.

Direction.—*The following abbreviations and those you have made must be committed to memory :—*

Acct. *or* acct.,	account.	bu.,	bushel.
Bbl. *or* bbl.,	barrel.	do.,	ditto (the same).
Chas.,	Charles.	doz.,	dozen. [ple].
Fla.,	Florida.	e. g.,	exempli gratia (for exam-
*LL. D.,	legum doctor	etc.,	et cætera (and others).
	(doctor of laws).	ft.,	foot, feet.
Messrs.,	messieurs	hhd.,	hogshead.
	(gentlemen).	hdkf.,	handkerchief.
Mme.,	madame.	i. e.,	id est (that is).
Mo.,	Missouri.	l.,	line.
Mrs.,	(pronounced missis)	ll.,	lines.
	mistress.	lb.,	libra (pound).
Mts.,	mountains.	oz.,	ounce.
Ph. D.,	philosophiæ doctor	p.,	page.
	(doctor of philosophy).	pp.,	pages.
Recd.,	received.	qt.,	quart.
Robt.,	Robert.	vs.,	versus (against).
Supt.,	superintendent.	viz.,	videlicet (namely).
Thos.,	Thomas.	yd.,	yard.

Remark.—In this Lesson we have given the abbreviations of the states as now regulated by the "U. S Official Postal Guide." In the "Guide" *Iowa* and *Ohio* are not abbreviated. They are, however, frequently abbreviated thus : *Iowa, Ia.* or *Io.; Ohio, O.*

The similarity, when hurriedly written, of the abbreviations *Cal., Col.; Ia., Io.; Neb., Nev.; Penn., Tenn.,* etc., has led to much confusion.

---

* The doubling of the *l* in *ll.* and *LL. D.*, and of *p* in *pp.*, with no period between the letters, comes from pluralizing the nouns *line, lex,* and *page.*

LESSON 11.

VERBS.

Introductory Hints.—We told you, Lesson 8, how, by noticing the essential likenesses in things and grouping the things thus alike, we could throw the countless objects around us into comparatively few classes.

We began to classify *words* according to their *use*, or *office*, in the sentence, and found one class that *name* things, and called them *nouns*.

But in all the sentences given you, we have had to use another class of words. These words, you notice, tell what the things *do*, or assert that they *are*, or *exist*.

When we say *Clocks tick*, *tick* is not the name of anything; it tells what clocks *do*; it asserts *action*.

When we say *Clocks are*, or *There are clocks*, *are* is not the *name* of anything, nor does it tell what clocks *do*; it simply asserts *existence*, or *being*.

When we say *Clocks hang, stand, last, lie*, or *remain*, these words *hang, stand, last*, etc., do not *name* anything, nor do they tell that clocks *act* or simply *exist*; they tell the *condition*, or *state*, in which clocks *are*, or *exist*; that is, they assert *state of being*.

All words that assert action, being, or state of being, we call **Verbs** (Lat. *verbum*, a word). The name was given to this class, because it was thought that they were the most important words in the sentence. They form the second part of speech.

Give a score of verbs that assert *action*. Give some that assert *being*, and some that assert *state of being*.

DEFINITION.—A *Verb* is a word that asserts action, being, or state of being.

There are two forms of the verb, the *participle* and the *infinitive* (see Lessons 37 and 40), that express action, being, or state of being, without asserting it.

Verbs.

Direction.—*Write after each of the following nouns as many appropriate verbs as you can think of :—*

Let some express *being* and some *state of being*.

Model.— Noun.

Fire
(or)
Fires
{ burns.
melt.
scorches.
keep.
spreads.
glow.
rages.
heat.
exists. }

Remark.—Notice that the simple form of the verb, as, *burn, melt, scorch*, adds *s* or *es* when its subject noun names but one thing.

Lawyers, mills, horses, books, education, birds, mind.

A verb may consist of two, three, or even four words; as, *is learning, may be learned, could have been learned*.

Direction.—*Unite the words in columns 2 and 3, and append the verbs thus formed to the nouns and pronouns in column 1:—*

Remark.—Notice that *is, was*, and *has* are used with nouns naming one thing, and with the pronouns *he, she*, and *it*; and that *are, were*, and *have* are used with nouns naming more than one thing, and with the pronouns *we, you*, and *they*. *I* may be used with *am, was*, and *have*.

1	2	3
Words	am	confused.
Cotton	is	exported.
Sugar	are	refined.
Air	was	coined.
Teas	were	delivered.
Speeches	has been	weighed.
I, we, you	have been	imported.
He, she, it, they		transferred.

As verbs are the only words that assert, **every predicate** must be a **verb**, or *must contain a verb*.

Naming the class to which a word belongs is the *first step in parsing.*

Direction.—*Parse five of the sentences you have written.*

Model.—*Poland was dismembered.*

Parsing.—*Poland* is a *noun*, because ——; *was dismembered* is a *verb*, because it asserts action.

LESSON 12.

MODIFIED SUBJECT.

ADJECTIVES.

Introductory Hints.—The subject noun and the predicate verb are not always or often the whole of the structure that we call the sentence, though they are the underlying timbers that support the rest of the verbal bridge. Other words may be built upon them.

We learned in Lesson 8 that things resemble one another and differ from one another. They resemble and they differ in what we call their *qualities*. Things are alike whose qualities are the same; as, two oranges having the same color, taste, and odor. Things are unlike, as, an orange and an apple, whose qualities are different.

It is by their qualities, then, that we know things, and are able to separate them or to group them.

Ripe apples are healthful. Unripe apples are hurtful. In these two sentences we have the same word *apples* to name the same *general class* of things; but the prefixed words *ripe* and *unripe*, marking opposite qualities in the apples, separate them into two kinds—the ripe ones and the unripe ones.

These prefixed words *ripe* and *unripe*, then, limit the word *apples* in its scope; *ripe apples* or *unripe apples* applies to fewer things than *apples* alone.

If we say *the, this, that* apple, or *an, no* apple, or *some, many, eight* apples, we do not mark any quality of the fruit; but *the, this,* or *that* points out a particular apple, and limits the word *apple* to the one pointed out; and *an, no, some, many,* or *eight* limits the word in respect to the number of apples that it denotes.

These and all such words as by marking quality, pointing out, or specifying number or quantity limit the scope or meaning of the noun, modify it, and are called **Modifiers**.

In the sentence above, *apples* is the **Simple Subject** and *ripe apples* is the **Modified Subject**.

Words modifying *nouns and pronouns* are called **Adjectives** (Lat. *ad*, to, and *jacere*, to throw), and form the fourth part of speech.

DEFINITION.—A *Modifier* is a word or group of words joined to some part of the sentence to qualify or limit the meaning.

The *Subject* with its *Modifiers* is called the *Modified Subject*. By some it is called the *Logical Subject*.

DEFINITION.—An *Adjective* is a word used to modify a noun or a pronoun.

Analysis and Parsing.

1. The cold November rain is falling.

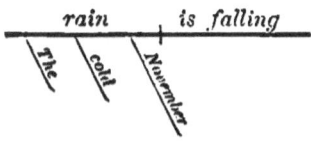

Explanation.—The two lines shaded alike and placed uppermost stand for the subject and the predicate, and show that these are of the same rank, and are the principal parts of the sentence. The lighter lines, placed under and joined to the subject line, stand for the less important parts, the modifiers, and show what is modified.*

---

* *To the Teacher.*—When several adjectives are joined to one noun, each adjective does not always modify the noun alone. *That old wooden house was burned.* Here *wooden* modifies *house*, *old* modifies *wooden house*, and *that* modifies *old wooden house*. This may be illustrated in the diagram by numbering the modifiers in the order of their rank, thus :—

Adverbs, and both phrase and clause modifiers often differ in rank in the same way, and in the diagram this difference may be indicated as above.

If the pupils are able to see these distinctions, it would be well to have them made in the analysis, as they often determine the punctuation and the arrangement. See Lessons 13 and 21.

Oral Analysis.—(Here and hereafter we shall omit from the *oral analysis* and *parsing* whatever has been provided for in previous Lessons.) *The, cold,* and *November* are modifiers of the subject. *The cold November rain* is the *modified subject.*

Parsing.—*The, cold,* and *November* are *adjectives* modifying *rain,*—*cold* and *November* expressing quality, and *the* pointing out.

2. The great Spanish Armada was destroyed.
3. A free people should be educated.
4. The old Liberty-Bell was rung.
5. The famous Alexandrian library was burned.
6. The odious Stamp Act was repealed.
7. Every intelligent American citizen should vote.
8. The long Hoosac Tunnel is completed.
9. I alone should suffer.
10. All nature rejoices.
11. Five large, ripe, luscious, mellow apples were picked.
12. The melancholy autumn days have come.
13. A poor old wounded soldier returned.
14. The oppressed Russian serfs have been freed.
15. Immense suspension bridges have been built.

LESSON 13.

COMPOSITION—ADJECTIVES.

Caution.—When two or more adjectives are used with a noun, care must be taken in their arrangement. If they differ in rank, place nearest the noun the one most closely modifying it. If of the same rank, place them where they will sound best—generally in the order of length, the shortest first.

Explanation.—*Two honest young men were chosen. A tall, straight,* *dignified person entered.* *Young* tells the kind of men, *honest* tells the kind of young men, and *two* tells the number of honest young men ; hence these adjectives are not of the same rank. *Tall, straight,* and *dignified* modify *person* independently—the person is tall and straight and dignified ; hence these adjectives are of the same rank.

Notice the comma after *tall* and *straight; and* may be supplied ; in the first sentence *and* cannot be supplied. See Lesson 21.

Direction.—*Arrange the adjectives, below, and give your reasons :—*

1. A Newfoundland pet handsome large dog. 2. Level low five the fields. 3. A wooden rickety large building. 4. Blind white beautiful three mice. 5. An energetic restless brave people. 6. An enlightened civilized nation.

Direction.—*Form sentences by prefixing modified subjects to these predicates :—*

1. —— have been invented.
2. —— were destroyed.
3. —— are cultivated.
4. —— may be abused.
5. —— was mutilated.
6. —— were carved.
7. —— have been discovered.
8. —— have fallen.
9. —— will be respected.
10. —— have been built.

Direction.—*Construct ten sentences, each of which shall contain a subject modified by three adjectives—one from each of these columns :—*

Let the adjectives be appropriate. For punctuation, see Lesson 21.

The	dark	sunny
That	bright	wearisome
This	dingy	commercial
Those	short	blue
These	soft	adventurous
Five	brave	fleecy
Some	tiny	parallel
Several	important	cheerless
Many	long	golden
A	warm	turbid

Direction.—*Prefix to each of these nouns several appropriate adjectives :—*

River, frost, grain, ships, air, men.

Direction.—*Couple those adjectives and nouns, below, that most appropriately go together:*—

Modest, lovely, flaunting, meek, patient, faithful, saucy, spirited, violet, dahlia, sheep, pansy, ox, dog, horse, rose, gentle, duck, sly, waddling, cooing, chattering, homely, chirping, puss, robin, dove, sparrow, blackbird, cow, hen, cackling.

LESSON 14.

MODIFIED PREDICATE.

ADVERBS.

Introductory Hints.—You have learned that the subject may be modified; let us see whether the predicate may be.

If we say, *The leaves fall*, we express a fact in a general way. But, if we wish to speak of the *time* of their falling, we can add a word and say, The leaves fall *early;* of the *place* of their falling, The leaves fall *here;* of the *manner*, The leaves fall *quietly;* of the *cause*, Why do the leaves fall?

We may join a word to any of these modifiers, and even another to that, and say, The leaves fall *so very* quietly. Here *very* modifies *quietly*, and *so* modifies *very* by telling the *degree*.

So very quietly is a group of words modifying the predicate. The predicate with its modifiers is called the **Modified Predicate**. Such words as *so*, *very*, *here*, and *quietly* form the fifth part of speech, and are called **Adverbs** (Lat. *ad*, to, and *verbum*, a word, or verb).

Adverbs may modify adjectives; as, *Very ripe* apples are healthful. Adverbs modify verbs just as adjectives modify nouns—by *limiting* them. The horse has a *proud step*, = The horse *steps proudly*.

The *Predicate* with its *Modifiers* is called the *Modified Predicate*. By some it is called the *Logical Predicate*.

Modified Predicate. 39

DEFINITION.—An *Adverb* is a word used to modify a verb, an adjective, or an adverb.

Analysis and Parsing.

1. The leaves fall very quietly.

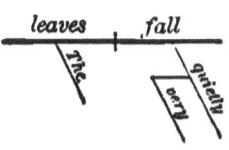

Explanation.—The two lines forming this group slant the same way to show that each stands for a modifying word. The line standing for the principal word of the group is joined to the predicate line. The end of the other is broken, and turned to touch its principal.

Oral Analysis.—*Very quietly* is a modifier of the predicate; *quietly* is the principal word of the group; *very* modifies *quietly*; *the leaves* is the modified subject; *fall very quietly* is the *modified predicate*.

Parsing.—*Quietly* is an *adverb* modifying *fall*, telling the manner; *very* is an *adverb* modifying *quietly*, telling the degree.

2. The old, historic Charter Oak was blown down.
3. The stern, rigid Puritans often worshiped there.
4. Bright-eyed daisies peep up everywhere.
5. The precious morning hours should not be wasted.
6. The timely suggestion was very kindly received.
7. We turned rather abruptly.
8. A highly enjoyable entertainment was provided.
9. The entertainment was highly enjoyed.
10. Why will people exaggerate so !
11. A somewhat dangerous pass had been reached quite unexpectedly.
12. We now travel still more rapidly.
13. Therefore he spoke excitedly.
14. You will undoubtedly be very cordially welcomed.
15. A furious equinoctial gale has just swept by.
16. The Hell Gate reef was slowly drilled away.

LESSON 15.

COMPOSITION—ADVERBS.

Caution.—Place adverbs where there can be no doubt as to what you intend them to modify. Have regard to the sound also.

Direction.—*Place the italicized words, below, in as many different positions as possible, and note the effect on the sound and the sense :—*

1. I *immediately* ran out. 2. *Only* one was left there. 3. She looked down *proudly*. 4. *Unfortunately,* this assistance came too late.

Direction.—*Construct on each of these subjects three sentences having modified subjects and modified predicates :—*

For punctuation, see Lesson 21.

Model.— —— clouds ——.

1. *Dark, heavy, threatening clouds are slowly gathering above.*
2. *Those brilliant, crimson clouds will very soon dissolve.*
3. *Thin, fleecy clouds are scudding over.*

   1. —— ocean ——. 2. —— breeze ——. 3. —— shadows ——.
   4. —— rock ——. 5. —— leaves ——.

Direction.—*Compose sentences in which these adverbs shall modify verbs :—*

Heretofore, hereafter, annually, tenderly, inaudibly, legibly, evasively, everywhere, aloof, forth.

Direction.—*Compose sentences in which five of these adverbs shall modify adjectives, and five shall modify adverbs :—*

Far, unusually, quite, altogether, slightly, somewhat, much, almost, too, rather.

LESSON 16.

REVIEW.

To the Teacher.—In all school work, but especially here, where the philosophy of the sentence and the principles of construction are developed in progressive steps, success depends largely on the character of the reviews.

Let reviews be, as far as possible, topical. Require frequent outlines of the work passed over, especially of what is taught in the "Introductory Hints." Except Rules and Definitions, the language should be the pupil's own, and the illustrative sentences should be original.

In oral recitation, such a topic as Classification of Words or Forms of Individual Names may be presented to the class and passed from one pupil to another till a full discussion is obtained.

Direction.—*Review from Lesson 8 to Lesson 15, inclusive.*

Give the substance of the "Introductory Hints" (tell, for example, what three things such words as *lick*, *are*, and *remain* do in the sentence, what office they have in common, what such words are called, and why; what common office such words as *ripe*, *the*, and *eight* have, in what three ways they perform it, what such words are called, and why, etc.). Memorize and illustrate definitions and rules; illustrate what is taught of the capitalization and abbreviation of names, and of the position of adjectives and adverbs.

LESSON 17.

PREPOSITIONAL PHRASES AND PREPOSITIONS.

Introductory Hints.—To express our thoughts with greater exactness we may need to expand a word modifier into several words; as, A *long* ride brought us *there* = A ride *of one hundred miles* brought us *to Chicago*. These groups of words, *of one hundred miles* and *to Chicago*,—the one substituted for the adjective *long*, the other for the adverb *there*—we call **Phrases**.

As adverbs modify adjectives and adverbs, they may modify their equivalent phrases; as, The train stops *only at the station*.

They sometimes modify only the introductory word of the phrase; as, He sailed *nearly around* the globe.

That we may learn the office of such words as *of, to,* and *at,* used to introduce these phrases, let us see how the relation of one idea to another may be expressed. *Wealthy men.* These two words express two ideas as related. We have learned to know this relation by the form and position of the words. Change these, and the relation is lost—*men wealth.* But by using *of* before *wealth* the relation is restored—*men of wealth.* The word *of,* then, shows the relation between the ideas expressed by the words *men* and *wealth.*

All such relation words are called **Prepositions** (Lat. *præ*, before, and *positus*, placed—their usual position being before the noun with which they form a phrase).

DEFINITION.—A *Phrase* is a group of words denoting related ideas but not expressing a thought.

DEFINITION.—A *Preposition* is a word that introduces a phrase modifier, and shows the relation, in sense, of its principal word to the word modified.

Analysis and Parsing.

1. The pitch of the musical note depends upon the rapidity of vibration.

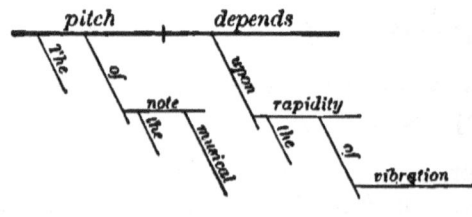

Explanation.—The diagram of the phrase is made up of a slanting line standing for the introductory word, and a horizontal line representing the principal word. Under the latter are drawn the lines which represent the modifiers of the principal word.

Oral Analysis.—*The* and the adjective phrase *of the musical note* are modifiers of the subject; the adverb phrase *upon the rapidity of vibration* is a modifier of the predicate. *Of* introduces the first phrase, and *note* is the principal word; *the* and *musical* are modifiers of *note*; *upon*

Prepositional Phrases and Prepositions.

introduces the second phrase, and *rapidity* is the principal word ; *the* and the adjective phrase *of vibration* are modifiers of *rapidity ; of* introduces this phrase, and *vibration* is the principal word.

Parsing.— *Of* is a *preposition* showing the relation, in sense, of *note* to *pitch ;* etc., etc.

To the Teacher.—Insist that, in parsing, the pupils shall give specific reasons instead of general definitions.

2. The Gulf Stream can be traced along the shores of the United States by the blueness of the water.
3. The North Pole has been approached in three principal directions.
4. In 1607, Hudson penetrated within six hundred miles of the North Pole.
5. The breezy morning died into silent noon.
6. The Delta of the Mississippi was once at St. Louis.
7. Coal of all kinds has originated from the decay of plants.
8. Genius can breathe freely only in the atmosphere of freedom.

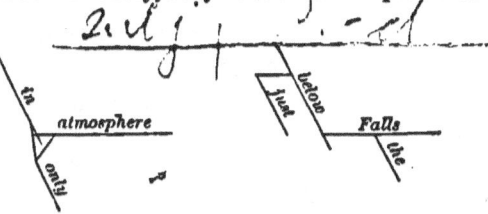

Explanation.—*Only* modifies the whole phrase ; and *just*, the preposition.

9. The Suspension Bridge is stretched across the Niagara river just below the Falls.
10. In Mother Goose the cow jumps clear over the moon.
11. The first standing army was formed in the middle of the fifteenth century.
12. The first astronomical observatory in Europe was erected at Seville by the Saracens.
13. The tails of some comets stretch to the distance of 100,000,000 miles.
14. The body of the great Napoleon was carried back from St. Helena to France.

LESSON 18.

COMPOSITION—PREPOSITIONAL PHRASES.

COMMA—RULE.—A Phrase out of its natural order* or not closely connected with the word it modifies, should be set off by the comma. †

Remark.—This rule must be applied with caution. Unless the phrase is to be made emphatic, or it breaks the continuity of the thought, the growing usage among writers is *not* to set it off.

Direction.—*Tell why the comma is, or is not, used in these sentences :—*

1. Between the two mountains lies a fertile valley.
2. Of the scenery along the Rhine, many travelers speak with enthusiasm.
3. He went, at the urgent request of the stranger, for the doctor.
4. He went from New York to Philadelphia on Monday.
5. In the dead of night, with a chosen band, under the cover of a truce, he approached.

Direction.—*Punctuate such of these sentences as need punctuation :—*

1. England in the eleventh century was conquered by the Normans.
2. Amid the angry yells of the spectators he died.
3. For the sake of emphasis a word or a phrase may be placed out of its natural order.
4. In the Pickwick Papers the conversation of Sam Weller is spiced with wit.
5. New York on the contrary abounds in men of wealth.
6. It has come down by uninterrupted tradition from the earliest times to the present day.

---

* For the natural order of words and phrases, see Lesson 51.

† An expression in the body of a sentence is *set off* by two commas; at the beginning or at the end, by one comma.

Composition—Prepositional Phrases.

Caution.—Place phrase modifiers where there can be no doubt as to what you intend them to modify. Have regard to the sound also.

Direction.—*Correct these errors in position, and use the comma when needed :—*

1. The honorable member was reproved for being intoxicated by the president.
2. That small man is speaking with red whiskers.
3. A message was read from the President in the Senate.
4. With his gun toward the woods he started in the morning.
5. On Monday evening on temperance by Mr. Gough a lecture at the old brick church was delivered.

Direction.—*Form a sentence out of each of these groups of words :—* Look sharply to the arrangement and the punctuation.

1. Of mind of splendor under the garb often is concealed poverty.
2. Of affectation of the young fop in the face impertinent an was seen smile.
3. Has been scattered Bible English the of millions by hundreds of the earth over the face.
4. To the end with no small difficulty of the journey at last through deep roads we after much fatigue came.
5. At the distance a flood of flame from the line from thirty iron mouths of twelve hundred yards of the enemy poured forth.

Direction.—*See into how many good, clear sentences you can convert these by transposing the phrases :—*

1. He went over the mountains on a certain day in early boyhood.
2. Ticonderoga was taken from the British by Ethan Allen on the tenth of May in 1775.

To the Teacher.—Examine the text-books frequently, and see that no pupil marks upon the page the punctuation of the sentences.

LESSON 19.

COMPOSITION—PREPOSITIONAL PHRASES.

Direction.—*Rewrite these sentences, changing the italicized words into equivalent phrases :—*

Model.—The sentence was *carefully* written.
   The sentence was written *with care.*

1. A *brazen* image was *then* set up.
2. Those *homeless* children were *kindly* treated.
3. Much has been said about the *Swiss* scenery.
4. An *aerial* trip to Europe was *rashly* planned.
5. The *American* Continent was *probably* discovered by Cabot.

Direction.—*Change these adjectives and adverbs into equivalent phrases; and then, attending carefully to the punctuation, use these phrases in sentences of your own :—*

1. Bostonian
2. why
3. incautiously
4. nowhere
5. there
6. hence
7. northerly
8. national
9. whence
10. here
11. Arabian
12. lengthy
13. historical
14. lucidly
15. earthward

Direction.—*Compose sentences, using these phrases as modifiers :—*

Of copper ; in Pennsylvania ; from the West Indies ; around the world ; between the tropics ; toward the Pacific ; on the 22d of December ; during the reign of Elizabeth ; before the application of steam to machinery ; at the Centennial Exposition of 1876.

To the Teacher.—If your pupils need more drill in the analysis and parsing of prepositional phrases, you can make up for them an exercise or two, from the sentences in Lesson 18 and those they are required to construct in Lesson 19.

LESSON 20.

COMPOUND SUBJECT AND COMPOUND PREDICATE.

CONJUNCTIONS AND INTERJECTIONS

Introductory Hints.—*Edward, Mary, and Elizabeth reigned in England.* The three words *Edward, Mary,* and *Elizabeth* have the same predicate—the same action being asserted of the king and the two queens. *Edward, Mary,* and *Elizabeth* are connected by *and,* and being understood between *Edward* and *Mary.* Connected subjects having the same predicate form a **Compound Subject**.

Charles I. was seized, was tried, and was beheaded. The three predicates *was seized, was tried,* and *was beheaded* have the same subject—the three actions being asserted of the same king. Connected predicates having the same subject form a **Compound Predicate**.

A sentence may have both a compound subject and a compound predicate; as, *Mary* and *Elizabeth lived* and *reigned* in England.

The words connecting the parts of a compound subject or of a compound predicate are called **Conjunctions** (Lat. *con* [*cum*], together, and *jungere,* to join), and form the seventh part of speech.

A conjunction may connect other parts of the sentence, as two word modifiers—*A dark and rainy* night follows. Some men sin *deliberately and presumptuously.*

It may connect two phrases; as, The equinox occurs *in March and in September.*

It may connect two clauses, that is, expressions that, standing alone, would be sentences; as, The leaves of the pine fall in spring, *but* the leaves of the maple drop in autumn.

Interjections (Lat. *inter,* between, and *jacere,* to throw) are the eighth and last part of speech.

Oh! ah! pooh! pshaw! etc., express bursts of feeling too sudden and violent for deliberate sentences.

Hail! fudge! indeed! amen! etc., once verbs, nouns, or adverbs, have lost their grammatical relation to other words. These express condensed thought as well as feeling.

Any part of speech may thus be wrenched from its construction with other words, and may lapse into an interjection; as, *Behold! shame! what!*

Two or more connected subjects having the same predicate form a **Compound Subject**.

Two or more connected predicates having the same subject form a **Compound Predicate**.

DEFINITION.—A *Conjunction* is a word used to connect words, phrases, or clauses.

DEFINITION.—An *Interjection* is a word used to express strong or sudden feeling.

Analysis and Parsing.

1. Ah! anxious wives, sisters, and mothers wait for the news.

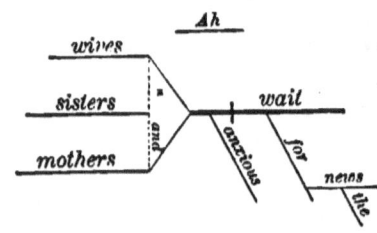

Explanation.—The three short horizontal lines represent each a part of the compound subject. They are connected by dotted lines, which stand for the connecting word. The x shows that a conjunction is understood. The line standing for the word modifier is joined to that part of the subject line which represents the *entire* subject. Turn this diagram about, and the connected horizontal lines will stand for the parts of a compound predicate.

Oral Analysis.—*Wives, sisters,* and *mothers* form the *compound subject; anxious* is a modifier of the compound subject; *and* connects *sisters* and *mothers*.

Parsing.—*And* is a *conjunction* connecting *sisters* and *mothers; ah* is an *interjection,* expressing a sudden burst of feeling.

2. In a letter we may advise, exhort, comfort, request, and discuss. (For diagram see the last sentence of the "Explanation" above.)

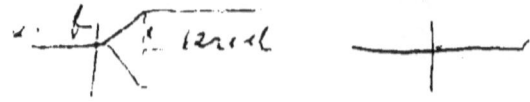

Compound Subject and Compound Predicate. 49

3. The mental, moral, and muscular powers are improved by use.

4. The hero of the Book of Job came from a strange land and of a strange parentage.
5. The optic nerve passes from the brain to the back of the eyeball, and there spreads out.
6. Between the mind of man and the outer world are interposed the nerves of the human body.
7. All forms of the lever and all the principal kinds of hinges are found in the body.
8. By perfection is meant the full and harmonious development of all the faculties.
9. Ugh! I look forward with dread to to-morrow.
10. From the Mount of Olives, the Dead Sea, dark and misty and solemn, is seen.
11. Tush! tush! 'twill not again appear.
12. A sort of gunpowder was used at an early period in China and in other parts of Asia.
13. Some men sin deliberately and presumptuously.
14. Feudalism did not and could not exist before the tenth century.

(The line on which *before* stands should touch the part of the predicate line that represents the *entire* predicate. Let ×, in place of *exist*, follow *did*.)

15. The opinions of the New York press are quoted in every port and in every capital.
16. Both friend and foe applauded.

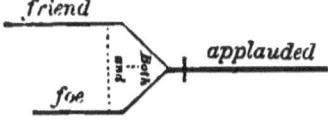

Explanation.—The conjunction *both* is used to strengthen the real connective *and*. So with *either—or, neither—nor*.

LESSON 21.

COMPOSITION—CONNECTED TERMS AND INTERJECTIONS.

COMMA—RULE.—Two or more words or phrases connected by conjunctions are separated from each other by the comma, unless all the conjunctions are expressed.

Remark.—When words and phrases stand in pairs, the pairs are separated according to the Rule, but the words of each pair are not.

When one term has a modifier that without the comma might be referred to both, or when the parts of compound predicates and of other phrases are long or differently modified, they are separated by the comma though no conjunction is omitted.

When two terms connected by *or* have the same meaning, the second is logically explanatory of the first, and is *set off* by the comma, *i. e.*, when it occurs in the body of the sentence a comma is placed after the explanatory word, as well as before *or*.

Direction.—*Justify the punctuation of these sentences:*—

1. Long, pious pilgrimages are made to Mecca.
2. Empires rise, flourish, and decay.
3. Cotton is raised in Egypt, in India, and in the United States.
4. The brain is protected by the skull, or cranium.
5. Nature and art and science were laid under tribute.
6. The room was furnished with a table, and a chair without legs.
7. The old oaken bucket hangs in the well.

Explanation.—No comma here, for no conjunction is omitted. *Oaken* limits *bucket*, *old* limits *oaken bucket*, and *the* limits *old oaken bucket*. See Lesson 13.

8. A Christian spirit should be shown to Jew or Greek, male or female, friend or foe.
9. We climbed up a mountain for a view.

Explanation.—No comma. *Up a mountain* tells where *we climbed*, and *for a view* tells why *we climbed up a mountain*.

Composition—Connected Terms and Interjections. 51

10. The boy hurries away from home, and enters upon a career of business or of pleasure.

11. The long procession was closed by the great dignitaries of the realm, and the brothers and sons of the king.

Direction.—*Punctuate such of these sentences as need punctuation, and give your reasons :—*

1. Men and women and children stare cry out and run.
2. Bright healthful and vigorous poetry was written by Milton.
3. Few honest industrious men fail of success in life.

(Where is the conjunction omitted ?)

4. Ireland or the Emerald Isle lies to the west of England.
5. *That* relates to the names of animals or things without sex.
6. The Hebrew is closely allied to the Arabic the Phœnician the Syriac and the Chaldee.
7. We sailed down the river and along the coast and into a little inlet.
8. The horses and the cattle were fastened in the same stables and were fed with abundance of hay and grain.
9. Spring and summer autumn and winter rush by in quick succession.
10. A few dilapidated old buildings still stand in the deserted village.

EXCLAMATION POINT—RULE.—**All *exclamatory expressions* must be followed by the exclamation point.**

Remark.—Sometimes an interjection alone and sometimes the interjection and the words following form the exclamatory expression ; as, *Oh ! it hurts. Oh, the beautiful snow*.

O is used in direct address ; as, *O father, listen to me*. *Oh* is used as a cry of pain, surprise, delight, fear, or appeal.

This distinction, however desirable, is not now strictly observed, *O* being frequently used in place of *Oh*.

CAPITAL LETTERS—RULE.—**The words *I* and *O* should be written in capital letters.**

Direction.—*Correct these violations of the two rules given above:*—

1. o noble judge o excellent young man. 2. Out of the depths have i cried unto thee. 3. Hurrah the field is won. 4. Pshaw how foolish. 5. Oh oh oh i shall be killed. 6. o life how uncertain o death how inevitable.

LESSON 22.

ANALYSIS AND PARSING.

Direction.—*Beginning with the 8th sentence of the first group of exercises in Lesson 21, analyze and parse thirteen, omitting (4), p. 51.*

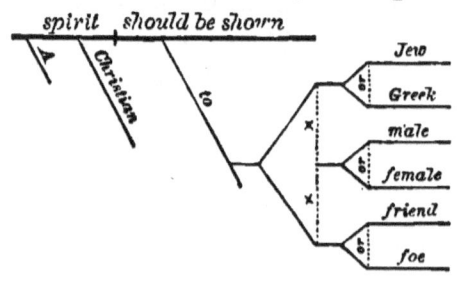

Model.—A Christian spirit should be shown to Jew or Greek, male or female, friend or foe.

LESSON 23.

COMPOSITION—CONNECTED TERMS.

Direction.—*Using the nouns below, compose sentences with compound subjects; compose others in which the verbs shall form compound predicates; and others in which the adjectives, the adverbs, and the phrases shall form compound modifiers:*—

In some let there be three or more connected terms. Observe Rule, Lesson 21, for punctuation. *Let your sentences mean something.*

NOUNS.

Washington, beauty, grace, Jefferson, symmetry, lightning, Lincoln, electricity, copper, silver, flowers, gold, rose, lily.

VERBS.

Examine, sing, pull, push, report, shout, love, hate, like, scream, loathe, approve, fear, obey, refine, hop, elevate, skip, disapprove.

ADJECTIVES.

Direction.—*See Caution, Lesson* 13.

Bright, acute, patient, careful, apt, forcible, simple, homely, happy, short, pithy, deep, jolly, mercurial, precipitous.

ADVERBS.

Direction.—*See Caution, Lesson* 15.

Neatly, slowly, carefully, sadly, now, here, never, hereafter.

PHRASES.

On sea ; in the city ; by day ; on land ; by night ; in the country ; by hook ; across the ocean ; by crook ; for weal ; over the lands ; for woe ; along the level road ; up the mountains.

LESSON 24.

REVIEW.

CAPITAL LETTERS AND PUNCTUATION.

Direction.—*Give the reason for every capital letter and for every mark of punctuation used below:*—

1. The sensitive parts of the body are covered by the cuticle, or skin. 2. The degrees of A.B., A.M., D.D., and LL.D. are conferred by the colleges and universities of the country. 3. Oh, I am so happy! 4. Fathers and mothers, sons and daughters rejoice at the news. 5. Plants are nourished by the earth, and the carbon of the air. 6. A tide of

American travelers is constantly flooding Europe. 7. The tireless, sleepless sun rises above the horizon, and climbs slowly and steadily to the zenith. 8. He retired to private life on half pay, and the income of a large estate in the South.

Direction.—*Write these expressions, using capital letters and marks of punctuation where they belong :—*

1. a fresh ruddy and beardless french youth replied 2. maj, cal, bu, p m, rev, no, hon, ft, w, e, oz, mr, n y, a b, mon, bbl, st 3. o father o father i cannot breathe here 4. ha ha that sounds well 5. the edict of nantes was established by henry the great of france 6. mrs, vs, co, esq, yd, pres, u s, prof, o, do, dr 7. hurrah good news good news 8. the largest fortunes grow by the saving of cents and dimes and dollars 9. the baltic sea lies between sweden and russia 10. the mississippi river pours into the gulf of mexico 11. supt, capt, qt, ph d, p, cr, i e, doz 12. benjamin franklin was born in boston in 1706 and died in 1790

Direction.—*Correct all these errors in capitalization and punctuation, and give your reasons :—*

1. Oliver cromwell ruled, over the english People, 2. halloo. I must speak to You ! 3. john Milton, went abroad in Early Life, and, stayed, for some time, with the Scholars of Italy, 4. Most Fuel consists of Coal and Wood from the Forests 5. books are read for Pleasure, and the Instruction and improvement of the Intellect, 6. In rainy weather the feet should be protected by overshoes or galoches 7. hark they are coming ! 8. A, neat, simple and manly style is pleasing to Us. 9. alas poor thing alas, 10. i fished on a, dark, and cool, and mossy, trout stream.

LESSON 25.

MISCELLANEOUS EXERCISES IN REVIEW.

ANALYSIS.

1. By the streets of By-and-by, one arrives at the house of Never.—*Span. Prov.*

2. The winds and waves are always on the side of the ablest navigators.—*Gibbon.*

3. The axis of the earth sticks out visibly through the center of each and every town or city.—*Holmes.*

4. The arrogant Spartan, with a French-like glorification, boasted forever of little Thermopylæ.—*De Quincey.*

5. The purest act of knowledge is always colored by some feeling of pleasure or pain.—*Hamilton.*

6. The thunder of the great London journals reverberates through every clime.—*Marsh.*

7. The cheeks of William the Testy were scorched into a dusky red by two fiery little gray eyes.—*Irving.*

8. The study of natural science goes hand in hand * with the culture of the imagination.—*Tyndall.*

9. The whole substance of the winds is drenched and bathed and washed and winnowed and sifted through and through by this baptism in the sea.—*Swain.*

10. The Arabian Empire stretched from the Atlantic to the Chinese Wall, and from the shores of the Caspian sea to those of the Indian Ocean.—*Draper.*

11. One half of all known materials consists of oxygen.—*Cooke.*

12. The range of thirty pyramids, even in the time of Abraham, looked down on the plain of Memphis.—*Stanley.*

---

* *Hand in hand* may be treated as one adverb, or *with* may be supplied.

LESSON 26.

WRITTEN PARSING.

Direction.—*Parse the sentences of Lesson 25 according to this* **Model for Written Parsing.**

	Nouns.	Pron.	Verbs.	Adj.	Adv.	Prep.	Conj.	Int
1st sentence.	streets, By-and-by, house, Never.	one.	arrives.	the, the.		By, of, at, of.		
2d sentence.								

To the Teacher.—Until the *Subdivisions* and *Modifications* of the parts of speech are reached, *Oral and Written Parsing* can be only a classification of the words in the sentence. You must judge how frequently a lesson like this is needed, and how much parsing should be done orally day by day. In their *Oral Analysis* let the pupils give *at first* the reasons for every statement, but guard against their doing this mechanically and in set terms; and, when you think it can safely be done, let them drop it. But ask now and then, whenever you think they have grown careless or are guessing, for the reason of this, that, or the other step taken.

LESSON 27.

REVIEW.

To the Teacher.—See suggestions, Lesson 16.

Direction.—*Review from Lesson 17 to Lesson 21, inclusive.*

Give the substance of the "Introductory Hints" (tell, for example, what such words as *long* and *there* may be expanded into, how these expanded forms may be modified, how introduced, what the introductory words are called, and why, etc.). Memorize and illustrate definitions and rules; illustrate fully what is taught of the position of phrases, and of the punctuation of phrases, connected terms, and exclamatory expressions. How many parts of speech are there?

LESSON 28.

NOUNS AS OBJECT COMPLEMENTS.

Introductory Hints.—In saying *Washington captured*, we do not fully express the action performed by Washington. If we add a noun and say, *Washington captured Cornwallis*, we complete the predicate by naming that which receives the action.

Whatever fills out, or completes, is a **Complement**. As *Cornwallis* completes the expression of the action by naming the thing acted upon —the object,—we call it the **Object Complement**. Connected objects completing the same verb form a **Compound Object Complement**; as, Washington captured *Cornwallis* and his *army*.

DEFINITION.—The *Object Complement of a Sentence* completes the predicate, and names that which receives the act.

The complement with all its modifiers is called the *Modified Complement*.

Analysis and Parsing

1. Clear thinking makes clear writing.

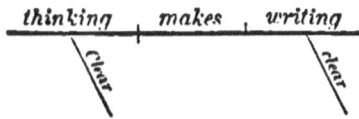

Explanation.—The line standing for the object complement is a continuation of the predicate line. The little vertical line only touches this without cutting it.

Oral Analysis.—*Writing* is the *object complement; clear writing* is the modified complement, and *makes clear writing* is the entire predicate.

2. Austerlitz killed Pitt.
3. The invention of gunpowder destroyed feudalism.
4. Liars should have good memories.
5. We find the first surnames in the tenth century.
6. God tempers the wind to the shorn lamb.

7. Benjamin Franklin invented the lightning-rod.

8. At the opening of the thirteenth century, Oxford took and held rank with the greatest schools of Europe.

9. The moon revolves, and keeps the same side toward us.

10. Hunger rings the bell, and orders up coals in the shape of bread and butter, beef and bacon, pies and puddings.

11. The history of the Trojan war rests on the authority of Homer, and forms the subject of the noblest poem of antiquity.

12. Every stalk, bud, flower, and seed displays a figure, a proportion, a harmony, beyond the reach of art.

13. The natives of Ceylon build houses of the trunk and thatch roofs with the leaves, of the cocoa-nut palm.

14. Richelieu exiled the mother, oppressed the wife, degraded the brother, and banished the confessor, of the king.

15. James and John study and recite grammar and arithmetic.

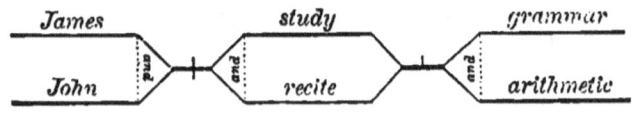

LESSON 29.

NOUNS AND ADJECTIVES AS ATTRIBUTE COMPLEMENTS.

Introductory Hints.—The subject presents one idea; the predicate, another, and asserts it of the first. *Corn is growing* presents the idea of the thing, corn, and the idea of the act, growing, and asserts the act of the thing. *Corn growing* lacks the asserting word, and *Corn is* lacks the word denoting the idea to be asserted.

In logic, the asserting word is called the *copula*—it shows that the two ideas are *coupled* into a thought,—and the word expressing the idea asserted is called the predicate. But, as one word often performs both offices, e. g., Corn *grows*, and, as it is in dispute whether any word can assert without expressing something of the idea asserted, we pass this distinction by as not essential in grammar, and call both that which asserts and that which expresses the idea asserted, by one name—the predicate.*

The maple leaves become. The verb *become* does not make a complete predicate; it does not fully express the idea to be asserted. The idea may be completely expressed by adding the adjective *red*, denoting the quality we wish to assert of leaves or attribute to them—*The maple leaves become red.*

Lizards are reptiles. The noun *reptiles,* naming the *class* of the animals called *lizards,* performs a like office for the asserting word *are*. *Rolfe's wife was Pocahontas.* *Pocahontas* completes the predicate by presenting a second idea, which *was* asserts to be *identical* with that of the subject.

When the completing word expressing the idea to be attributed does not unite with the asserting word to make a single verb, we distinguish it as the **Attribute Complement.** Connected attribute complements of the same verb form a **Compound Attribute Complement.**

Most grammarians call the adjective and the noun, when so used, the **Predicate Adjective** and the **Predicate Noun.**

DEFINITION.—The *Attribute Complement of a Sentence* completes the predicate and belongs to the subject.

Analysis and Parsing.

1. Slang is vulgar.

Slang | is ╲ vulgar

Explanation.—The line standing for the attribute complement is, like the object line, a continuation of the predicate line; but notice that the line which sepa-

---

* We may call the *verb* the *predicate;* but, when it is followed by a complement, it is an *incomplete* predicate.

rates the incomplete predicate from the complement slants toward the subject to show that the complement is an attribute of it.

Oral Analysis.—*Vulgar* is the *attribute complement*, completing the predicate and expressing a quality of slang; *is vulgar* is the entire predicate.

 2. The sea is fascinating and treacherous.
 3. The mountains are grand, tranquil, and lovable.
 4. The Saxon words in English are simple, homely, and substantial.
 5. The French and the Latin words in English are elegant, dignified, and artificial.
 6. The ear is the ever-open gateway of the soul.
 7. The verb is the life of the sentence.
 8. Good-breeding is surface-Christianity.
 9. A dainty plant is the ivy green.

Explanation.—The subject names that of which the speaker says something. The *terms* in which he says it,—the predicate,—he, of course, assumes that the hearer already understands. Settle, then, which—plant or ivy—Dickens supposed the reader to know least about, and which, therefore, Dickens was telling him about; and you settle which word—*plant* or *ivy*—is the subject. (Is it not the writer's poetical conception of "the green ivy" that the reader is supposed not to possess?)

 10. The highest outcome of culture is simplicity.
 11. Stillness of person and steadiness of features are signal marks of good-breeding.
 12. The north wind is full of courage, and puts the stamina of endurance into a man.
 13. The west wind is hopeful, and has promise and adventure in it.
 14. The east wind is peevishness and mental rheumatism and grumbling, and curls one up in the chimney-corner.
 15. The south wind is full of longing and unrest and effeminate suggestions of luxurious ease.

LESSON 30.

ATTRIBUTE COMPLEMENTS—CONTINUED.

ANALYSIS AND PARSING.

1. He went out as mate and came back captain.

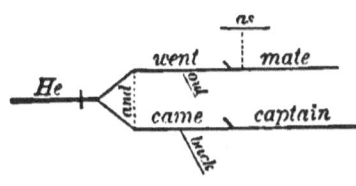

Explanation.—*Mate*, like *captain*, is an attribute complement. Some would say that the conjunction *as* connects *mate* to *he;* but we think this connection is made through the verb *went*, and that *as* is simply introductory. This is indicated in the diagram.

2. The sun shines bright and hot at midday.
3. Velvet feels smooth, and looks rich and glossy.
4. She grew tall, queenly, and beautiful.
5. Plato and Aristotle are called the two head-springs of all philosophy.
6. Under the Roman law, every son was regarded as a slave.
7. He came a foe and returned a friend.
8. I am here. I am present.

Explanation.—The office of an adverb sometimes fades into that of an adjective attribute and cannot be distinguished from it. *Here*, like an adjective, seems to complete *am*, and, like an adverb, to modify it. From their form and usual function, *here* should, in this sentence, be called an adverb, and *present* an adjective.

9. This book is presented to you as a token of esteem and gratitude.
10. The warrior fell back upon the bed a lifeless corpse.
11. The apple tastes and smells delicious.
12. Lord Darnley turned out a dissolute and insolent husband.
13. In the fable of the Discontented Pendulum, the weights hung speechless.
14. The brightness and freedom of the New Learning seemed incarnate in the young and scholarly Sir Thomas More.
15. Sir Philip Sidney lived and died the darling of the Court, and the gentleman and idol of the time.

LESSON 31.

OBJECTIVE COMPLEMENTS.

Introductory Hints.—*He made the wall white.* Here *made* does not fully express the action performed upon the wall. We do not mean to say, He *made* the *white wall*, but, He *made-white (whitened)* the wall. *White* helps *made* to express the action, and at the same time it denotes the quality attributed to the wall as the result of the action.

They made Victoria queen. Here *made* does not fully express the action performed upon Victoria. They did not *make* Victoria, but *made-queen (crowned)* Victoria. *Queen* helps *made* to express the action, and at the same time denotes the office to which the action raised Victoria.

A word that, like the adjective *white* or the noun *queen*, helps to complete the predicate and at the same time belongs to the object complement, differs from an attribute complement by belonging not to the subject but to the *object complement*, and so is called an **Objective Complement**.

As the *objective complement* denotes what the receiver of the act is *made* to be, in fact or in thought, it is sometimes called the *factitive* complement or the *factitive* object (Lat. *facere*, to make).

Some of the other verbs which are thus completed are *call*, *think*, *choose*, and *name*.

DEFINITION.—The *Objective Complement* completes the predicate and belongs to the object.

Analysis and Parsing.

1. They made Victoria queen.

They | made ╱ queen ╲ Victoria

Explanation.—The line that separates *made* from *queen* slants toward the *object* complement to show that *queen* belongs to the object.

Oral Analysis.—*Queen* is an *objective complement* completing *made* and belonging to *Victoria ; made Victoria queen* is the complete predicate.

2. Some one has called the eye the window of the soul.
3. Destiny had made Mr. Churchill a schoolmaster.
4. President Hayes chose the Hon. Wm. M. Evarts Secretary of State.
5. After a break of sixty years in the ducal line of the English nobility, James I. created the worthless Villiers Duke of Buckingham.
6. We should consider time as a sacred trust.

Explanation.—*As,* may be used simply to introduce an objective complement.

7. Ophelia and Polonius thought Hamlet really insane.
8. The President and the Senate appoint certain men ministers to foreign courts.
9. Shylock would have struck Jessica dead beside him.
10. Custom renders the feelings blunt and callous.
11. Socrates styled beauty a short-lived tyranny.
12. Madame de Stael calls beautiful architecture frozen music.
13. They named the state New York from the Duke of York.
14. Henry the Great consecrated the Edict of Nantes as the very ark of the constitution.

LESSON 32.

COMPOSITION—COMPLEMENTS.

Caution.—Be careful to distinguish an adjective complement from an adverb modifier.

Explanation.—Mary arrived *safe.* We here wish to tell the *condition* of Mary on her arrival, and *not* the *manner* of her arriving. My head feels *bad* (*is* in a bad condition, as perceived by the sense of feeling). The sun shines *bright* (*is* bright—quality,—as perceived by its shining).

When the idea of *being* is prominent in the verb, as in the examples above, you see that the adjective, and not the adverb, follows.

Direction.—*Justify the use of these adjectives and adverbs :—*
1. The boy is running wild.
2. The boy is running wildly about.
3. They all arrived safe and sound.
4. The day opened bright.
5. He felt awkward in the presence of ladies.
6. He felt around awkwardly for his chair.
7. The sun shines bright.
8. The sun shines brightly on the tree-tops.
9. He appeared prompt and willing.
10. He appeared promptly and willingly.

Direction.—*Correct these errors and give your reasons :—*
1. My head pains me very bad.
2. My friend has acted very strange in the matter.
3. Don't speak harsh.
4. It can be bought very cheaply.
5. I feel tolerable well.
6. She looks beautifully.

Direction.—*Join to each of the nouns, below, three appropriate adjectives expressing the qualities as a s s u m e d, and then make complete sentences by a s s e r t i n g these qualities :—*

Model.—{ Hard, brittle, transparent } glass.   Glass is hard, brittle, and transparent.

Coal, iron, Niagara Falls, flowers, war, ships.

Direction.—*Compose sentences containing these nouns as attribute complements :—*

Emperor, mathematician, Longfellow, Richmond.

Direction.—*Compose sentences, using these verbs as predicates, and these pronouns as attribute complements :—*

Is, was, might have been; I, we, he, she, they.

Remark.—Notice that these forms of the pronouns—*I, we, thou, he, she, ye, they*, and *who*—are never used as object complements or as principal words in prepositional phrases; and that *me, us, thee, him, her, them*, and *whom* are never used as subjects or as attribute complements of sentences.

Direction.—*Compose sentences in which each of the following verbs shall have two complements—the one an object complement, the other an objective complement :—*

Let some object complements be pronouns, and let some objective complements be introduced by *as*.

Model.—They call *me chief.* We regard composition *as* very *important.*

Make, appoint, consider, choose, call.

LESSON 33.

NOUNS AS ADJECTIVE MODIFIERS.

Introductory Hints.—*Solomon's temple was destroyed. Solomon's* limits *temple* by telling what or whose temple is spoken of, and is, therefore, a modifier of it.

The relation of Solomon to the temple is expressed by the apostrophe and *s* ('s) added to the noun *Solomon*. When *s* has been added to the noun to denote more than one, this relation of possession is expressed by the apostrophe alone ('); as, *boys'* hats. This same relation of possession may be expressed by the preposition *of ; Solomon's temple = the temple of Solomon.*

Dom Pedro, the emperor, was welcomed by the Americans. The noun *emperor* modifies *Dom Pedro* by telling what Dom Pedro is meant. Both words name the same person.

Solomon's and *emperor*, like adjectives, modify nouns; but they are *names* of things, and, besides, when modified, are modified by adjectives and not by adverbs; as, *the wise* Solomon's temple, etc.; Dom Pedro, the *Brazilian* emperor, etc. These are conclusive reasons for calling them nouns.

They represent two kinds of **Noun Modifiers**—the **Possessive** and the **Explanatory**.

Analysis and Parsing.

1. Elizabeth's favorite, Raleigh, was beheaded by James I.

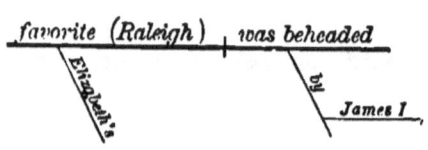

Explanation.—*Raleigh* is written on the subject line, because it and *favorite* name the same person; but *Raleigh* is enclosed within curves to show that *favorite* is the proper grammatical subject.

Oral Analysis.—*Elizabeth's* and *Raleigh* are modifiers of the subject, the first telling *whose* favorite is meant, the second *what* or *which* favorite. *Elizabeth's favorite, Raleigh* is the modified subject.

2. The best features of King James's translation of the Bible are derived from Tyndale's version.
3. St. Paul, the apostle, was beheaded in the reign of Nero.
4. A fool's bolt is soon shot.
5. The tadpole, or polliwog, becomes a frog.
6. An idle brain is the devil's workshop.
7. Mahomet, or Mohammed, was born in the year 569 and died in 632.
8. They scaled Mount Blanc—a daring feat.

Explanation.—*Feat* is explanatory of the sentence, *They scaled Mount Blanc*, and in the diagram it stands, enclosed in curves, on a short line placed after the sentence line.

9. Bees communicate to each other the death of the queen, by a rapid interlacing of the antennæ.

Explanation.—*Each other* may be treated as one term, or *each* may be made explanatory of *bees*.

10. The lamp of a man's life has three wicks—brain, blood, and breath.

Explanation.—Several words may together be explanatory of one.

11. The turtle's back-bone and breast-bone—its shell and coat of armor—are on the outside of its body.

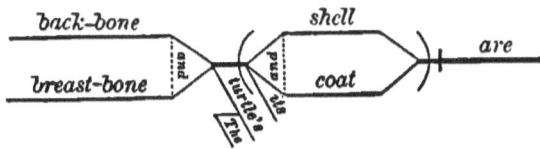

12. Cromwell's rule as Protector began in the year 1653 and ended in 1658.

Explanation.—*As, namely, to wit, viz., i. e., e. g.,* and *that is* may introduce explanatory modifiers, but they do not seem to connect them to the words modified. In the diagram they stand like *as* in Lesson 30. *Protector* is explanatory of *Cromwell's*.

13. In the latter half of the eighteenth century, three powerful nations, namely, Russia, Austria, and Prussia, united for the dismemberment of Poland.

14. John, the beloved disciple, lay on his Master's breast.

15. The petals of the daisy, *day's-eye*, close at night and in rainy weather.

LESSON 34.

COMPOSITION—NOUNS AS ADJECTIVE MODIFIERS.

COMMA—RULE.—An *Explanatory Modifier*, when it does not restrict the modified term or combine closely with it, is set off* by the comma.

---

* See foot-note, Lesson 18.

Explanation.—*The words I and O should be written in capital letters.* The phrase *I and O* restricts *words,* that is, limits its application, and no comma is needed.

Jacob's favorite sons, Joseph and Benjamin, were Rachel's children. The phrase *Joseph and Benjamin* explains *sons* without restricting, and, therefore, should be set off by the comma.

In each of these expressions, *I myself, we boys, William the Conqueror,* the explanatory term combines closely with the word explained, and no comma is needed.

Direction.—*Give the reasons for the insertion or the omission of commas in these sentences:*—

1. My brother Henry and my brother George belong to a boat-club.
2. The author of Pilgrim's Progress, John Bunyan, was the son of a tinker.
3. Shakespeare, the great dramatist, was careless of his literary reputation.
4. The conqueror of Mexico, Cortez, was cruel in his treatment of Montezuma.
5. Pizarro, the conqueror of Peru, was a Spaniard.
6. The Emperors Napoleon and Alexander met and became fast friends on a raft at Tilsit.

Direction.—*Insert commas, below, where they are needed, and give your reasons:*—

1. The Franks a warlike people of Germany gave their name to France.
2. My son Joseph has entered college.
3. You blocks! You stones! O you hard hearts!
4. Mecca a city in Arabia is sacred in the eyes of Mohammedans.
5. He himself could not go.
6. The poet Spenser lived in the reign of Elizabeth.
7. Elizabeth Queen of England ruled from 1558 to 1603.

Direction.—*Compose sentences containing these expressions as explanatory modifiers:*—

The most useful metal ; the capital of Turkey ; the Imperial City the great English poets ; the hermit ; a distinguished American statesman.

Direction.—*Punctuate these expressions, and employ each of them in a sentence :—*

See Remark, Lesson 21. Omit *or,* and note the effect.

1. Palestine or the Holy Land ——. 2. New York or the Empire State ——. 3. New Orleans or the Crescent City ——. 4. The five Books of Moses or the Pentateuch.

Remember that ('s) and (') are the possessive signs, (') being used when *s* has been added to denote more than one, ('s) in other cases.

Direction.—*Copy the following, and note the use of the possessive sign :—*

The lady's fan ; the girl's bonnet ; a dollar's worth ; Burns's poems ; Brown & Co.'s business ; a day's work ; men's clothing ; children's toys ; those girls' dresses ; ladies' calls ; three years' interest ; five dollars' worth.

Direction.—*Make possessive modifiers of the following words, and join them to appropriate nouns :—*

Woman, women ; mouse, mice ; buffalo, buffaloes ; fairy, fairies ; hero, heroes ; baby, babies ; calf, calves.

Caution.—Do not use ('s) or (') with the pronouns *its, his, ours, yours, hers, theirs.*

LESSON 35.

NOUNS AS ADVERB MODIFIERS.

Introductory Hints.—*He gave me a book.* Here we have what many grammarians call a *double object. Book,* naming the *thing* acted upon, they call the *direct* object ; and *me,* naming the *person* toward whom the act is directed, the *indirect,* or *dative,* object.

You see that *me* and *book* do not, like *Cornwallis* and *army,* in *Washington captured Cornwallis and his army,* form a compound object complement ; they cannot be connected by a conjunction, for they do not stand in the same relation to the verb *gave.* The meaning is not, He gave me *and* the book.

We prefer to treat these so-called indirect objects, which generally name the person to or for whom something is done, as phrase modifiers without the preposition. If we change the order of the words, the preposition must be supplied ; as, He gave a *book to me.* He bought *me a book ;* He bought a *book for me.* He asked *me* a *question ;* He asked a *question of me.*

Teach, tell, send, and *lend* are other examples of verbs said to be followed by double objects.

Besides these so-called indirect objects, nouns denoting measure, quantity, weight, time, value, distance, or direction are often used adverbially, being equivalent to phrase modifiers without the preposition. We walked four *miles* an *hour.* It weighs one *pound.* It is worth a *dollar* a *yard.* I went *home* that *way.* The wall is ten *feet,* six *inches* high.

The idiom of the language does not often admit a preposition before nouns denoting measure, direction, etc. In your analysis you need not supply one.

Analysis and Parsing.

1. They offered Cæsar the crown three times.

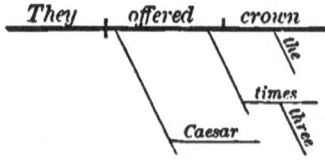

Explanation.—Cæsar, the so-called dative object, and *times,* the noun denoting measure, stand in the diagram on lines representing the principal words of prepositional phrases. But there are no prepositions on the slanting lines, nor is there an × to mark the omission, there being no preposition understood.

Oral Analysis.—Cæsar and *times,* without prepositions, perform the office of adverb phrases modifying the predicate *offered.*

2. We pay the President of the United States $50,000 a year.

3. He sent his daughter home that way.

4. I gave him a dollar a bushel for his wheat, and ten cents a pound for his sugar.

5. Shakespeare was fifty-two years old the very day of his death.

6. Serpents cast their skin once a year.

7. The famous Charter Oak of Hartford, Conn., fell Aug. 21, 1856.

8. Good land should yield its owner seventy-five bushels of corn an acre.

9. On the fatal field of Zutphen, Sept. 22, 1586, his attendants brought the wounded Sir Philip Sidney a cup of cold water.

10. He magnanimously gave a dying soldier the water.

11. The frog lives several weeks as a fish, and breathes by means of gills.

12. Queen Esther asked King Ahasuerus a favor.

13. Aristotle taught Alexander the Great philosophy.

14. The pure attar of roses is worth twenty or thirty dollars an ounce.

15. Puff-balls have grown six inches in diameter in a single night.

LESSON 36.

REVIEW.

To the Teacher.—See suggestions, Lesson 16.

Direction.—*Review from Lesson 28 to Lesson 35, inclusive:*—

Give the substance of the "Introductory Hints" (for example, show clearly what two things are essential to a complete predicate; explain what is meant by a complement; distinguish clearly the three kinds of complements; show what parts of speech may be employed for each, and tell what general idea—action, quality, class, or identity—is expressed by each attribute or objective complement in your illustrations, etc.). Memorize and illustrate definitions and rules; explain and illustrate fully the distinction between an adjective complement and an adverb modifier; illustrate what is taught of the forms *I*, *we*, etc.; *me*, *us*, etc.; explain and illustrate the use of the possessive sign.

LESSON 37.

VERBS AS ADJECTIVES AND AS NOUNS—PARTICIPLES.

Introductory Hints.—*Corn grows; Corn growing.* Here *growing* differs from *grows* in lacking the power to assert. *Growing* is a form of the verb that cannot, like *grows*, make a complete predicate, because it only *assumes* the act—*implies* that the corn does the act. *Corn* may be called its *assumed subject.*

Birds, singing, delight us. Here *singing* does duty (1) as an *adjective,* describing birds by assuming or implying an action, and (2) as a *verb* by expressing the act of singing as going on at the time they delight us.

By singing their songs birds delight us. Here *singing* has the nature of a verb and that of a noun. As a verb it has an object complement, *songs;* and as a noun it *names* the action, and stands as the principal word in a prepositional phrase.

Their singing so sweetly delights us. Here, also, *singing* has the nature of a verb and that of a noun. As a verb it has an adverb modifier, *sweetly,* and as a noun it names an act and takes a possessive modifier.

This form of the verb is called the **Participle** (Lat. *pars*, a part, and *capere*, to take), because it partakes of two natures and performs two offices—those of a verb and an adjective, or those of a verb and a noun. (For definition see Lesson 131.)

Singing birds delight us. Here *singing* has lost its verbal nature, and expresses a permanent quality of birds—telling what kind of birds,—and so is a mere adjective. *The singing of the birds delights us.* Here *singing* is simply a noun, naming the act and taking adjective modifiers.

You see that there are two * kinds of participles; one sharing the nature of the verb and that of the adjective; the other, the nature of the

---

* Many grammarians restrict the name *participle* to the first kind, calling words of the second kind *gerunds*, or *verbal nouns*, because they suppose all verbal forms used as nouns to have a different origin, and to have once had a different ending. But the original participles, like other adjectives, are freely used as nouns.

verb and that of the noun. The common endings of the participle are *ing*, *ed*, and *en*.

The participle, like other forms of the verb, may be followed by an object complement or an attribute complement.

Analysis and Parsing.

The *participle* may be used as an *adjective modifier*.

'1. Hearing a step, I turned.

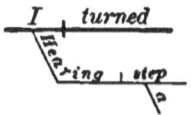

Explanation.—The line standing for the participle is broken; one part slants to represent the adjective nature of the participle, and the other is horizontal to represent its verbal nature.

Oral Analysis.—The phrase *hearing a step* is a modifier of the subject;* the principal word is *hearing*, which is completed by the noun *step; step* is modified by *a*.

Parsing.—*Hearing* is a form of the verb called participle, because the action expressed by it is merely assumed, and it shares the nature of an adjective and that of a verb.

2. The fat of the body is fuel laid away for use.

Explanation.—The complement is here modified by a participle phrase.

3. The spinal marrow, proceeding from the brain, extends downward through the back-bone.
4. Van Twiller sat in a huge chair of solid oak, hewn in the celebrated forest of the Hague.

Explanation.—The principal word of a prepositional phrase is here modified by a participle phrase.

5. Lentulus, returning with victorious legions, had amused the populace with the sports of the amphitheater.

---

* Logically, or in sense, *hearing a step* modifies the predicate also. *I turned when* or *because* I heard a step. See Lesson 79.

The *participle* may be used as an *attribute complement*.

6. The natives came crowding around.

Explanation.—*Crowding* here completes the predicate *came*, and belongs to the subject *natives*. The natives are represented as performing the act of coming and the accompanying act of crowding. The assertive force of the predicate *came* seems to extend over both verbs.

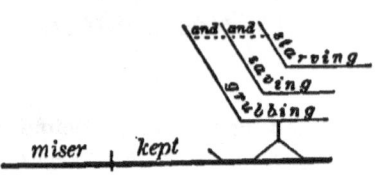

7. The city lies sleeping.
8. They stood terrified.
9. The philosopher sat buried in thought.
10. The old miser kept grubbing and saving and starving.

The *participle* may be used as an *objective complement*.

11. He kept me waiting.

Explanation.—*Waiting* completes *kept* and relates to the object complement *me*. *Kept-waiting* expresses the complete action performed upon me. *He kept-waiting me = He detained me.* The relation of *waiting* to *me* may be seen by changing the form of the verb; as, I *was kept waiting*. See Lesson 31.

12. I found my book growing dull.

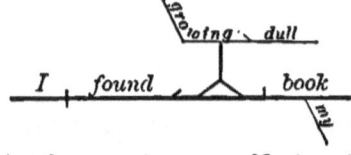

Explanation.—The diagram representing the phrase complement is drawn above the complement line, on which it is made to rest by means of a support. All that stands on the complement line is regarded as the complement. Notice that the little mark before the phrase points toward the object complement. The adjective *dull* completes *growing* and belongs to *book*, the assumed subject of *growing*.

13. He owned himself defeated.
14. No one ever saw fat men heading a riot or herding together in turbulent mobs.
15. I felt my heart beating faster.
16. You may imagine me sitting there.
17. Saul, seeking his father's asses, found himself suddenly turned into a king.

LESSON 38.

PARTICIPLES—CONTINUED.

ANALYSIS AND PARSING.

The *participle* may be used as *principal word* in a *prepositional phrase.*

1. We receive good by doing good.

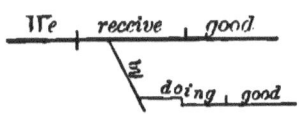

Explanation.—The line representing the participle here is broken; the first part represents the participle as a noun, and the other as a verb. (Nouns and verbs are both written on horizontal lines.)

Oral Analysis.—The phrase *by doing good* is a modifier of the predicate; *by* introduces the phrase; the principal word is *doing*, which is completed by the noun *good*.

Parsing.—*Doing* is a participle; like a noun, it follows the preposition *by;* and, like a verb, it takes an object complement.

2. Portions of the brain may be cut off without producing any pain.
3. The Coliseum was once capable of seating ninety thousand persons.
4. Success generally depends on acting prudently, steadily, and vigorously.
5. You cannot fully sympathize with suffering without having suffered. (*Suffering* is here a noun.)

The *participle* may be the *principal word* in a phrase used as a *subject* or as an *object complement.*

6. Your writing that letter so neatly secured the position.

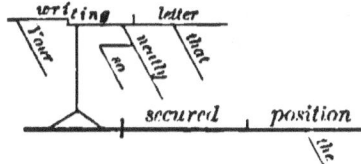

Explanation.—The diagram of the subject phrase is drawn above the subject line. All that rests on the subject line is regarded as the subject.

Oral Analysis.—The phrase *your writing that letter so neatly* is the subject; the principal word of it is *writing*, which is completed by *letter; writing*, as a noun, is modified by *your*, and, as a verb, by the adverb phrase *so neatly*.

7. We should avoid injuring the feelings of others.
8. My going there will depend upon my father's giving his consent.
9. Good reading aloud is a rare accomplishment.

The *participle* may be used as a *mere noun* or a *mere adjective*.

10. The cackling of geese saved Rome.
11. Such was the exciting campaign, celebrated in many * a long-forgotten song.

Explanation.—*Many* modifies *song* as modified by *a* and *long-forgotten*.

12. All silencing of discussion is an assumption of infallibility.
13. He was a squeezing, grasping, hardened old sinner.

The *participle* may be used in *independent* or *absolute phrases*.

14. The bridge at Ashtabula giving way, the train fell into the river.

Explanation.—The diagram of the absolute phrase, which consists of a noun used independently with a participle, stands by itself. See Lesson 44.

15. Talking of exercise, you have heard, of course, of Dickens's "constitutionals."

---

* "*Manig man* in Anglo-Saxon was used like German *mancher mann*, Latin *multus vir*, and the like, until the thirteenth century; when the article was inserted to emphasize the distribution before indicated by the singular number."—*Prof. F. A. March.*

LESSON 39.

COMPOSITION—PARTICIPLES.

COMMA—RULE.—The Participle used as an adjective modifier, with the words belonging to it, is set off* by the comma unless restrictive.

Explanation.—*A bird, lighting near my window, greeted me with a song. The bird sitting on the wall is a wren.* Lighting describes without restricting; *sitting* restricts—limits the application of *bird* to a particular bird.

Direction.—*Justify the punctuation of the participle phrases in Lesson* 37.

Caution.—In using a participle be careful to leave no doubt as to what you intend it to modify.

Direction.—*Correct these errors in arrangement, and punctuate, giving your reasons:*—

1. A gentleman will let his house going abroad for the summer to a small family containing all the improvements.
2. The town contains fifty houses and one hundred inhabitants built of brick.
3. Suits ready made of material cut by an experienced tailor handsomely trimmed and bought at a bargain are offered cheap.
4. Seated on the topmost branch of a tall tree busily engaged in gnawing an acorn we espied a squirrel.
5. A poor child was found in the streets by a wealthy and benevolent gentleman suffering from cold and hunger.

Direction.—*Recast these sentences, making the reference of the participle clear, and punctuating correctly:*—

---

* An expression in the body of a sentence is *set off* by two commas; at the beginning or at the end, by one comma.

Model.—Climbing to the top of the hill the Atlantic ocean was seen. Incorrect, because it appears that the ocean did the climbing. Climbing to the top of the hill, we saw the Atlantic ocean.

1. Entering the next room was seen a marble statue of Apollo.
2. By giving him a few hints he was prepared to do the work well.
3. Desiring an early start the horse was saddled by five o'clock.

Direction.—*Compose sentences in which each of these three participles shall be used as an adjective modifier, as the principal word in a prepositional phrase, as the principal word in a phrase used as a subject or as an object complement, as a mere adjective, as a mere noun, and in an absolute phrase :—*

Buzzing, leaping, waving.

LESSON 40.

VERBS AS NOUNS—INFINITIVES.

Introductory Hints.—*I came to see you.* Here the verb *see*, like the participle, lacks the asserting power—*I to see* asserts nothing. *See*, following the preposition *to*,* names the act and is completed by *you*, and so does duty as a noun and as a verb. In office it is like the second kind of participles, described in Lesson 37, and from some grammarians has received the same name—some calling both *gerunds*, and others calling both *infinitives*. It differs from this participle in form, and in following only the preposition *to*. *Came to see = came for seeing.*

This form of the verb is frequently the principal word of a phrase used as a subject or as an object complement ; as, *To read good books is profitable ; I like to read good books.* Here also the form with *to* is equivalent to the participle form *reading*. *Reading good books is profitable.*

As this form of the verb names the action in an indefinite way, without limiting it to a subject, we call it the **Infinitive** (Lat. *infinitus*, without limit). For definition, see Lesson 131.

---

* For the discussion of *to* with the infinitive, see Lesson 134.

Verbs as Nouns—Infinitives. 79

Frequently the infinitive expresses purpose, as in the first example given above, and in such cases *to* expresses relation, and performs its full function as a preposition; but when the infinitive phrase is used as subject or as object complement, the *to* expresses no relation. It serves only to introduce the phrase, and in no way affects the meaning of the verb.

The infinitive, like other forms of the verb, may be followed by the different complements.

Analysis and Parsing.

The *infinitive phrase* may be used as an *adjective modifier* or an *adverb modifier*.

1. The hot-house is a trap to catch sunbeams.

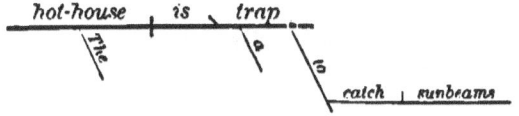

Oral Analysis.—*To* introduces the phrase; *catch* is the principal word, and *sunbeams* completes it.

Parsing.—*To* is a preposition, introducing the phrase and showing the relation, in sense, of the principal word to *trap*; *catch* is a form of the verb called *infinitive*; like a noun, it follows the preposition *to* and names the action, and, like a verb, it is completed by *sunbeams*.

2. Richelieu's title to command rested on sublime force of will and decision of character.

3. Many of the attempts to assassinate William the Silent were defeated.

4. We will strive to please you.

Explanation.—The infinitive phrase is here used adverbially to modify the predicate.

5. Ingenious Art steps forth to fashion and refine the race.
6. These harmless delusions tend to make us happy.

Explanation.—*Happy* completes *make* and relates to *us*.

7. Wounds made by words are hard to heal.

Explanation.—The infinitive phrase is here used adverbially to modify the adjective *hard*. *To heal=to be healed.*

8. The representative Yankee, selling his farm, wanders away to seek new lands, to clear new cornfields, to build another shingle palace, and again to sell off and wander.

9. These apples are not ripe enough to eat.

Explanation.—The infinitive phrase is here used adverbially to modify the adverb *enough*. *To eat=to be eaten.*

The *infinitive phrase* may be used as *subject* or *complement*.

10. To be good is to be great.

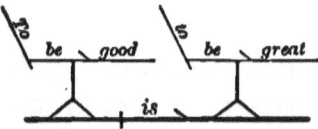

Explanation.—*To*, in each of these phrases, shows no relation—it serves merely to introduce. The complements *good* and *great* are adjectives used abstractly, having no noun to relate to.

11. To bear our fate is to conquer it.
12. To be entirely just in our estimate of others is impossible.
13. The noblest vengeance is to forgive.
14. He seemed to be innocent.

Explanation.—The infinitive phrase here performs the office of an adjective. *To be innocent=innocent.*

15. The blind men's dogs appeared to know him.
16. We should learn to govern ourselves.

Explanation.—The infinitive phrase is here used as an object complement.

17. Each hill attempts to ape her voice.

LESSON 41.

INFINITIVES—CONTINUED.

ANALYSIS.

The *infinitive phrase* may be used *after a preposition* as the *principal term* of another phrase.

1. My friend is about to leave me.

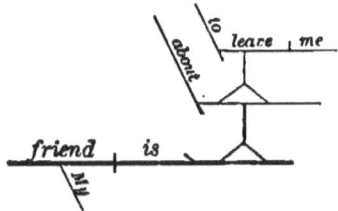

Explanation.—The preposition *about* introduces the phrase used as attribute complement; the principal part is the infinitive phrase *to leave me*.

2. Paul was now about to open his mouth.
3. No way remains but to go on.

Explanation.—*But* is here used as a preposition.

The *infinitive* and its *assumed subject* may form the *principal term* in a phrase introduced by the preposition *for*.

4. For us to know our faults is profitable.

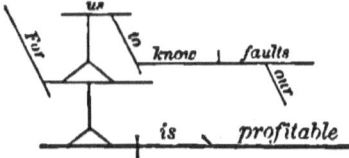

Explanation.—*For* introduces the subject phrase; the principal part of the entire phrase is *us to know our faults;* the principal word is *us*, which is modified by the phrase *to know our faults*.

5. God never made his work for man to mend.

Explanation.—The principal term of the phrase *for man to mend* is not *man*, but *man to mend*.

6. For a man to be proud of his learning is the greatest ignorance.

The *infinitive phrase* may be used as an *explanatory modifier*.

7. It is easy to find fault.

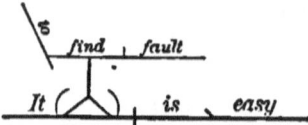

Explanation.—The infinitive phrase *to find fault* explains the subject *it*. Read the sentence without *it*, and you will see the real nature of the phrase. This use of *it* as a substitute for the real subject is a very common idiom of our language. It allows the real subject to follow the verb, and thus gives the sentence balance of parts.

8. It is not the way to argue down a vice to tell lies about it.
9. It is natural to man to indulge in the illusions of hope.
10. It is not all of life to live.
11. This task, to teach the young, may become delightful.

The *infinitive phrase* may be used as *objective complement*.

12. He made me wait.

Explanation.—The infinitive *wait* (here used without *to*) completes *made* and relates to *me*. *He made-wait me = He detained me.*

See "Introductory Hints," Lesson 31, and participles used as objective complements, Lesson 37. Compare *I saw him do it* with *I saw him doing it*. Compare also *He made the stick bend*—equaling *He made-bend (= bent) the stick*—with *He made the stick straight*—equaling *He made-straight (= straightened) the stick.*

The relation of these objective complements to *me*, *him*, and *stick* may be more clearly seen by changing the form of the verb, thus: I was made *to wait*, He was seen *to do it*, He was seen *doing it*, The stick was made *to bend*, The stick was made *straight.*

13. We found the report to be true.*

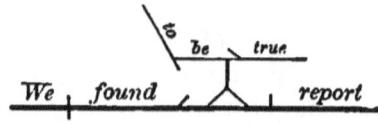

---

* Some prefer to treat *the report to be true* as an object *clause*, because it is equivalent to the clause *that the report is true*. But many expressions logically equivalent are entirely different in grammatical construction.

If, in "I desire him to be promoted," *him to be promoted* is a clause because equiv-

Infinitives—Continued. 83

14. He commanded the bridge to be lowered.*
15. I saw the leaves stir.

Explanation.—*Stir* is an infinitive without the *to.*

16. Being persuaded by Poppæa, Nero caused his mother, Agrippina, to be assassinated.

LESSON 42.

INFINITIVES—CONTINUED.

ANALYSIS.

The *infinitive phrase* may be used *independently*.†

Explanation.—In the diagram, the independent element must stand by itself.

1. England's debt, to put it in round numbers, is $4,000,000,000.
2. Every object has several faces, so to speak.
3. To make a long story short, Louis XVI. and Marie Antoinette were executed.

---

alent to *that he should be promoted,* why is not *his promotion* a clause in "I desire his promotion"?

"I saw *the sun rising.*" "I saw the *rising of the sun.*" If we must call *sun rising* a clause, why not call *the rising of the sun* a clause? In both expressions *sun* names the actor and *rising* denotes the act.

Besides, when the pupil has learned that *he* is a subject form and *him* an object form, and that participles and infinitives lack the asserting element, necessary to a true predicate, we prefer not to confuse him by calling *him* the *subject* and *to be promoted* the *predicate* of a *clause.*

* Notice the difference, in construction, between this sentence and the sentence *He commanded him to lower the bridge. Him* represents the one *to whom* the command is given, and *to lower the bridge* is the object complement. This last sentence = He commanded *him that he should lower the bridge.* Compare *He told me to go* with *He told (to) me a story;* also *He taught me to read* with *He taught (to) me reading.*

† These infinitive phrases can be expanded into dependent clauses. See Lesson 79.
For the infinitive after *as, than,* etc., see Lesson 63. Participles and infinitives unite with other verbs to make compound forms; as, have *walked,* shall *(to) walk.*

Infinitives and Participles.
MISCELLANEOUS.

4. It is a good thing to give thanks unto the Lord.
5. We require clothing in the summer to protect the body from the heat of the sun.
6. Rip Van Winkle could not account for everything's having changed so.
7. This sentence is not too difficult for me to analyze.
8. The fog came pouring in at every chink and keyhole.
9. Conscience, her first law broken, wounded lies.
10. To be, or not to be,—that is the question.
11. I supposed him to be a gentleman.
12. Food, keeping the body in health by making it warm and repairing its waste, is a necessity.
13. I will teach you the trick to prevent your being cheated another time.
14. She threatened to go beyond the sea, to throw herself out of the window, to drown herself.
15. Busied with public affairs, the council would sit for hours smoking and watching the smoke curl from their pipes to the ceiling.

LESSON 43.
COMPOSITION—THE INFINITIVE.

Direction.—*Change the infinitives in these sentences into participles, and the participles into infinitives :—*

Notice that *to*, the only preposition used with the infinitive, is changed to *toward, for, of, at, in,* or *on,* when the infinitive is changed to a participle.

1. I am inclined to believe it.
2. I am ashamed to be seen there.
3. She will be grieved to hear it.
4. They trembled to hear such words.
5. It will serve for amusing the children.
6. There is a time to laugh.
7. I rejoice to hear it.
8. You are prompt to obey.
9. They delight to do it.
10. I am surprised at seeing you.
11. Stones are used in ballasting vessels.

Words and Phrases Used Independently.

Direction.—*Improve these sentences by changing the participles into infinitives, and the infinitives into participles:*—

1. We began ascending the mountain.
2. He did not recollect to have paid it.
3. I commenced to write a letter.
4. It is inconvenient being poor.
5. It is not wise complaining.

Direction.—*Vary these sentences as in the model:*—

Model.—*Rising* early is healthful, *To rise* early is healthful, *It* is healthful *to rise* early, *For one to rise* early is healthful.
(Notice that the explanatory phrase after *it* is not set off by the comma.)

1. Reading good books is profitable.
2. Equivocating is disgraceful.
3. Slandering is base.
4. Indorsing another's paper is dangerous.
5. Swearing is sinful.

Direction.—*Write nine sentences, in three of which the infinitive shall be used as an adjective, in three as an adverb, and in three as a noun.*

Direction.—*Write eight sentences in which these verbs shall be followed by an infinitive without to:*—

Model.—We *saw* the sun *sink* behind the mountain.

Bid, dare, feel, hear, let, make, need, and see.

LESSON 44.

WORDS AND PHRASES USED INDEPENDENTLY.

Introductory Hints.—In this Lesson we wish to notice words and phrases that in certain uses have no grammatical connection with the rest of the sentence.

The fault, dear Brutus, is not in our stars. *Dear Brutus* serves only to arrest attention, and is independent by *address*.

Poor man! he never came back again. *Poor man* is independent by *exclamation*.

Thy rod and thy staff, they comfort me. *Rod* and *staff* simply call attention to the objects before anything is said of them, and are independent by *pleonasm*—a construction used sometimes for rhetorical effect, but out of place and improper in ordinary speech.

His master being absent, the business was neglected. *His master being absent* logically modifies the verb *was neglected* by assigning the cause, but the phrase has no connective expressed or understood, and so is *grammatically* independent. This is called the *absolute phrase*.

His conduct, generally speaking, was honorable. *Speaking* is a participle without connection, and with the adverb *generally* forms an independent phrase.

To confess the truth, I was wrong. The infinitive phrase is independent.

The adverbs, *well, now, why, there* are sometimes independent, as; *Well,* life is an enigma; *Now,* that is strange; *Why,* it is already noon; *There* are pitch-pine Yankees and white-pine Yankees.

Interjections are without grammatical connection, as you have learned, and so are independent.

Whatever is enclosed within marks of parenthesis is also independent of the rest of the sentence; as, I stake my fame (*and I had fame*), my heart, my hope, my soul, upon this cast.

Analysis and Parsing.

1. The loveliest things in life, Tom, are but shadows.

Explanation.—*Tom* is independent by address, and in the diagram must stand by itself. *But* is used as an adjective modifying *shadows*.

2. There are one story intellects, two story intellects, and three story intellects with sky-lights.

Explanation.—Often, as here, *there* is used idiomatically, merely to throw the subject after the verb, the idea of place having faded out of it. To express place another *there* may follow the predicate; as, *There is gold there.*

3. Ah! then and there was hurrying to and fro.
4. Hope lost, all is lost.
5. The smith, a mighty man is he.
6. Why, this is not revenge.
7. Well, this is the forest of Arden.
8. Now, there is at Jerusalem, by the sheep-market, a pool.
9. To speak plainly, your habits are your worst enemies.
10. No accident occurring, we shall arrive to-morrow.
11. The teacher being sick, there was no school Friday.
12. Mr. President, I shall enter on no encomium upon Massachusetts.
13. Properly speaking, there can be no chance in our affairs.
14. But the enemies of tyranny—their path leads to the scaffold.

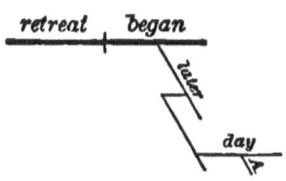

15. She (oh, the artfulness of the woman !) managed the matter extremely well.

16. A day later (Oct. 19, 1812) began the fatal retreat of the Grand Army, from Moscow.

See Lesson 35.

LESSON 45.

COMPOSITION—INDEPENDENT WORDS AND PHRASES.

COMMA—RULE.—Words and phrases independent or nearly so are set off by the comma.

Remark.—Interjections, as you have seen, are usually followed by the *exclamation point;* and *there,* used merely to introduce, is never set off by the comma. When the break after pleonastic expressions is slight, as in (5), Lesson 44, the comma is used; but if it is more abrupt, as in (14), the dash is required. If the independent expression can be omitted without affecting the sense, it may be enclosed within marks of parenthesis, as in (15) and (16). (For the uses of the dash and the marks of parenthesis, see Lesson 148.)

Words and phrases *nearly* independent are those which like *however, of course, indeed, in short, by the bye, for instance,* and *accordingly* do not modify any word or phrase alone, but rather the sentence as a whole; as, *Lee did not, however, follow Washington's orders.*

Direction.—*Write sentences illustrating the several kinds of independent expressions, and punctuate according to the Rule as explained.*

Direction.—*Write short sentences in which these words and phrases, used in a manner n e a r l y independent, shall occur, and punctuate them properly:*—

In short, indeed, now and then, for instance, accordingly, moreover, however, at least, in general, no doubt, by the bye, by the way, then, too, of course, in fine, namely, above all, therefore.

Direction.—*Write short sentences in which these words shall modify some particular word or phrase so closely as not to be set off by the comma:*—

Indeed, surely, too, then, now, further, why, again, still.

LESSON 46.

SENTENCES CLASSIFIED WITH RESPECT TO MEANING.

Introductory Hints.—In the previous Lessons we have considered the sentence with respect to the words and phrases composing it. Let us now look at it as a whole.

The mountains lift up their heads. This sentence simply affirms or declares a fact, and is called a **Declarative Sentence.**

Do the mountains lift up their heads? This sentence asks a question, and is called an **Interrogative Sentence.**

Lift up your heads. This sentence expresses a command, and is called an **Imperative Sentence.** Such expressions as *You must go, You shall go* are equivalent to imperative sentences, though they have not the imperative form.

How the mountains lift up their heads! In this sentence the thought is expressed with strong emotion. It is called an **Exclamatory Sentence.** *How* and *what* usually introduce such sentences; but a declarative, an interrogative, or an imperative sentence may become exclamatory when the speaker uses it mainly to give vent to his feelings; as, *It is impossible! How can I endure it! Talk of hypocrisy after this!*

DEFINITION.—A *Declarative Sentence* is one that affirms or denies.

DEFINITION.—An *Interrogative Sentence* is one that expresses a question.

DEFINITION.—An *Imperative Sentence* is one that expresses a command or an entreaty.

DEFINITION.—An *Exclamatory Sentence* is one that expresses sudden thought or strong feeling.

INTERROGATION POINT—RULE.—Every direct interrogative sentence should be followed by an interrogation point.

Analysis and Parsing.

Direction.—*Before analyzing these sentences classify them, and justify the terminal marks of punctuation:—*

1. There are no accidents in the providence of God.
2. Why does the very murderer, his victim sleeping before him, and his glaring eye taking the measure of the blow, strike wide of the mortal part?
3. Suffer not yourselves to be betrayed with a kiss.
    (The subject is *you* understood.)

4. How wonderful is the advent of spring!
5. Oh! a dainty plant is the ivy green!
6. Six days shalt thou labor and do all thy work.
7. Alexander the Great died at Babylon in the thirty-third year of his age.
8. How sickness enlarges the dimensions of a man's self to himself!
9. Thou shalt not take the name of the Lord thy God in vain.
10. Lend me your ears.
11. What brilliant rings the planet Saturn has!
12. What power shall blanch the sullied snow of character?
13. The laws of nature are the thoughts of God.
14. How beautiful was the snow, falling all day long, all night long, on the roofs of the living, on the graves of the dead!
15. Who, in the darkest days of our Revolution, carried your flag into the very chops of the British Channel, bearded the lion in his den, and woke the echoes of old Albion's hills by the thunders of his cannon and the shouts of his triumph?

LESSON 47.

MISCELLANEOUS EXERCISES IN REVIEW.

ANALYSIS AND PARSING.

1. Poetry is only the eloquence and enthusiasm of religion.—*Wordsworth.*

Explanation.—*Only*, usually an adverb, here modifies *eloquence* and *enthusiasm*.

2. Refusing to bare his head to any earthly potentate, Richelieu would permit no eminent author to stand bareheaded in his presence.—*Stephen.*

3. The Queen of England is simply a piece of historic heraldry; a flag, floating grandly over a Liberal ministry yesterday, over a Tory ministry to-day.—*Conway.*

4. The vulgar intellectual palate hankers after the titillation of foaming phrase.—*Lowell.*

5. Two mighty vortices, Pericles and Alexander the Great, drew into strong eddies about themselves all the glory and the pomp of Greek literature, Greek eloquence, Greek wisdom, Greek art.—*De Quincey.*

6. Reason's whole pleasure, all the joys of sense lie in three words—health, peace, and competence.—*Pope.*

7. Extreme admiration puts out the critic's eye.—*Tyler.*

8. The setting of a great hope is like the setting of the sun.—*Longfellow.*

9. Things mean, the Thistle, the Leek, the Broom of the Plantagenets, become noble by association.—*F. W. Robertson.*

10. Prayer is the key of the morning and the bolt of the night.—*Beecher.*

11. In that calm Syrian afternoon, memory, a pensive Ruth, went gleaning the silent fields of childhood, and found the scattered grain still golden, and the morning sunlight fresh and fair.—*Curtis.*

LESSON 48.

MISCELLANEOUS EXERCISES IN REVIEW.

ANALYSIS AND PARSING.

1. By means of steam man realizes the fable of Æolus's bag, and carries the two-and-thirty winds in the boiler of his boat.—*Emerson.*

2. The Angel of Life winds our brains up once for all, then closes the case, and gives the key into the hands of the Angel of Resurrection.—*Holmes.*

3. I called the New World into existence to redress the balance of the Old.—*Canning.*

4. The prominent nose of the New Englander is evidence of the constant linguistic exercise of that organ.—*Warner.*

5. Every Latin word has its function as noun or verb or adverb ticketed upon it.—*Earle.*

6. The Alps, piled in cold and still sublimity, are an image of despotism.—*Phillips.*

7. I want my husband to be submissive without looking so.—*Gail Hamilton.*

8. I love to lose myself in other men's minds.—*Lamb.*

9. Cheerfulness banishes all anxious care and discontent, soothes and composes the passions, and keeps the soul in a perpetual calm.—*Addison.*

10. To discover the true nature of comets has hitherto proved beyond the power of science.—*Brown's Gram.*

Explanation.—*Beyond the power of science=impossible,* and so is an attribute complement. The preposition *beyond* shows the relation, in sense, of *power* to the subject phrase.

11. Authors must not, like Chinese soldiers, expect to win victories by turning somersets in the air.—*Longfellow.*

LESSON 49.

REVIEW OF PUNCTUATION.

Direction.—*Give the reason, as far as you have been taught, for the marks of punctuation used in Lessons 44, 46, 47, and 48.*

LESSON 50.

REVIEW.

To the Teacher.—See suggestions, Lesson 16.

Direction.—*Review from Lesson 37 to Lesson 46 inclusive :—*

Give, in some such way as we have outlined in preceding Review Lessons, the substance of the "Introductory Hints;" memorize and illustrate definitions and rules; illustrate the different uses of the participle and the infinitive, and the Caution regarding the use of the participle; illustrate the different ways in which words and phrases may be grammatically independent, and the punctuation of these independent elements.

LESSON 51.
ARRANGEMENT—NATURAL ORDER.

To the Teacher.—If, from lack of time or from the necessity of conforming to a prescribed course of study, it is found desirable to abridge these Lessons on Arrangement and Contraction, the exercises to be written may be omitted, the pupil may be required to name and illustrate the positions of the different parts, in both the Natural and the Transposed order, and then to read the examples given, making the required changes orally.

The eight following Lessons may thus be reduced to two.

Let us recall the *Natural Order* of words and phrases in a simple declarative sentence.

The verb follows the subject, and the object complement follows the verb.

Example.—*Drake circumnavigated* the *globe.*

Direction.—*Observing this order, write three sentences each with an object complement.*

An adjective or a possessive modifier precedes its noun, and an explanatory modifier follows it.

Examples.—*Man's life* is *a brief span. Moses, the lawgiver,* came down from the Mount.

Direction.—*Observing this order, write four sentences, two with possessive modifiers and two with explanatory, each sentence containing an adjective.*

The attribute complement, whether noun or adjective, follows the verb, the objective complement follows the object complement, and the so-called indirect object precedes the direct.

Examples.—Egypt *is the valley* of the Nile. Eastern life *is dreamy.* They made *Bonaparte consul.* They offered *Cæsar a crown.*

Direction.—*Observing this order, write four sentences illustrating the positions of the noun and the adjective when they perform these offices.*

If adjectives are of unequal rank, the one most closely modifying the noun stands nearest to it; if of the same rank, they stand in the order of their length—the shortest first.

Examples.—*Two honest young* men enlisted. Cassius has a *lean* and *hungry* look. A rock, *huge* and *precipitous*, stood in our path.

Direction.—*Observing this order, write three sentences illustrating the relative position of adjectives before and after the noun.*

An adverb precedes the adjective, adverb, or phrase which it modifies; precedes or follows (more frequently follows) the simple verb or the verb with its complement; and follows one or more words of the verb if the verb is compound.

Examples.—The light *far in the distance* is *so very bright.* I *soon* found him. I hurt him *badly.* He *had often been* there.

Direction.—*Observing this order, write sentences illustrating these several positions of the adverb.*

Phrases follow the words they modify; if a word has two or more phrases, those most closely modifying it stand nearest to it.

Examples.—*Facts once established* are facts forever. He *sailed for Liverpool on Monday.*

Direction.—*Observing this order, write sentences illustrating the positions of participle and prepositional phrases.*

LESSON 52.

ARRANGEMENT—TRANSPOSED ORDER.

Introductory Hints.—The common and natural order, spoken of in the preceding Lesson, is not the only order admissible in an English sentence; on the contrary, great freedom in the placing of words and phrases is sometimes allowable. Let the *relation of the words be kept obvious* and, consequently, the *thought clear,* and in poetry, in impassioned oratory, in excited speech of any kind, one may deviate widely from this order.

Arrangement—Transposed Order. 95

One's meaning is never distributed evenly among his words; more of it lies in some words than in others. Under the influence of strong feeling, one may use words out of their accustomed place, and, by thus attracting attention to them, give them additional importance to the reader or hearer.

When any word or phrase in the predicate stands out of its usual place, appearing either at the front of the sentence or at the rear, we have what we may call the **Transposed Order**. *I dare not venture to go down into the cabin—Venture to go down into the cabin I dare not. You shall die—Die you shall. Their names will forever live on the lips of the people—Their names will, on the lips of the people, forever live.*

When the word or phrase moved to the front carries the verb, or the principal word of it, before the subject, we have the *extreme* example of the transposed order; as, *A yeoman had he. Strange is the magic of a turban.* The whole of a verb is not placed at the beginning of a declarative sentence except in poetry; as, *Flashed all their sabres bare.*

To the Teacher.—Where, in our directions in these Lessons on Arrangement and Contraction, we say *change, transpose,* or *restore,* the pupils need not write the sentences. They should study them and be able to *read* them. Require them to show what the sentence has lost or gained in the change.

Direction.—*Change these sentences from the natural to the transposed order by moving words or phrases to the front, and explain the effect:—*

1. He could not avoid it.
2. They were pretty lads.
3. The great Queen died in the year 1603.
4. He would not escape.
5. I must go.
6. She seemed young and sad.
7. He cried, "My son, my son!"
8. He ended his tale here.
9. The moon shone bright.
10. A frozen continent lies beyond the sea.
11. He was a contentious man.
12. It stands written so.
13. Monmouth had never been accused of cowardice.

Direction.—*Change these sentences from the transposed order to the natural, and explain the effect:—*

1. Him the Almighty Power hurled headlong.
2. Volatile he was.
3. Victories, indeed, they were.
4. Of noble race the lady came.
5. Slowly and sadly we laid him down.
6. Once again we'll sleep secure.
7. This double office the participle performs.

8. That gale I well remember.
9. Churlish he often seemed.
10. One strong thing I find here below.
11. Overhead I heard a murmur.
12. To their will we must succumb.
13. Him they hanged.
14. Freely ye have received.

Direction.— *Write five sentences, each with one of the following nouns or adjectives as a complement; and five, each with one of the adverbs or phrases as predicate modifier; then transpose the ten with these same words moved to the front, and explain the effect :—*

Giant, character, happy, him, serene, often, in the market, long and deeply, then, under foot.

Direction.—*Transpose these sentences by placing the italicized words last, and note the effect :—*

1. The clouds lowering upon our house are *buried* in the deep bosom of the ocean.
2. Æneas did *bear* from the flames of Troy upon his shoulder the old Anchises.
3. Such a heart *beats* in the breast of my people.
4. The great fire *roared* up the deep and wide chimney.

Direction.—*Change these to the natural order :—*

1. No woman was ever in this wild humor wooed and won.
2. Let a shroud, stripped from some privileged corpse, be, for its proper price, displayed.
3. An old clock, early one summer's morning, before the stirring of the family, suddenly stopped.
4. Treasures of gold and of silver are, in the deep bosom of the earth, concealed.
5. Ease and grace in writing are, of all the acquisitions made in school, the most difficult and valuable.

Direction.—*Write three sentences, each with the following noun or adjective or phrase in its natural place in the predicate, and then transpose, placing these words wherever they can properly go :—*

Mountains, glad, by and by.

LESSON 53.

ARRANGEMENT—TRANSPOSED ORDER.

Direction.—*Restore these sentences to their natural order by moving the object complement and the verb to their usual places, and tell what is lost by the change :—*

1. Thorns and thistles shall the earth bring forth.
2. "Exactly so," replied the pendulum.
3. Me restored he to mine office.
4. A changed France have we.
5. These evils hath sin wrought.

Direction.—*Transpose these sentences by moving the object complement and the verb, and tell what is gained by the change :—*

1. The dial-plate exclaimed, "Lazy wire!"
2. The maiden has such charms.
3. The English character has faults and plenty of them.
4. I will make one effort more to save you.
5. The king does possess great power.
6. You have learned much in this short journey.

Direction.—*Write six transposed sentences with these nouns as object complements, and then restore them to their natural order :—*

Pause, cry, peace, horse, words, gift.

Direction.—*Restore these sentences to their natural order by moving the attribute complement and verb to their usual places, and tell what is lost by the change :—*

1. A dainty plant is the ivy green.
2. Feet was I to the lame.
3. A mighty man is he.
4. As a mark of respect was the present given.
5. A giant towered he among men.

Direction.—*Transpose these sentences by moving the attribute complement and the verb, and tell what is gained by the change :—*

1. We are merry brides.

2. Washington is styled the "Father of his Country."
3. He was a stark mosstrooping Scot.
4. The man seemed an incarnate demon.
5. Henry VIII. had become a despot.

Direction.—*Using these nouns as attribute complements, write three sentences in the natural order, and then transpose them :—*

Rock, desert, fortress.

Direction.—*Restore these sentences to their natural order by moving the adjective complement and verb to their usual places :—*

1. Happy are we to-night, boys.
2. Good and upright is the Lord.
3. Hotter grew the air.
4. Pale looks your Grace.
5. Dark rolled the waves.
6. Louder waxed the applause.
7. Blood-red became the sun.
8. Doubtful seemed the battle.
9. Wise are all his ways.
10. Wide open stood the doors.
11. Weary had he grown.
12. Faithful proved he to the last.

Direction.—*Transpose these sentences by moving the adjective complement and the verb :—*

1. My regrets were bitter and unavailing.
2. The anger of the righteous is weighty.
3. The air seemed deep and dark.
4. She had grown tall and queenly.
5. The peacemakers are blessed.
6. I came into the world helpless.
7. The untrodden snow lay bloodless.
8. The fall of that house was great.
9. The uproar became intolerable.
10. The secretary stood alone.

Direction.—*Write five transposed sentences, each with one of these adjectives as attribute complement, and then restore them to the natural order :—*

Tempestuous, huge, glorious, lively, fierce.

LESSON 54.

ARRANGEMENT—TRANSPOSED ORDER.

Direction.—*Restore these sentences to the natural order by moving the adverb and verb to their usual places, and note the loss:—*

1. Then burst his mighty heart.
2. Here stands the man.
3. Crack! went the ropes.
4. Down came the masts.
5. So died the great Columbus of the skies.
6. Tictac! tictac! go the wheels of thought.
7. Away went Gilpin.
8. Off went his bonnet.
9. Well have ye judged.
10. On swept the lines.
11. There dozed the donkeys.
12. Boom! boom! went the guns.
13. Thus waned the afternoon.
14. There thunders the cataract age after age.

Direction.—*Transpose these sentences by moving the adverb and the verb:—*

1. I will never desert Mr. Micawber.
2. The great event occurred soon after.
3. The boy stood there with dizzy brain.
4. The Spaniard's shot went whing! whing!
5. Catiline shall no longer plot her ruin.
6. A sincere word was never utterly lost.
7. It stands written so.
8. Venus was yet the morning star.
9. You must speak thus.
10. Lady Impudence goes up to the maid.
11. Thy proud waves shall be stayed here.

Direction.—*Write ten sentences in the transposed order, using these adverbs:—*

Still, here, now, so, seldom, there, out, yet, thus, never.

Direction.—*Restore these sentences to the natural order by moving the phrase and the verb to their usual places, and note the loss:—*

1. Behind her rode Lalla Rookh.
2. Seven years after the Restoration appeared Paradise Lost.
3. Into the valley of death rode the six hundred.
4. To such straits is a kaiser driven.

5. Upon such a grating hinge opened the door of his daily life.
6. In purple was she robed.
7. Between them lay a mountain ridge.
8. Near the surface are found the implements of bronze.
9. Through the narrow bazaar pressed the demure donkeys.
10. In those days came John the Baptist.
11. On the 17th of June, 1775, was fought the Battle of Bunker Hill.
12. Three times were the Romans driven back.

Direction.—*Transpose these sentences by moving the phrase and the vb :*—

1. The disciples came at the same time.
2. The dreamy murmur of insects was heard over our heads.
3. An ancient and stately hall stood near the village.
4. His trusty sword lay by his side.
5. Pepin eventually succeeded to Charles Martel.
6. The house stands somewhat back from the street.
7. Our sphere turns on its axis.
8. The bridle is red with the sign of despair.
9. I have served in twenty campaigns.
10. Touch proper lies in the finger-tips and in the lips.

Direction.—*Write ten sentences in the natural order, using these prepositions to introduce phrases, and then transpose them, and compare the two orders :*—

Beyond, upon, toward, of, by, into, between, in, at, to.

Direction.—*Write six sentences in the transposed order, beginning them with these words :*—

There (independent), nor, neither.

LESSON 55.

ARRANGEMENT—INTERROGATIVE SENTENCES.

If the interrogative word is subject or a modifier of it, the order is natural.

Examples.— *Who came* last evening ? *What star* shines brightest ?

Direction.— *Write five interrogative sentences, using the first word below as a subject; the second as a subject and then as a modifier of the subject; the third as a subject and then as a modifier of the subject :—*
Who, which, what.

If the interrogative word is object or attribute complement or a modifier of either, the order is transposed.

Examples.— *Whom did you* see ? *What are* personal *consequences?* *Which course will you* choose ?

Direction.— *Write an interrogative sentence with the first word below as object complement, and another with the second word as attribute complement. Write four with the third and the fourth as complements, and four with the third and the fourth as modifiers of the complement :—*
Whom, who, which, what.

If the interrogative word is an adverb, the order is transposed.

Examples.— *Why is the forum* crowded ? *Where are the flowers*, the fair young flowers ?

Direction.— *Write five interrogative sentences, using these adverbs :—*
How, when, where, whither, why.

If there is no interrogative word, the subject stands after the verb when this is simple ; after the first word of it when it is compound.

Examples.—Have you your lesson ? *Has the gentleman* finished ?

Direction.—*Write six interrogative sentences, using these verbs :—*
Is, has, can learn, might have gone, could have been found, must see.

Direction.—*Change the sentences you have written in this Lesson into declarative sentences.*

LESSON 56.

ARRANGEMENT—IMPERATIVE AND EXCLAMATORY SENTENCES.

The subject is usually omitted in the imperative sentence; but, when it is expressed, the sentence is in the transposed order.

Examples.—*Praise* ye the Lord. *Give* (*thou*) me three grains of corn.

Direction.—*Using these verbs, write ten sentences, in five of which the subject shall be omitted; and in five, expressed:—*

Remember, listen, lend, love, live, choose, use, obey, strive, devote.

Although any sentence may without change of order become exclamatory (Lesson 46), yet exclamatory sentences ordinarily begin with *how* or *what,* and are usually in the transposed order.

Examples.—*How quietly* the child sleeps! *How excellent* is thy loving kindness! *What visions* have I seen! *What a life* his was!

Direction.—*Write six exclamatory sentences with the word* how *modifying (1) an adjective, (2) a verb, and (3) an adverb—in three sentences let the verb follow, and in three precede, the subject. Write four sentences with the word* what *modifying (1) an object complement and (2) an attribute complement—in two sentences let the verb follow, and in two precede, the subject.*

LESSON 57.

CONTRACTION OF SENTENCES.

Direction.—*Contract these sentences by omitting the repeated modifiers and prepositions, and all the conjunctions except the last:—*

1. Webster was a great lawyer, a great statesman, a great debater, and a great writer.

2. By their valor, by their policy, and by their matrimonial alliances, they became powerful.

3. Saml. Adams's habits were simple and frugal and unostentatious.
4. Flowers are so fragile, so delicate, and so ornamental!
5. They are truly prosperous and truly happy.
6. The means used were persuasions and petitions and remonstrances and resolutions and defiance.
7. Carthage was the mistress of oceans, of kingdoms, and of nations.

Direction.—*Expand these by repeating the adjective, the adverb, the preposition, and the conjunction :—*

1. He was a good son, father, brother, friend.
2. The tourist traveled in Spain, Greece, Egypt, and Palestine.
3. Bayard was very brave, truthful, and chivalrous.
4. Honor, revenge, shame, and contempt inflamed his heart.

Direction.—*Write eight sentences, each with one of these words used four times; and then contract them, as above, and note the effect of the repetition and omission :—*

Poor, colossal, how, thus, with, through, or, and.

Direction.—*Expand these sentences by supplying subjects :—*

1. Give us this day our daily bread.
2. Why dost stare so?
3. Thank you, sir.
4. Hear me for my cause.
5. Where hast been these six months?
6. Bless me!
7. Save us.

Direction.—*Expand these by supplying the verb or some part of it :—*

1. Nobody there.
2. Death to the tyrant.
3. All aboard!
4. All hands to the pumps!
5. What to me fame?
6. Short, indeed, his career.
7. When Adam thus to Eve.
8. I must after him.
9. Thou shalt back to France.
10. Whose footsteps these?

Direction.—*Expand these by supplying both subject and verb, and note the loss in vivacity :—*

1. Upon them with the lance.
2. At your service, sir.
3. Why so unkind?
4. Forward, the light brigade!
5. Half-past nine.
6. Off with you.
7. My kingdom for a horse!
8. Hence, you idle creatures!
9. Coffee for two.
10. Shine, sir?

11. Back to thy punishment, false fugitive.
12. On with the dance.
13. Strange, strange!
14. Once more unto the breach.
15. Away, away!
16. Impossible!

Direction.—*Contract these by omitting the subject or the verb:*—

1. Art thou gone?
2. Will you take your chance?
3. His career was ably run.
4. Are you a captain?
5. May long life be to the republic.
6. How great is the mystery!
7. Canst thou wonder?
8. May a prosperous voyage be to you.
9. Are you here?

Direction.—*Contract these by omitting both subject and verb, and note the gain in force and animation:*—

1. I offer a world for sale.
2. Now, then, go you to breakfast.
3. Sit you down, soothless insulter.
4. I want a word with you, wife.
5. Those are my sentiments, madam.
6. Bring ye lights there.
7. It is true, sir.
8. We will drink a health to Preciosa.
9. I offer a penny for your thoughts.
10. Whither are you going so early?

Direction.—*Construct ten full sentences, using, in each, one of these adverbs or phrases or nouns, and then contract them by omitting both subject and verb:*—

Why, hence, to arms, silence, out, to your tents, peaches, room, for the guns, water.

LESSON 58.
REVIEW.

To the Teacher.—See suggestions, Lesson 16.

Direction.—*Review from Lesson 51 to Lesson 57, inclusive.*

Illustrate the different positions—Natural and Transposed—that the words and phrases of a declarative sentence may take; illustrate the different positions of the parts of an interrogative, an imperative, and an exclamatory sentence; illustrate the different ways of contracting sentences.

LESSON 59.

COMPLEX SENTENCE—ADJECTIVE CLAUSE.

Introductory Hints.—*A discreet youth makes friends.* In Lesson 17 you learned that you could expand the adjective *discreet* into a phrase, and say, A youth *of discretion* makes friends. You are now to learn that you can expand it into an expression that asserts, and say, A youth *that is discreet* makes friends. This part of the sentence and the other, *A youth makes friends*, containing each a subject and a predicate, we call **Clauses**.

The adjective clause *that is discreet*, performing the office of a single word, we call a **Dependent Clause**, and *A youth makes friends*, not performing such office, we call an **Independent Clause**.

The whole sentence, composed of an independent and a dependent clause, we call a **Complex Sentence**.

Analysis and Parsing.

1. They that touch pitch will be defiled.

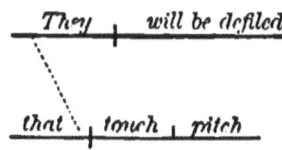

Explanation.—The relative importance of the two clauses is shown by their position, by their connection, and by the difference in the shading of the lines. The pronoun *that* is written on the subject line of the dependent clause. *That* performs the office of a conjunction also. This office is shown by the dotted line. As modifiers are joined by slanting lines to the words they modify, you learn from this diagram that *that touch pitch* is a modifier of *they*.

Oral Analysis.—This is a complex sentence, because it consists of an independent clause and a dependent clause. *They will be defiled* is the independent clause, and *that touch pitch* is the dependent. *That touch pitch* is a modifier of *they*, because it limits its meaning; the dependent clause is connected by its subject *that* to *they*.

To the Teacher.—Illustrate the connecting force of *who*, *which*, and *that* by substituting for them the words for which they stand, and noting the loss of connection.

2. The lever which moves the world of mind is the printing-press.

3. Wine makes the face of him who drinks it to excess blush for his habits.

Explanation.—The adjective clause does not always modify the subject.

4. Photography is the art which enables common-place mediocrity to look like genius.

5. In 1685, Louis XIV. signed the ordinance that revoked the Edict of Nantes.

6. The thirteen colonies were welded together by the measures which Samuel Adams framed.

Explanation.—The pronoun connecting an adjective clause is not always a subject.

7. The guilt of the slave-trade, which sprang out of the traffic with Guinea, rests with John Hawkins.

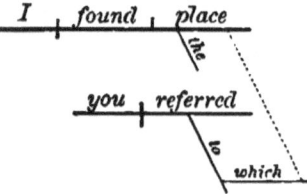

8. I found the place to which you referred.

9. The spirit in which we act is the highest matter.

10. It was the same book that I referred to.

Explanation.—The phrase *to that* modifies *referred*. *That* connects the adjective clause. When the pronoun *that* connects an adjective clause, the preposition never precedes. The diagram is similar to that of (8).

11. She that I spoke to was blind.

12. Grouchy did not arrive at the time that Napoleon most needed him.

Explanation.—A preposition is wanting. *That* = *in which*.

13. Attention is the stuff that memory is made of.

Adjective Clauses—Continued.

14. It is to you that I speak.

Explanation.—Here the preposition, which naturally would stand last in the sentence, is found before the complement of the independent clause. In analysis restore the preposition to its natural place—It is you that I speak *to*. *That I speak to* modifies the subject.

15. It was from me that he received the information.

(*Me* must be changed to *I* when *from* is restored to its natural position.)

16. Islands are the tops of mountains whose base is in the bed of the ocean.

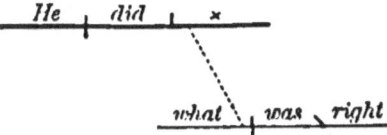

Explanation.—The connecting pronoun is here a possessive modifier of *base*.

17. Unhappy is the man whose mother does not make all mothers interesting.

LESSON 60.
ADJECTIVE CLAUSES—CONTINUED.
ANALYSIS.

1. Trillions of waves of ether enter the eye and hit the retina in the time you take to breathe.

Explanation.—The connecting pronoun is omitted. Supply *that*.

2. The *smith* takes his name from his *smoothing* the metals he works on.

3. Socrates was one of the greatest sages the world ever saw.

4. Whom the Lord loveth he chasteneth.

Explanation.—The adjective clause modifies the omitted antecedent of *whom*. Supply *him*.

5. He did what was right.

Explanation.—The adjective clause modifies the omitted word *thing*, or some word whose meaning is general or indefinite.*

---

* Many grammarians prefer to treat *what was right* as a noun clause (see Lesson 71), the object of *did*. They would treat in the same way clauses introduced by *whoever, whatever, whichever*.

" *What* was originally an interrogative and introduced substantive clauses. Its use

6. What is false in this world below betrays itself in a love of show.
7. The swan achieved what the goose conceived.
8. What men he had were true.

Explanation.—*Men* is here taken from its natural position before *what*, and placed after it, as if the relative were an adjective. In analysis restore *men* to its place—*Men what* (= *that*) *he had were true.*

9. Whoever does a good deed is instantly ennobled.

Explanation.—The adjective clause modifies the omitted subject (*man* or *he*) of the independent clause.

10. I told him to bring whichever was the lightest.
11. Whatever crushes individuality is despotism.
12. A dépôt is a place where stores are deposited.

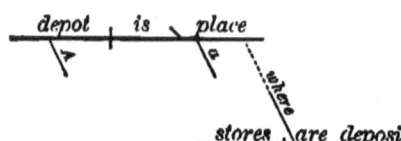

Explanation.—The line representing *where* is made up of two parts. The upper part represents *where* as a conjunction connecting the adjective clause to *place*, and the lower part represents it as an adverb modifying *are deposited*. As *where* performs these two offices, it may be called a *conjunctive adverb*. By changing *where* to the equivalent phrase *in which*, and using a diagram similar to (8), Lesson 59, the double nature of the conjunctive adverb will be seen.

13. He raised the maid from where she knelt.
   (Supply *the place* before *where*.)
14. Youth is the time when the seeds of character are sown.
15. Shylock would give the duke no reason why he followed a losing suit against Antonio.
16. Mark the majestic simplicity of those laws whereby the operations of the universe are conducted.

---

as a compound relative is an extension of its use as an indirect interrogative; it is confined to clauses which may be parsed as substantives, and before which no antecedent is needed, or permitted to be expressed. Its possessive *whose* has, however, attained the full construction of a relative."—*Prof. F. A. March.*

LESSON 61.

COMPOSITION—ADJECTIVE CLAUSE.

COMMA—RULE.—The *Adjective Clause*, when not restrictive, is set off by the comma.

Explanation.—I picked the apple *that was ripe*. I picked the apple, *which was ripe*. In the first sentence the adjective clause restricts or limits *apple*, telling which one was picked; in the second the adjective clause is added merely to describe the apple picked, being nearly equivalent to, I picked the apple, *and it* was ripe. This difference in meaning is shown by the punctuation.

Caution.—The adjective clause should be placed as near as possible to the word it modifies.

Direction.—*Correct the following errors of position, and insert the comma when needed:—*

1. The Knights of the Round Table flourished in the reign of King Arthur who vied with their chief in chivalrous exploits.
2. Solomon was the son of David who built the Temple.
3. My brother caught the fish on a small hook baited with a worm which we had for breakfast.
4. You have no right to decide who are interested.

Direction.—*Construct five complex sentences, each containing an adjective clause equivalent to one of the following adjectives:—*

Ambitious, respectful, quick-witted, talkative, lovable.

Direction.—*Change the following simple sentences into complex sentences by expanding the participle phrases into adjective clauses:—*

1. Those fighting custom with grammar are foolish.
2. The Constitution framed by our fathers is the sheet-anchor of our liberties.

3. I am thy father's spirit, doomed for a certain term to walk the night.

4. Some people, having lived abroad, undervalue the advantages of their native land.

5. A wife and children, threatened with widowhood and orphanage, have knelt at your feet on the very threshold of the Senate Chamber.

Direction.—*Change these simple sentences to complex sentences by expanding the infinitive phrases into adjective clauses:*—

1. I have many things to tell you
2. There were none to deliver.
3. He had an ax to grind.
4. It was a sight to gladden the heart.
5. It was a din to fright a monster's ear.

Direction.—*Form complex sentences in which these pronouns and conjunctive adverbs shall be used to connect adjective clauses:*—

Who, which, that, what, whoever, and whatever.
When, where, and why.

Direction.—*Change* that which *in the following sentences to* what, *and* what *to* that which; *whoever to* he who, *and* whatever *to* anything *or* everything which; *where and when to* at, on, *or* in which; *wherein to* in which; *and* whereby *to* by which:—

1. *That which* is seen is temporal.
2. *What* God hath joined together let not man put asunder.
3. *Whoever* lives a pious life blesses his race.
4. *Whatever* we do has an influence.
5. Scholars have grown old and blind, striving to put their hands on the very spot *where* brave men died.
6. The year *when* Chaucer was born is uncertain.
7. The play's the thing *wherein* I'll catch the conscience of the king.
8. You take my life in taking the means *whereby* I live.

Direction.—*Expand these possessive and explanatory modifiers into adjective clauses:*—

1. A *man's* heart deviseth *his* way.
2. *Reason's* whole pleasure, all the joys of sense,
   Lie in three words—*health, peace,* and *competence.*

LESSON 62.

Direction.—*Analyze the first nine sentences in the preceding Lesson, and write illustrative sentences as here directed:*—

Give an example of an adjective clause modifying a subject; one modifying a complement; one modifying the principal word of a phrase; one modifying some word omitted; one the connective of which is a subject; one whose connective is a complement; one whose connective is the principal word of a phrase; one whose connective is a possessive modifier; one whose connective is omitted; one whose connective is an adverb.

LESSON 63.

COMPLEX SENTENCE—ADVERB CLAUSE.

Introductory Hints.—*He arrived late.* You have learned that you could expand the adverb *late* into a phrase, and say, He arrived *at midnight.* You are now to learn that you can expand it into a clause of **Time**, and say, He arrived *when the clock struck twelve.*

He stood where I am. The adverb clause, introduced by *where*, is a clause of **Place**, and is equivalent to the adverb *here* or to the phrase *in this place.*

This exercise is as profitable as it is pleasant. The adverb clause, introduced by *as . . . as,* modifies *profitable,* telling the **Degree of the** quality expressed by it.

Analysis and Parsing.

The *adverb clause* may express *time*.

1. When pleasure calls, we listen.

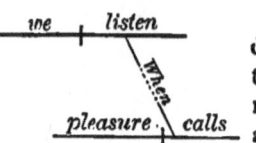

Explanation.— *When* modifies both *listen* and *calls*, denoting that the two actions take place at the same time. It also connects *pleasure calls*, as an adverb modifier, to *listen*. The offices of the conjunctive adverb *when* may be better understood by expanding it into two phrases thus: We listen *at the time at which* pleasure calls. *At the time* modifies *listen*, *at which* modifies *calls*, and *which* connects.

The line representing *when* is made up of three parts to picture these three offices. The part representing it as a modifier of *calls* is, for convenience, placed above its principal line instead of below it.

2. While Louis XIV. reigned, Europe was at war.
3. When my father and my mother forsake me, then the Lord will take me up.

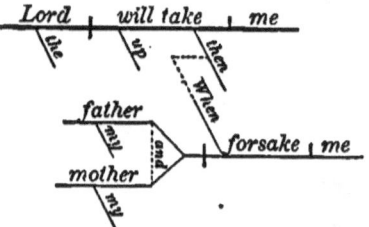

Explanation.—By changing *then* into *at the time*, and *when* into *at which*, the offices of these two words will be clearly seen. For explanation of the line representing *when*, see Lesson 14 and (1) above.

4. Cato, before* he durst give himself the fatal stroke, spent the night in reading "Plato's Immortality."
5. Many † a year is in its grave since I crossed this restless wave.

Explanation.—*Many* here modifies *year*, or, rather, *year* as modified by *a*.

6. Blucher arrived on the field of Waterloo just as Wellington was meeting the last onslaught of Napoleon.

---

* Some prefer, in constructions like this, to treat *before, ere, after, till, until,* and *since* as prepositions followed by noun clauses.

† See foot-note p. 76.

Explanation.—Just may be treated as a modifier of the dependent clause. A closer analysis, however, would make it a modifier of *as*. *Just as* = *just at the time at which*. *Just* here modifies *at the time*. *At the time* is represented in the diagram by the first element of the *as* line.

The *adverb clause* may express *place*.

7. Where the snow falls, there is freedom.
8. Pope skimmed the cream of good sense and expression wherever he could find it.
9. The wind bloweth where it listeth.

The *adverb clause* may express *degree*.

10. Washington was as good as he was great.

Explanation.—The adverb clause *as he was great* modifies the first *as*, which is an adverb modifying *good*. The first *as*, modified by the adverb clause, answers the question, Good to what extent or degree? The second *as* modifies *great* and performs the office of a conjunction, and is, therefore, a conjunctive adverb. Transposing, and expanding *as . . . as* into two phrases, we have, Washington was good *in the degree in which* he was great. See diagram of (3).

11. The wiser he grew, the humbler he became.

Explanation. — The words *the . . . the* are similar in office to *as . . . as*—He became humbler *in that degree in which* he became wiser.

12. Gold is heavier than iron.

Explanation.—*Heavier* = *heavy beyond the degree*, and *than* = *in which*. The sentence = Gold is heavy beyond the degree in which iron is heavy. *Is* and *heavy* are omitted. Frequently words are omitted after *than* and *as*. *Than* modifies *heavy* (understood) and connects the clause expressing degree to *heavier*, and is, therefore, a conjunctive adverb.

13. To be right is better than to be president.

Explanation.—To be right is better (good in a greater degree) than to be president (would be good).

14. It was so cold that the mercury froze.*

Explanation.—The degree of the cold is here shown by the effect it produced. The adverb *so*, modified by the adverb clause *that the mercury froze*, answers the question, Cold to what degree? The sentence = It was cold *to that degree in which* the mercury froze. *That*, as you see, modifies *froze* and connects the clauses; it is, therefore, a conjunctive adverb.

15. It was so cold as to freeze the mercury.

Explanation.—It was so cold as to freeze the mercury *would indicate* or *require*; or, It was as cold *as it would be* to freeze the mercury. This phrase may be resolved into the clause *that the mercury froze*.

16. Dying for a principle is a higher degree of virtue than scolding for it.

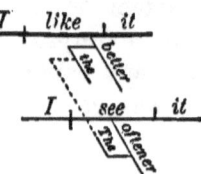

17. He called so loud that all the hollow deep of hell resounded.

18. To preach is easier than to practice.

19. One's breeding shows itself nowhere more than in his religion.

20. The oftener I see it, the better I like it.

---

* In this sentence, also in (15) and (17), the dependent clause is sometimes termed a clause of Result or Consequence. Clauses of Result express different logical relations, and cannot always be classed under Degree.

The following are somewhat peculiar:—

I had heard of it before, *so that I was not surprised*. I never go this way *that I do not think of it*. Who is he *that he should be so honored?*

LESSON 64.

ADVERB CLAUSE—CONTINUED.

Introductory Hints.—*He lived as the fool lives.* The adverb clause, introduced by *as*, is a clause of **Manner**, and is equivalent to the adverb *foolishly* or to the phrase *in a foolish manner*.

The ground is wet, because it has rained. The adverb clause, introduced by *because*, assigns the **Real Cause** of the ground's being wet.

It has rained, for the ground is wet. The adverb clause, introduced by *for*, does not assign the cause of the raining, but the cause of our believing that it has rained; it gives the **Reason** for the assertion or the **Evidence** of what is asserted.*

Analysis and Parsing.

The *adverb clause* may express *manner*.

1. He died as he lived.

Explanation.—He died *in the manner in which* he lived. For diagram, see (1), Lesson 63.

2. The upright man speaks as he thinks.
3. As the upright man thinks so he speaks.

(For diagram of *as . . . so*, see *when . . . then* (3), Lesson 63.)

4. As is the boy so will be the man.
5. The waves of conversation roll and shape our thoughts as the surf rolls and shapes the pebbles on the shore.

The *adverb clause* may express *real cause*.

---

* Reason or Evidence should be carefully distinguished from Cause. Cause produces an effect, Reason or Evidence produces knowledge of an effect.

Reason, Evidence, and *Proof* have been used to name this element. Evidence, however, is not Proof till conclusive. In some sentences the term *Reason* will best apply: in others, *Evidence*.

Clauses of Reason or Evidence are sometimes treated as independent.

6. The ground is wet, because it has rained.

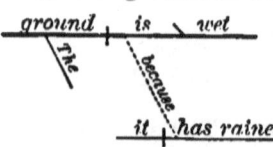

Explanation.—Because, being a mere conjunction, stands on a line wholly dotted.

7. Slang is always vulgar, as it is an affected way of talking.
8. We keep the pores of the skin open, for through them the blood throws off its impurities.
9. Since the breath contains poisonous carbonic acid, wise people ventilate their sleeping rooms.
10. Sea-bathing is the most healthful kind of washing, as it combines fresh air and vigorous exercise with its other benefits.
11. Wheat is the most valuable of grains, because bread is made from its flour.

The *adverb clause* may express *reason* or *evidence*.

12. God was angry with the children of Israel, for he overthrew them in the wilderness.
13. Tobacco and the potato are American products, since Raleigh found them here.
14. It rained last night, because the ground is wet this morning.
15. We Americans must all be cuckoos, for we build our homes in the nests of other birds.

LESSON 65.

ADVERB CLAUSE—CONTINUED.

Introductory Hints.—*If it rains, the ground will be wet.* The adverb clause, introduced by *if*, assigns what, if it occurs, *will be* the cause of the ground's being wet, but, as here expressed, is only a **Condition** ready to become a cause.

He takes exercise that he may get well. The adverb clause, introduced by *that*, assigns the cause or motive, or, better, the **Purpose**, of his exercising.

The ground is dry, although it has rained. The adverb clause, introduced by *although*, expresses a Concession. It is conceded that a cause for the ground's *not* being dry exists ; but, *in spite of this opposing cause*, it is asserted that the ground *is dry.*

All these dependent clauses of *real cause, reason, condition, purpose,* and *concession* come, as you see, under the general head of Cause, although only the first assigns the cause proper.

Analysis and Parsing.

The *adverb clause* may express *condition.*

1. If the air is quickly compressed, enough heat is evolved to produce combustion.

2. Unless your thought packs easily and neatly in verse, always use prose.

(*Unless* = *if not.*)

3. If ever you saw a crow with a king-bird after him, you have an image of a dull speaker and a lively listener.

4. Were it not for the warm waters of the Gulf Stream, the harbors and the rivers of Britain would be blocked up with ice for a great part of the year.

Explanation.—The relative position of the subject and the verb renders the *if* unnecessary. This omission of *if* is a common idiom.

5. Should the calls of hunger be neglected, the fat of the body is thrown into the grate to keep the furnace in play.

The *adverb clause* may express *purpose.*

6. Language was given us that we might say pleasant things to each other.

Explanation.—*That,* introducing a clause of purpose, is a mere conjunction.

7. Spiders have eyes all over their heads in order that they may see in many directions at one time.

Explanation.—The phrases *in order that, so that* = *that*.

8. The ship-canal across the Isthmus of Suez was dug so that European vessels need not sail around the Cape of Good Hope to reach the Orient.

9. The air draws up vapors from the sea and the land, and retains them dissolved in itself or suspended in cisterns of clouds, that it may drop them as rain or dew upon the thirsty earth.

The *adverb clause* may express *concession*.

10. Although the brain is only one fortieth of the body, about one sixth of the blood is sent to it.

11. Though the atmosphere presses on us with a load of fifteen pounds on every square inch of surface, still we do not feel its weight.

12. Though thou shouldst bray a fool in a mortar, yet will not his foolishness depart from him.

13. If the War of Roses did not utterly destroy English freedom, it arrested its progress for a hundred years.

Explanation.—*If* here = *even if* = *though*.

14. Though many rivers flow into the Mediterranean, they are not sufficient to make up the loss caused by evaporation.

LESSON 66.

COMPOSITION—ADVERB CLAUSES.

COMMA—RULE.—An *Adverb Clause* is set off by the comma unless it closely follows and restricts the word it modifies.

Explanation.—I met him in Paris, *when I was last abroad.* I will not call him villain, *because it would be unparliamentary.* Paper was invented in China, *if the Chinese tell the truth.* In these sentences the adverb clauses are not restrictive, but are supplementary, and are added almost as afterthoughts.

Glass bends easily *when it is red-hot.* Leaves do not turn red *because the frost colors them.* It will break *if you touch it.* Here the adverb clauses are restrictive ; each is very closely related in thought to the independent clause, and may almost be said to be the essential part of the sentence.

When the adverb clause precedes, it is set off.

Direction.—*Tell why the adverb clauses are or are not set off in Lessons 63 and 64.*

Direction.—*Write, after these independent clauses, adverb clauses of time, place, degree, etc. (for connectives, see Less. 100), and punctuate according to the Rule :—*

1. The leaves of the water-maple turn red—*time.*
2. Our eyes cannot bear the light—*time.*
3. Millions of soldiers sleep—*place.*
4. The Bunker Hill Monument stands—*place.*
5. Every spire of grass was so edged and tipped with dew—*degree.*
6. Vesuvius threw its lava so far—*degree.*
7. The tree is inclined—*manner.*
8. The lion springs upon his prey—*manner.*
9. 123 persons died in the Black Hole of Calcutta—*cause.*
10. Dew does not form in a cloudy night—*cause.*
11. That thunderbolt fell a mile away—*reason.*
12. We dream in our sleep—*reason.*
13. Peter the Great worked in Holland in disguise—*purpose.*
14. We put salt into butter and upon meat—*purpose.*
15. Iron bends and moulds easily—*condition.*
16. Apples would not fall to the ground—*condition.*
17. Europe conquered Napoleon at last—*concession.*
18. Punishment follows every violation of nature's laws—*concession.*

LESSON 67.

COMPOSITION—ADVERB CLAUSES.

ARRANGEMENT.

The adverb clause may stand before the independent clause, between the parts of it, or after it.

Direction.—*Think, if you can, of another adverb clause for each independent clause in the preceding Lesson, and by means of a caret (∧) indicate where it may properly stand in the sentence. Note its force in its several positions, and attend to the punctuation. Some of these adverb clauses can stand only at the end.*

LESSON 68.

COMPOSITION—ADVERB CLAUSES.

An adverb clause may be contracted into a participle or a participle phrase.

Example.—*When he saw me, he stopped* = *Seeing me, he stopped.*

Direction.—*Contract these complex sentences to simple ones:—*

1. Coral insects, when they die, form vast islands with their bodies.
2. The water will freeze, for it has cooled to 32°.
3. Truth, though she may be crushed to earth, will rise again.
4. Error, if he is wounded, writhes with pain, and dies among his worshipers.
5. Black clothes are too warm in summer, because they absorb heat.

An adverb clause may be contracted to an absolute phrase.

Example.—*When night came on, we gave up the chase* = *Night coming on, we gave up the chase.*

Composition—Adverb Clauses.

Direction.—*Contract these complex sentences to simple ones :—*
1. When oxygen and carbon unite in the minute blood-vessels, heat is produced.
2. It will rain to-morrow, for "Probabilities" predicts it.
3. Washington retreated from Long Island, because his army was outnumbered.
4. If Chaucer is called the father of our later English poetry, Wycliffe should be called the father of our later English prose.

An adverb clause may be contracted to a prepositional phrase having for its principal word (1) a participle, (2) an infinitive, or (3) a noun.

Direction.—*Contract each of these adverb clauses to a prepositional phrase having a participle for its principal word :—*

Model.—They will call *before they leave* the city = They will call *before leaving* the city.

1. The Gulf Stream reaches Newfoundland before it crosses the Atlantic.
2. If we use household words, we shall be better understood.
3. He grew rich, because he attended to his business.
4. Though they persecuted the Christians, they did not exterminate them.

Direction.—*Contract each of these adverb clauses to an infinitive phrase :—*

Model.—She stoops *that she may conquer* = She stoops *to conquer*.

1. The pine tree is so tall that it overlooks all its neighbors.
2. Philip II. built the Armada that he might conquer England.
3. He is foolish, because he leaves school so early in life.
4. What would I give, if I could see you happy !
5. We are pained when we hear God's name used irreverently.

Direction.—*Contract each of these adverb clauses to a prepositional phrase having a noun for its principal word :—*

Model.—He fought *that he might obtain glory* = He fought *for glory*.

1. Luther died where he was born.

2. A fish breathes, though it has no lungs.
3. The general marched as he was ordered.
4. Criminals are punished that society may be safe.
5. If you are free from vices, you may expect a happy old age.

An adverb clause may be contracted by simply omitting such words as may easily be supplied.

Example.—*When you are right,* go ahead = *When right,* go ahead.

Direction.—*Contract these adverb clauses:*—

1. Chevalier Bayard was killed while he was fighting for Francis I.
2. Error must yield, however strongly it may be defended.

Explanation.—*However* modifies *strongly,* and connects a concessive clause.

3. Much wealth is corpulence, if it is not disease.
4. No other English author has uttered so many pithy sayings as Shakespeare has uttered.

(Frequently, clauses introduced by *as* and *than* are contracted.)

5. The sun is many times larger than the earth is large.

(Sentences like this never appear in the full form.)

6. This is a prose era rather than it is a poetic era.

An adverb clause may sometimes be changed to an adjective clause or phrase.

Example.—This man is to be pitied, *because he has no friends* = This man, *who has no friends,* is to be pitied = This man, *having no friends,* is to be pitied = This man, *without friends,* is to be pitied.

Direction.—*Change each of the following adverb clauses first to an adjective clause and then to an adjective phrase:*—

1. A man is to be pitied if he does not care for music.
2. When a man lacks health, wealth, and friends, he lacks three good things.

LESSON 69.

ANALYSIS.

Direction.—*Tell the kind of adverb clause in each of the sentences in Lesson 68, and note the different positions in which these clauses stand.*

Select two sentences containing t i m e clauses; one, a p l a c e clause; two, d e g r e e; one, m a n n e r; two, r e a l c a u s e; two, r e a s o n; two, p u r p o s e; two, c o n d i t i o n; and two, c o n c e s s i o n, and analyze them.

LESSON 70.

REVIEW.

Direction.—*Compose sentences illustrating the different kinds of adverb clauses named in Lessons 63, 64, 65, and explain fully the office of each. For connectives, see Lesson 100. Tell why the adverb clauses in Lesson 68 are or are not set off by the comma. Compose sentences illustrating the different ways of contracting adverb clauses.*

LESSON 71.

THE COMPLEX SENTENCE—NOUN CLAUSE.

Introductory Hints.—In Lessons 40 and 41 you learned that an infinitive phrase may perform many of the offices of a noun. You are now to learn that a clause may do the same.

Obedience is better than sacrifice = *To obey* is better than sacrifice = *That men should obey* is better than sacrifice. The dependent clause *that men should obey* is equivalent to a noun, and is the **Subject of** *is*.

Many people believe that the beech tree is never struck by lightning. The dependent clause, introduced by *that*, is equivalent to a noun, and is the **Object Complement** of *believe*.

The fact that mould, mildew, and yeast are plants is wonderful. The clause introduced by *that* is equivalent to a noun, and is **Explanatory** of *fact*.

A peculiarity of English is, that it has so many borrowed words. The clause introduced by *that* is equivalent to a noun, and is an **Attribute Complement** relating to *peculiarity*.

Your future depends very much on who your companions are. The clause *who your companions are* is equivalent to a noun, and is the **Principal Term of a Phrase** introduced by the preposition *on*.

Analysis and Parsing.

The *noun clause* may be used as *subject*.

1. That the earth is round has been proved.

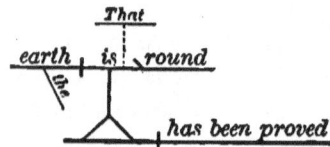

Explanation.—The clause *that the earth is round* is used like a noun as the subject of *has been proved*. The conjunction *that** simply introduces the noun clause.

This is a peculiar kind of complex sentence. Strictly speaking, there is here no principal clause, for the *whole sentence* cannot be called a clause, *i. e.*, *a part of a sentence*. We may say that it is a complex sentence in which the whole sentence takes the place of a principal clause.

2. That the same word is used for the soul of man and for a glass of gin is singular.
3. "What have I done?" is asked by the knave and the thief.
4. Who was the discoverer of America is not yet fully determined by historians.

Explanation.—The subject clause is here an indirect question. See Lesson 74.

---

* " *That* was originally the neuter demonstrative pronoun, used to point to the fact stated in an independent sentence ; as, It was good ; he saw *that*. By an inversion of the order this became, He saw *that* (namely) it was good, and so passed into the form *He saw that it was good*, where *that* has been transferred to the accessory clause, and has become a mere sign of grammatical subordination."—*C. P. Mason.*

5. When letters were first used is not certainly known.
6. "Where is Abel, thy brother?" smote the ears of the guilty Cain.
7. When to quit business and enjoy their wealth is a problem never solved by some.

Explanation.—*When to quit business and enjoy their wealth* is an indirect question. A question, fully stated, requires a subject and a predicate. *When to quit business* = *When they are to quit business*, or *When they ought to quit business.* Such constructions may be expanded into clauses, or they may be treated as phrases equivalent to clauses.

The *noun clause* may be used as *object complement.*

8. Galileo taught that the earth moves.

Explanation.—Here the clause introduced by *that* is used like a noun as the object complement of *taught.*

9. The Esquimau feels intuitively that bear's grease and blubber are the dishes for his table.
10. The world will not anxiously inquire who you are.
11. It will ask of you, "What can you do?"
12. The peacock struts about, saying, "What a fine tail I have!"
13. He does not know which to choose.
  (See explanation of (7), above.)
14. No one can tell how or when or where he will die.
15. Philosophers are still debating whether the will has any control over the current of thought in our dreams.

LESSON 72.

NOUN CLAUSE—CONTINUED.

ANALYSIS AND PARSING.

The *noun clause* may be used as *attribute complement.*

1. A peculiarity of English is, that it has so many borrowed words.
2. Tweed's defiant question was, "What are you going to do about it?"
3. The question ever asked and never answered is, "Where and how am I to exist in the Hereafter?"
4. Hamlet's exclamation was, "What a piece of work is man!"
5. The myth concerning Achilles is, that he was invulnerable in every part except the heel.

The *noun clause* may be used as *explanatory modifier*.

6. It has been proved that the earth is round.

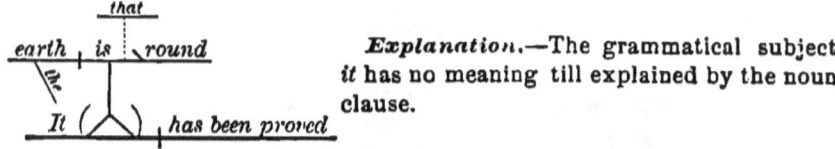

Explanation.—The grammatical subject *it* has no meaning till explained by the noun clause.

7. It is believed that sleep is caused by a diminution in the supply of blood to the brain.
8. The fact that mould, mildew, and yeast are plants is wonderful.
9. Napoleon turned his Simplon road aside in order that he might save a tree mentioned by Cæsar.

Explanation.—Unless *in order that* is taken as a conjunction connecting an adverb clause of purpose (see (7), Lesson 65), the clause introduced by *that* is a noun clause explanatory of *order*.*

10. Shakespeare's metaphor, "Night's candles are burnt out," is one of the finest in literature.
11. The advice that St. Ambrose gave St. Augustine in regard to conformity to local custom was, in substance, this: "When in Rome, do as the Romans do."
12. This we know, that our future depends on our present.

The *noun clause* may be used as *principal term* of a *prepositional phrase* or of an *absolute phrase*.

---

* A similar explanation may be made of *on condition that, in case that,* introducing adverb clauses expressing condition.

13. Have birds any sense of why they sing?

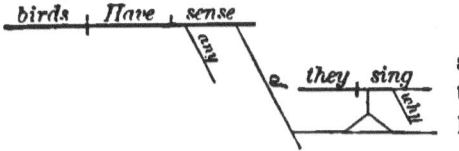

Explanation.—*Why they sing* is an indirect question, here used as the principal term of a prepositional phrase.

14. There has been some dispute about who wrote "Shakespeare's Plays."
15. We are not certain that an open sea surrounds the Pole.

Explanation.—By supplying *of* before *that*, the noun clause may be treated as the principal term of a prepositional phrase modifying the adjective *certain*. By supplying *of the fact*, the noun clause will become *explanatory*.

16. We are all anxious that the future shall bring us success and triumph.
17. The Sandwich Islander is confident that the strength and valor of his slain enemy pass into himself.
18. That the earth is round being proved, we can easily account for these phenomena.

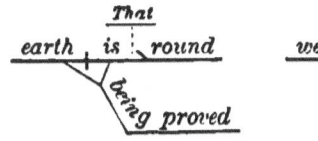

Explanation.—The noun clause is here the assumed subject of "being proved," forming with this participle an absolute phrase. See Lesson 44. The diagram of the participle is made to touch both elements of the clause line.

LESSON 73.

COMPOSITION—NOUN CLAUSE.

COMMA—RULE.—The noun clause used as attribute complement is generally set off by the comma.

Remark.—Present usage seems to favor the omission of the comma with the clause used as subject or as object complement, except where it would contribute to clearness of construction.

The punctuation of the explanatory clause is like that of other explanatory modifiers. See Lesson 34. But the real subject made explanatory of *it* is seldom set off. See next Lesson for the punctuation of noun clauses that are questions or quotations.

Direction.—*Give the reasons for the use or the omission of the comma with the noun clauses in the preceding Lesson.*

By using *it* as a substitute for the subject clause, this clause may be placed last.

Example.—*That the story of William Tell is a myth* is now believed= It is now believed *that the story of William Tell is a myth.*

Direction.—*By the aid of the expletive it, transpose five subject clauses in Lesson 71.*

Often the clause used as object complement may be placed first.

Direction.—*Transpose such of the clauses used as object complements, in the preceding Lessons, as admit transposition. Punctuate them if they need it.*

The noun clause may be made prominent by separating it, and inserting the independent clause between its parts.

Example.—The story of William Tell, *it is now believed,* is a myth.
(Notice that the principal clause, used parenthetically, is set off by the comma.)

Direction.—*Write the following sentences, using the independent clauses parenthetically :—*

1. We believe that the first printing-press in America was set up in Mexico in 1536.
2. I am aware that refinement of mind and clearness of thinking usually result from grammatical studies.
3. It is true that the glorious sun pours down his golden flood as cheerily on the poor man's cottage as on the rich man's palace.

Composition—Noun Clause.

Direction.—*Vary the following sentence so as to illustrate the six different kinds of noun clauses :—*

Model.—1. *That stars are suns* is the belief of astronomers.
    2. Astronomers believe *that stars are suns.*
    3. The belief of astronomers is, *that stars are suns.*
    4. The belief *that stars are suns* is held by astronomers.
    5. Astronomers are confident *that stars are suns.*
    6. *That stars are suns* being the belief of astronomers, we accept the theory.

1. Our conclusion is, that different forms of government suit different stages of civilization.

The noun clause may be contracted by changing the predicate to a participle, and the subject to a possessive.

Example.—*That he was brave* cannot be doubted = *His being brave* cannot be doubted.

Direction.—*Make the following complex sentences simple by changing the noun clauses to phrases :—*

1. That the caterpillar changes to a butterfly is a curious fact.
2. Everybody admits that Cromwell was a great leader.
3. A man's chief objection to a woman is, that she has no respect for the newspaper.
4. The thought that we are spinning around the sun at the rate of twenty miles a second makes us dizzy.
5. She was aware that I appreciated her situation.

The noun clause may be contracted by making the predicate, when changed to an infinitive, the objective complement, and the subject the object complement.

Direction.—*Make the following complex sentences simple by changing the predicates of the noun clauses to objective complements, and the subjects to object complements :—*

Model.—King Ahasuerus commanded *that Haman should be hanged* = King Ahasuerus commanded *Haman to be hanged.*

1. I believe that he is a foreigner.
2. The Governor ordered that the prisoner should be set free.
3. Many people believe that Webster was the greatest of American statesmen.
4. How wide do you think that the Atlantic ocean is?
5. They hold that taxation without representation is unjust.

Direction.—*Expand into complex sentences such of the sentences in Lesson 41 as contain an objective complement and an object complement that together are equivalent to a clause.*

A noun clause may be contracted to an infinitive phrase.

Example.—*That he should vote* is the duty of every American citizen = *To vote* is the duty of every American citizen.

Direction.—*Contract these noun clauses to infinitive phrases:*—
1. That we guard our liberty with vigilance is a sacred duty.
2. Every one desires that he may live long and happily.
3. The effect of looking upon the sun is, that the eye is blinded.
4. Cæsar Augustus issued a decree that all the world should be taxed.
5. We are all anxious that we may make a good impression.
6. He does not know whom he should send.
7. He can not find out how he is to go there.

LESSON 74.

COMPOSITION—NOUN CLAUSE—CONTINUED.

QUOTATION MARKS—RULE.—Quotation marks (" ") inclose a copied word or passage.

Remark.—Single marks (' ') inclose a quotation within a quotation. If, within the quotation having single marks, still another quotation is made, the double marks are again used; as, "The incorrectness of the dispatches led Bismarck to declare, 'It will soon come to be said, "He lies like the telegraph."'" This introduction of a third quotation should generally be avoided, especially where the three marks come at the end, as above.

When a quotation is divided by a parenthetical expression, each part of the quotation is inclosed ; as, "I would rather be right," said Clay, "than be president."

CAPITAL LETTER—RULE.—The first word of a direct quotation making complete sense or of a direct question introduced into a sentence should begin with a capital letter.

Remark.—A direct quotation is one whose exact words, as well as thought, are copied ; as, Nathan said to David, "*Thou art the man.*" An indirect quotation is one whose thought, but not whose exact words, is copied ; as, Nathan told David *that he was the man.*

The direct quotation is set off by the comma, begins with a capital letter, and is inclosed within quotation marks—though these *may be* omitted. The indirect quotation is not generally set off by the comma, does not necessarily begin with a capital letter, and is not inclosed within quotation marks.

A direct question introduced into a sentence is one in which the exact words and their order in an interrogative sentence (see Lesson 55) are preserved, and which is followed by an interrogation point ; as, Cain asked, "*Am I my brother's keeper?*" An indirect question is one which is referred to as a question, but not directly asked or quoted as such, and which is not followed by an interrogation point ; as, Cain asked *whether he was his brother's keeper.*

The direct question introduced into a sentence is set off by the comma (but no comma is used after the interrogation point), begins with a capital letter, and is inclosed within quotation marks—though these *may be* omitted. An indirect question is not generally set off by a comma, does not necessarily begin with a capital letter, and is not inclosed within quotation marks.

If the direct quotation, whether a question or not, is formally introduced (see Lesson 147), it is preceded by the colon ; as, Nathan's words to David were these: "*Thou art the man.*" He put the question thus : "*Can you do it?*"

Direction.—*Point out the direct and indirect quotations and questions in the sentences of Lesson 71, tell why they do or do not begin with capital letters, and justify the use or the omission of the comma, the interrogation point, and the quotation marks.*

Direction.—*Rewrite these same sentences, changing the direct quotations and questions to indirect, and the indirect to direct.*

Direction.— *Write five sentences containing direct quotations, some of which shall be formally introduced, and some of which shall be questions occurring at the beginning or in the middle of the sentence. Change these to the indirect form, and look carefully to the punctuation and the capitalization.*

LESSON 75.

ANALYSIS.

Direction.—*Analyze the sentences given for arrangement and contraction in Lesson 73.*

LESSON 76.

THE COMPOUND SENTENCE.

Introductory Hints.—*Cromwell made one revolution, and Monk made another.* The two clauses are independent of each other. The second clause, added by the conjunction *and* to the first, *continues the line of thought* begun by the first.

Man has his will, but woman has her way. Here the conjunction connects independent clauses whose thoughts stand *in contrast to each other*—the sentence faces, so to speak, half way about on *but*.

The Tudors were despotic, or history belies them. The independent clauses, connected by *or*, present thoughts between which you may choose, but *either, accepted, excludes the other.*

The ground is wet, therefore it has rained. Here the inferred fact, the raining, *really* stands to the other fact, the wetness of the ground, as cause to effect—the raining *made* the ground wet. *It has rained, hence the ground is wet.* Here the inferred fact, the wetness of the ground, *really* stands to the other fact, the raining, as effect to cause—the ground *is made* wet by the raining. But this the *real*, or *logical*, relation between the facts in either sentence is expressed in a sentence of the compound form—an *and* may be placed before *therefore* and *hence*. Unless the *connecting word* expresses the dependence of one of the clauses, the grammarian regards them both as independent.

Temperance promotes health, intemperance destroys it. Here the independent clauses are joined to each other by their very position in the sentence—connected without any conjunction. This kind of connection is common.

Sentences made up of independent clauses we call **Compound Sentences.**

DEFINITION.—A *Clause* is a part of a sentence containing a subject and its predicate.

DEFINITION.—A *Dependent Clause* is one used as an adjective, an adverb, or a noun.

DEFINITION.—An *Independent Clause* is one not dependent on another clause.

SENTENCES CLASSIFIED WITH RESPECT TO FORM.

DEFINITION.—A *Simple Sentence* is one that contains but one subject and one predicate, either or both of which may be compound.

DEFINITION.—A *Complex Sentence* is one composed of an independent clause and one or more dependent clauses.

DEFINITION.—A *Compound Sentence* is one composed of two or more independent clauses.

Analysis and Parsing.

Independent Clauses in the *same line* of thought.

1. Light has spread, and bayonets think.

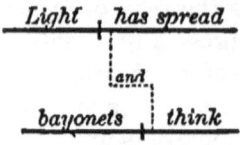

Explanation.—The clauses are of equal rank, and so the lines on which they stand are shaded alike, and the line connecting them is not slanting. As one entire clause is connected with the other, the connecting line is drawn between the *predicates* merely for convenience.

Oral Analysis.—This is a *compound sentence*, because it is made up of independent clauses.

2. Hamilton smote the rock of the national resources, and abundant streams of revenue gushed forth.

3. Some are born great, some achieve greatness, and some have greatness thrust upon them.

Independent Clauses expressing thoughts in *contrast*.

4. The man dies, but his memory lives.
5. Put not your trust in money, but put your money in trust.
6. Ready writing makes not good writing, but good writing brings on ready writing.

Independent Clauses expressing thoughts in *alternation*.

7. Be temperate in youth, or you will have to be abstinent in old age.
8. Places near the sea are not extremely cold in winter, nor are they extremely warm in summer.

(Here a choice is denied.)

9. Either Hamlet was mad, or he feigned madness admirably.

(See (16), Less. 20.)

Independent Clauses expressing thoughts one of which is an *inference* from the other.

10. People in the streets are carrying umbrellas, hence it must be raining.

11. I have seen, therefore I believe.

Explanation.—In such constructions *and* may be supplied, or the *adverb* may be regarded as the connective. The diagram illustrates *therefore* as connective.

Independent Clauses joined in the sentence *without a conjunction*.

12. The camel is the ship of the ocean of sand, the reindeer is the camel of the desert of snow.
13. Of thy unspoken word thou art master, thy spoken word is master of thee.
14. The ship leaps, as it were, from billow to billow.

Explanation.—*As it were* is an independent clause, used parenthetically. *As* simply introduces it.

15. Religion—who can doubt it?—is the noblest of themes for the exercise of intellect.
16. What grave (these are the words of Wellesley, speaking of the two Pitts) contains such a father and such a son !

LESSON 77.

COMPOSITION—COMPOUND SENTENCE.

COMMA and SEMICOLON—RULE.—Independent clauses, when short and closely connected, are separated by the comma; but, when the clauses are slightly connected, or when they are themselves divided into parts by the comma, the semicolon is used.

Remark.—A parenthetical clause may be set off by the comma or by the dash, or it may be inclosed within marks of parenthesis—the marks of parenthesis showing the least degree of connection in sense. See the last three sentences in the preceding Lesson.

Examples.—1. We must conquer our passions, or our passions will conquer us. 2. The prodigal robs his heirs ; the miser robs himself. 3. There is a fierce conflict between good and evil ; but good is in the ascendant, and must triumph at last.

(The rule above is another example.)

Direction.—*Punctuate the following sentences, and give your reasons :—*

1. The wind and the rain are over the clouds are divided in heaven over the green hill flies the inconstant sun.
2. The epic poem recites the exploits of a hero tragedy represents a disastrous event comedy ridicules the vices and follies of mankind pastoral poetry describes rural life and elegy displays the tender emotions of the heart.
3. Wealth may seek us but wisdom must be sought.
4. The race is not to the swift nor the battle to the strong.
5. Occidental manhood springs from self-respect Oriental manhood finds its greatest satisfaction in self-abasement.
6. The more discussion the better if passion and personality be avoided and discussion even if stormy often winnows truth from error.

Direction.—*Assign reasons for the punctuation of the independent clauses in the preceding Lesson.*

Direction.—*Using the copulative a n d, the adversative b u t, and the alternative o r or n o r, form compound sentences out of the following simple sentences, and give the reasons for your choice of connectives :—*

Read not that you may find material for argument and conversation. The rain descended. Read that you may weigh and consider the thoughts of others. Can the Ethiopian change his skin ? Righteousness exalteth a nation. The floods came. Great was the fall of it. Language is not the dress of thought. Can the leopard change his spots ? The winds blew and beat upon that house. Sin is a reproach to any people. It is not simply its vehicle. It fell.

Compound sentences may be contracted by using but once the parts common to all the clauses, and compounding the remaining parts.

Composition—Compound Sentence.

Example.—*Time* waits for no man, and *tide waits for no man* = *Time* and *tide wait for no man.*

Direction.—*Contract these compound sentences, attending carefully to the punctuation :—*

1. Lafayette fought for American independence, and Baron Steuben fought for American independence.
2. The sweet but fading graces of inspiring autumn open the mind to benevolence, and the sweet but fading graces of inspiring autumn dispose the mind for contemplation.
3. The Spirit of the Almighty is within us, the Spirit of the Almighty is around us, and the Spirit of the Almighty is above us.

A compound sentence may be contracted by simply omitting from one clause such words as may readily be supplied from the other.

Example.—He is witty, *but he is vulgar* = He is witty, *but vulgar.*

Direction.—*Contract these sentences :—*

1. Mirth should be the embroidery of conversation, but it should not be the web.
2. It is called so, but it is improperly called so.
3. Was Cabot the first discoverer of America, or was he not the first discoverer of America?
4. William the Silent has been likened to Washington, and he has justly been likened to him.
5. It was his address that pleased me, and it was not his dress that pleased me.

A compound sentence may sometimes be changed to a complex sentence without materially changing the sense.

Example.—*Take care of the minutes,* and the hours will take care of themselves = *If you take care of the minutes,* the hours will take care of themselves.

Direction.—*Change these compound sentences to complex sentences :—*

1. Resist the devil, and he will flee from you.

2. Govern your passions, or they will govern you.
3. I heard that you wished to see me, and I lost no time in coming.
4. He converses, and at the same time he plays a difficult piece of music.
5. He was faithful, and he was rewarded.

Direction.—*Change one of the independent clauses in each of these sentences to a dependent clause, and then change the dependent clause to a participle phrase :—*

Model.—The house *was built* upon a rock, *and therefore* it did not fall =
The house did not fall, *because it was built* upon a rock =
The house, *being built* upon a rock, did not fall.

1. He found that he could not escape, and so he surrendered.
2. Our friends heard of our coming, and they hastened to meet us.

Direction.—*Using a n d, b u t, and o r for connectives, compose three compound sentences, each containing three independent clauses.*

LESSON 78.

COMPLEX AND COMPOUND CLAUSES.

Introductory Hints.—*Sun and moon and stars* obey. Peter the Great went *to Holland, to England,* and *to France. I came, I saw, I conquered.* Here we have co-ordinate words, co-ordinate phrases, and co-ordinate clauses, that is, words, phrases, and clauses of equal rank, or order.

Leaves fall *so very quietly.* They ate *of the fruit from the tree in the garden.* Regulus would have paused *if he had been the man that he was before captivity had unstrung his sinews.* Here just as the word modifier *quietly* is itself modified by *very,* and *very* by *so ;* and just as *fruit,* the principal word in a modifying phrase, is modified by another phrase, and the principal word of that by another: so *man,* in the adverb clause which modifies *would have paused*, is itself modified by the adjective clause *that he was*, and *was* by the adverb clause *before captivity had unstrung his sinews*. These three dependent clauses in the complex clause modifier, like the three words and the three phrases in the complex word modifier and the complex phrase modifier, are not co-ordinate, or of equal rank.

Mary married Philip; but Elizabeth would not marry, although Parliament frequently urged it, and the peace of England demanded it. This is a compound sentence, composed of the simple clause which precedes *but* and the complex clause which follows it—the complex clause being composed of an independent clause and two dependent clauses, one co-ordinate with the other, and the two connected by *and*.

Analysis.

The *clauses* of *complex* and *compound* sentences may themselves be *complex* or *compound*.

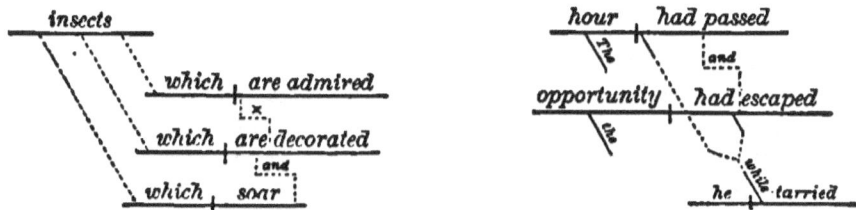

Explanation.—The first diagram illustrates the analysis of the compound adjective clause in (3), below. Each adjective clause is connected to *insects* by *which*. *And* connects the co-ordinate clauses. The second diagram shows that the clause *while he tarried* modifies both predicates of the independent clauses. *While* modifies *had passed, had escaped,* and *tarried,* as illustrated by the short lines under the first two verbs and the one over *tarried*. The office of *while* as connective is shown by the dotted lines. The third diagram illustrates the analysis of a complex sentence, containing a compound noun clause.

1. Sin has a great many tools, but a lie is a handle which fits them all.

2. Some one has said that the milkman's favorite song should be, "Shall we gather at the river?"

3. Some of the insects which are most admired, which are decorated with the most brilliant colors, and which soar on the most ethereal wings, have passed the greater portion of their lives in the bowels of the earth.

4. Still the wonder grew, that one small head could carry all he knew.

5. When a man becomes overheated by working, running, rowing, or making furious speeches, the six or seven millions of perspiration tubes pour out their fluid, and the whole body is bathed and cooled.

6. Milton said that he did not educate his daughters in the languages, because one tongue was enough for a woman.

7. Glaciers, flowing down mountain gorges, obey the law of rivers; the upper surface flows faster than the lower, and the center faster than the adjacent sides.

8. Not to wear one's best things every day is a maxim of New England thrift, which is as little disputed as any verse in the catechism.

9. In Holland the stork is protected by law, because it eats the frogs and worms that would injure the dikes.

10. It is one of the most marvelous facts in the natural world that, though hydrogen is highly inflammable, and oxygen is a supporter of combustion, both, combined, form an element, water, which is destructive to fire.

11. In your war of 1812, when your arms on shore were covered by disaster, when Winchester had been defeated, when the Army of the Northwest had surrendered, and when the gloom of despondency hung, like a cloud, over the land, who first relit the fires of national glory, and made the welkin ring with the shouts of victory?

LESSON 70.

EXPANSION.

Participles may be expanded into different kinds of clauses.

Direction.—*Expand the participles in these sentences into the clauses indicated:—*

1. Simon Peter, having a sword, drew it. (Adj. clause.)
2. Desiring to live long, no one would be old. (Concession.)
3. They went to the temple, suing for pardon. (Purpose.)
4. White garments, reflecting the rays of the sun, are cool in summer. (Cause.)
5. Loved by all, he must have a genial disposition. (Reason.)
6. Writing carefully, you will learn to write well. (Condition.)
7. Sitting there, I heard the cry of "fire!" (Time.)
8. She regrets not having read it. (Noun clause.)
9. The icebergs floated down, cooling the air for miles around. (Ind. clause.)

Absolute phrases may be expanded into different kinds of clauses.

Direction.—*Expand these absolute phrases into the clauses indicated:—*

1. Troy being taken by the Greeks, Æneas came into Italy. (Time.)
2. The bridges having been swept away, we returned. (Cause.)
3. A cause not preceding, no effect is produced. (Condition.)
4. All things else being destroyed, virtue could sustain itself. (Concession.)
5. There being no dew this morning, it must have been cloudy or windy last night. (Reason.)
6. The infantry advanced, the cavalry remaining in the rear. (Ind. Clause.)

Infinitives may be expanded into different kinds of clauses.

Direction.—*Expand these infinitives into the clauses indicated:*—

1. They have nothing to wear. (Adj. clause.)
2. The weather is so warm as to dissolve the snow. (Degree.)
3. Herod will seek the young child to destroy it. (Purpose.)
4. The adversative sentence faces, so to speak, half way about on *but*. (Condition.)
5. He is a fool to waste his time so. (Cause.)
6. I shall be happy to hear of your safe arrival. (Time.)
7. He does not know where to go. (Noun clause.)

Direction.—*Complete these elliptical expressions:*—

1. And so shall Regulus, though dead, fight as he never fought before. 2. Oh, that I might have one more day! 3. He is braver than wise. 4. What if he is poor? 5. He handles it as if it were glass. 6. I regard him more as a historian than as a poet. 7. He is not an Englishman, but a Frenchman. 8. Much as he loved his wealth, he loved his children better. 9. I will go whether you go or not. 10. It happens with books as with mere acquaintances. 11. No examples, however awful, sink into the heart.

LESSON 80.

MISCELLANEOUS EXERCISES IN REVIEW.

ANALYSIS AND PARSING.

1. Whenever the wandering demon of Drunkenness finds a ship adrift, he steps on board, takes the helm, and steers straight for the Maelstrom.—*Holmes.*

2. The energy which drives our locomotives and forces our steamships through the waves comes from the sun.—*Cooke.*

3. No scene is continually loved but one rich by joyful human labor; smooth in field, fair in garden, full in orchard.—*Ruskin.*

4. What is bolder than a miller's neck-cloth, which takes a thief by the throat every morning?—*German Proverb.*

5. The setting sun stretched his celestial rods of light across the level

landscape, and smote the rivers and the brooks and the ponds, and they became as blood.—*Longfellow.*

6. Were the happiness of the next world as closely apprehended as the felicities of this, it were a martyrdom to live.—*Sir T. Browne.*

7. There is a good deal of oratory in me, but I don't do as well as I can, in any one place, out of respect to the memory of Patrick Henry. —*Nasby.*

8. Van Twiller's full-fed cheeks, which seemed to have taken toll of everything that went into his mouth, were curiously mottled and streaked with dusky red, like a spitzenberg apple.—*Irving.*

9. The evil of silencing the expression of an opinion is, that it is robbing the human race.—*Mill.*

10. There is no getting along with Johnson; if his pistol misses fire, he knocks you down with the butt of it.—*Goldsmith.*

11. We think in words; and when we lack fit words, we lack fit thoughts.—*White.*

12. To speak perfectly well one must feel that he has got to the bottom of his subject.—*Whately.*

13. Office confers no honor upon a man who is worthy of it, and it will disgrace every man who is not.—*Holland.*

14. The men whom men respect, the women whom women approve are the men and women who bless their species.—*Parton.*

LESSON 84.

MISCELLANEOUS EXERCISES IN REVIEW.

Analysis and Parsing.

1. A ruler who appoints any man to an office when there is in his dominions another man better qualified for it sins against God and against the state.—*Koran.*

2. We wondered whether the saltness of the Dead Sea was not Lot's wife in solution.—*Curtis.*

3. There is a class among us so conservative that they are afraid the roof will come down if you sweep off the cobwebs.—*Phillips.*

4. Kind hearts are more than coronets, and simple faith than Norman blood.—*Tennyson*.

5. All those things for which men plough, build, or sail obey virtue.—*Sallust*.

6. The sea licks your feet, its huge flanks purr very pleasantly for you ; but it will crack your bones and eat you for all that.—*Holmes*.

7. Of all sad words of tongue or pen the saddest are these : "It might have been."—*Whittier*.

8. I fear three newspapers more than a hundred-thousand bayonets.—*Napoleon*.

9. He that allows himself to be a worm must not complain if he is trodden on.—*Kant*.

10. It is better to write one word upon the rock than a thousand on the water or the sand.—*Gladstone*.

11. A breath of New England's air is better than a sup of Old England's ale.—*Higginson*.

12. We are as near to heaven by sea as by land.—*Sir H. Gilbert*.

13. No language that cannot suck up the feeding juices secreted for it in the rich mother-earth of common folk can bring forth a sound, lusty book.—*Lowell*.

14. Commend me to the preacher who has learned by experience what are human ills and what is human wrong.—*Country Parson*.

15. He prayeth best who loveth best all things both* great and small; for the dear God who loveth us, he made and loveth all.—*Coleridge*.

LESSON 82.

REVIEW.

Show that an adjective may be expanded into an equivalent phrase or clause. Give examples of adjective clauses connected by *who, whose, which, what, that, whichever, when, where, why,* and show that each connective performs also the office of a pronoun or that of an adverb. Give and illustrate fully the Rule for punctuating the adjective clause,

---

* See Lesson 20.

and the Caution regarding the position of the adjective clause. Show that an adjective clause may be equivalent to an infinitive phrase or a participle phrase.

Show that an adverb may be expanded into an equivalent phrase or clause. Illustrate the different kinds of adverb clauses, and explain the office of each and the fitness of the name. Give and explain fully the Rule for the punctuation of adverb clauses. Illustrate the different positions of adverb clauses. Illustrate the different ways of contracting adverb clauses.

LESSON 83.

REVIEW.

Illustrate the six different offices of a noun clause. Explain the two different ways of treating clauses introduced by *in order that*, etc. Explain the office of the expletive *it*. Illustrate the different positions of a noun clause used as object complement. Show how the noun clause may be made prominent. Illustrate the different ways of contracting noun clauses. Give and illustrate fully the Rule for quotation marks. Illustrate and explain fully the distinction between direct and indirect quotations, and the distinction between direct and indirect questions introduced into a sentence. Tell all about their capitalization and punctuation.

LESSON 84.

REVIEW.

Illustrate and explain the distinction between a dependent and an independent clause. Illustrate and explain the different ways in which independent clauses connected by *and, but, or,* and *hence* are related in sense. Show how independent clauses may be joined in sense without a connecting word. Define a clause. Name and define the different kinds of clauses. Name and define the different classes of sentences with regard to form. Give the Rule for the punctuation of independent clauses, and illustrate fully. Illustrate the different ways of contracting independent clauses. . Show how an independent clause may be changed to an equivalent dependent clause and then to an equivalent phrase.

Illustrate and explain the difference between compound and complex word modifiers; between compound and complex phrases; between compound and complex clauses.

Give two or more participle phrases, two or more absolute phrases, and two or more infinitive phrases, and expand them into different kinds of clauses.

What three parts of speech may connect clauses?

To the Teacher.—It would be well to exercise the pupils here in the grouping of simple sentences into complex and compound, and the resolving of complex and compound sentences into simple ones. Any reading-book will furnish good material.

Models.—In the desert a route through the sand is always preferred. In sandy tracts springs are more likely to be found. The sand presents a soft, dry bed. The traveler can repose upon it after the fatigues of the day =

In the desert a route through the sand is always preferred, *because* in sandy tracts springs are more likely to be found, *and because* the sand presents a soft, dry bed *on which* the traveler can repose after the fatigues of the day.

The breath of the ocean is sweet. The winds fill their mighty lungs with it. They strike their wings for the shore. They reach it. They breathe health and vigor along all the fainting, waiting hosts =

The winds fill their mighty lungs *with the sweet breath of ocean, and, striking* their wings for the shore, they *go breathing* health and vigor along all the fainting hosts *that wait for it.*

How to turn complex and compound sentences into simple ones is here suggested, of course.

It might be well, before taking up *" Parts of Speech Subdivided,"* to turn over to *"Composition,"* the fourth division, and exercise the pupils in the grouping of sentences into *Paragraphs,* and of *Paragraphs* into *Themes.*

GENERAL REVIEW.

To the Teacher.—This scheme will be found very helpful in a general review. The pupils should be able to reproduce it, in part or entire, except the Lesson numbers.

Scheme for the Sentence.

(The numbers refer to Lessons.)

PARTS.

- **Subject.**
  - Noun or Pronoun (8).
  - Phrase (38, 40).
  - Clause (71).

- **Predicate.** Verb (11).

- **Complements.**
  - **Object.**
    - Noun or Pronoun (28).
    - Phrase (38, 40).
    - Clause (71).
  - **Attribute.**
    - Adjective (29, 30).
    - Participle (37).
    - Noun or Pronoun (29, 30).
    - Phrase (37, 40).
    - Clause (72).
  - **Objective.**
    - Adjective (31).
    - Participle (37).
    - Noun (31).
    - Phrase 37, 41).

- **Modifiers.**
  - Adjectives (12).
  - Adverbs (14).
  - Participles (37).
  - Nouns and Pronouns (33, 35).
  - Phrases (17, 37, 38, 40, 41).
  - Clauses (59, 60, 63, 64, 65).

- **Connectives.**
  - Conjunctions (20, 64, 65, 71, 78).
  - Pronouns (59, 60).
  - Adverbs (60, 63, 64).

- **Independent Parts** (44).

Classes. Meaning. Declarative, Interrogative, Imperative, Exclamatory (46).

Classes. Form. Simple, Complex, Compound (76).

Additional Selections.

To the Teacher.—We believe that you will find the preceding pages unusually full and rich in illustrative selections; but, should additional work be needed for reviews or for maturer classes, the following selections will afford profitable study. Let the pupils translate these passages into prose, and discuss the thought and the poetic form, as well as the logical construction.

>Speak clearly, if you speak at all;
>Carve every word before you let it fall.—*Holmes.*

>The robin and the blue-bird, piping loud,
>   Filled all the blossoming orchards with their glee;
>The sparrows chirped as if they still were proud
>   Their race in Holy Writ should mentioned be;
>And hungry crows, assembled in a crowd,
>   Clamored their piteous prayer incessantly,
>Knowing who hears the ravens cry, and said,
>"Give us, O Lord, this day our daily bread!"—*Longfellow.*

>Better to stem with heart and hand
> The roaring tide of life than lie,
>Unmindful, on its flowery strand,
> Of God's occasions drifting by.
> Better with naked nerve to bear
> The needles of this goading air
>Than, in the lap of sensual ease, forego
>The godlike power to do, the godlike aim to know.
>   —*Whittier.*

>Then to side with Truth is noble when we share her
>   wretched crust,
>Ere her cause bring fame and profit, and 't is prosperous
>   to be just;
>Then it is the brave man chooses, while the coward
>   stands aside,
>Doubting in his abject spirit, till his Lord is
>   crucified.—*Lowell.*

PARTS OF SPEECH SUBDIVIDED

LESSON 85.

CLASSES OF NOUNS AND PRONOUNS.

Introductory Hints.—You have now reached a point where it becomes necessary to divide the eight great classes of words into subclasses.

You have learned that nouns are the names of things; as, *girl, Sarah*. The name *girl* is held in common by all girls, and so does not distinguish one girl from another. The name *Sarah* is not thus held in common; it does distinguish one girl from other girls. Any name which belongs in common to all things of a class we call a **Common Noun**; and any particular name of an individual, distinguishing this individual from others of its class, we call a **Proper Noun**. The "proper, or individual, names" which in Rule 1, Lesson 8, you were told to begin with capital letters are proper nouns.

Such a word as *wheat, music,* or *architecture* does not distinguish one thing from others of its class; there is but one thing in the class denoted by each, each thing forms a class by itself; and so we call these words common nouns.

In Lesson 8 you learned that pronouns are not names, but words used instead of names. Any one speaking of *himself* may use *I, my,* etc., instead of his own name; speaking *to one,* he may use *you, thou, your, thy,* etc., instead of that person's name; speaking *of one,* he may use *he, she, it, him, her,* etc., instead of that one's name. These little words that by their form denote the speaker, the one spoken to, or the one spoken of are called **Personal Pronouns**.

By adding *self* to *my, thy, your, him, her,* and *it,* and *selves* to *our, your,* and *them,* we form what are called **Compound Personal Pronouns**, used either for emphasis or to reflect the action of the verb back upon the actor ; as, *Xerxes himself* was the last to cross the Hellespont ; The *mind* cannot see *itself*.

If the speaker wishes to modify a noun, or some word or words used like a noun, by a clause, he introduces the clause by *who, which, what*, or *that ;* as, I know the man *that* did that. These words, relating to words in another clause, and binding the clauses together, are called **Relative Pronouns**. By adding *ever* and *soever* to *who, which*, and *what*, we form what are called the **Compound Relative Pronouns** *whoever, whosoever, whichever, whatever*, etc., used in a general way, and without any word expressed to which they relate.

If the speaker is ignorant of the name of a person or a thing and asks for it, he uses *who, which*, or *what ;* as, *Who* did that ? These pronouns, used in asking questions, are called **Interrogative Pronouns**.

Instead of naming things a speaker may indicate them by words pointing them out as near or remote ; as, Is *that* * a man ? What is *this?* or telling something of their number, order, or quantity : as, *None* are perfect ; The *latter* will do ; *Much* has been done. Such words we call **Adjective Pronouns**.

DEFINITIONS.

A *Noun* is the name of anything.

A *Common Noun* is a name which belongs to all things of a class.

A *Proper Noun* is the particular name of an individual.

Remark.—It may be well to note two classes of common nouns— *collective* and *abstract*. A **Collective Noun** is the name of a number of things taken together ; as, *army, flock, mob, jury*. An **Abstract Noun** is the name of a quality, an action, a being, or a state ; as, *whiteness, beauty, wisdom*, (the) *singing, movement,* (the) *sleep*.

---

* Such words as *this* and *that* may be called *demonstrative* pronouns ; and such words as *none, latter*, and *much, indefinite* pronouns.

"The difference between nouns and pronouns starts from the roots. Common substantives and adjectives are formed from verbal roots, and denote quality and attributes. Pronominal roots denote relations, and from them are formed those substantive and adjective words which indicate things by their relations. The demonstrative roots are the most important of all."—*Prof. F. A. March.*

A *Pronoun* is a word used for a noun.*

A *Personal Pronoun* is one that, by its form, denotes the speaker, the one spoken to, or the one spoken of.

A *Relative Pronoun* is one that relates to some preceding word or words, and connects clauses.

An *Interrogative Pronoun* is one with which a question is asked.

An *Adjective Pronoun* is one that performs the offices of both an adjective and a noun.

The simple personal pronouns are:—
I, thou, you, he, she, and *it.*

The compound personal pronouns are:—
Myself, thyself, yourself, himself, herself, and *itself*

The simple relative pronouns are:—
Who, which,† that, and *what.‡*

The compound relative pronouns are:—
Whoever or *whosoever, whichever* or *whichsoever, whatever* or *whatsoever.*

The interrogative pronouns are:—
Who, which, and *what.*

---

* In our definition and general treatment of the pronoun, we have conformed to the traditional views of grammarians; but it may be well for the student to note that pronouns are something more than mere substitutes for nouns, and that their primary function is not to prevent the repetition of nouns.

Unlike common nouns, which denote things by their qualities, pronouns denote things by their relations. In the sentence " *I* will help *you*," *I* and *you* mark the relations of the persons to the act of speaking, *I* denoting the person *speaking* and *you* the one *spoken to*—a function that does not belong to nouns.

The relation of the clauses in the sentence "Whales are the largest animals *that* swim" cannot be expressed by a noun, nor even by a noun and a conjunction.

In the sentence " *What* did you say ?" the speaker finds *what* something more than a substitute for a noun.

† *Which,* retaining its office as connective, may accompany its noun as an adjective; as, " I gave him definite instruction, *which* instruction he has followed."

‡ *As,* in such sentences as this : *Give such things as you can spare,* may be treated as a relative pronoun. But by expanding the sentence *as* is seen to be a conjunctive adverb—Give such things *as those are which* you can spare.

Some of the more common adjective pronouns are:—

All, another, any, both, each, either, enough, few, former, latter, little, many, much, neither, none, one, other, same, several, such, that, these, this, those, whole, etc.*

The word, phrase, or clause in the place of which a pronoun is used is called an *Antecedent*.

Direction.—*Point out the pronouns and their antecedents in these sentences:—*

Jack was rude to Tom, and always knocked off his hat when he met him. To lie is cowardly, and every boy should know it. Daniel and his companions were fed on pulse, which was to their advantage. To lie is to be a coward, which one should scorn to be. To sleep soundly, which is a blessing, is to repair and renew the body.

Who † (or *whose* and *whom*), *which*, and *what* are interrogative pronouns when the sentence or clause in which they stand asks a question directly or indirectly; they are relatives when they connect adjective clauses.

Direction.—*Analyze these sentences, and parse all the pronouns:—*

1. Who steals my purse steals trash. 2. I myself know who stole my purse. 3. They knew whose house was robbed. 4. He heard what was said. 5. You have guessed which belongs to me. 6. Whom the gods would destroy they first make mad. 7. What was said, and who said it? 8. It is not known to whom the honor belongs. 9. She saw one of them, but she cannot positively tell which. 10. Whatever is done must be done quickly.

---

* But for the fact that such words as *brave, good,* etc., in the phrases *the brave, the good,* etc., *describe*—which pronouns never do—we might call them adjective pronouns. They may be treated as nouns, or as adjectives modifying nouns to be supplied.

The is not always used with these adjectives; as, for *better* or *worse*, in *general*, at *random*, in *vain*, in *particular*.

Some adjectives preceded by *the* are abstract nouns; as, the *grand*, the *sublime*, the *beautiful*.

† See Lessons 60, 61, and 71, for further treatment of these words.

LESSON 86.

CONSTRUCTION OF PRONOUNS.

To the Teacher.—In the recitation of all Lessons containing errors for correction, the pupils' books should be closed, and the examples should be read by you. To insure care in preparation and close attention in the class, read some of the examples in their *correct* form. Require specific reasons.

Caution.—Avoid *he, it, they,* or any other pronoun when its reference to an antecedent would not be clear. Repeat the noun instead, quote the speaker's exact words, or recast the sentence.

Direction.—*Study the Caution, and relieve these sentences of their ambiguity :—*

Model.—The lad cannot leave his father ; for, if he should leave *him, he* would die = The lad cannot leave his father ; for, if he should leave *his father, his father* would die. Lysias promised his father never to abandon *his* friends = Lysias gave his father this promise : "I will never abandon *your* (or *my*) friends."

1. Dr. Prideaux says that, when he took his commentary to the bookseller, he told him it was a dry subject. 2. He said to his friend that, if he did not feel better soon, he thought he had better go home.

(This sentence may have four meanings. Give them all, using what you may suppose were the speaker's words.)

3. A tried to see B in the crowd, but could not, because he was so short. 4. Charles's duplicity was fully made known to Cromwell by a letter of his to his wife, which he intercepted. 5. The farmer told the lawyer that his bull had gored his ox, and that it was but fair that he should pay him for his loss.

Caution.—Do not use pronouns needlessly.

Direction.—*Write these sentences, omitting needless pronouns :—*

1. It isn't true what he said. 2. The father he died, the mother she followed, and the children they were taken sick. 3. The cat it mewed,

and the dogs they barked, and the man he shouted. 4. Let every one turn from his or her evil ways. 5. Napoleon, Waterloo having been lost, he gave himself up to the English.

Caution.—In addressing one, do not, in the same sentence, use the two styles of the pronoun.

Direction.—*Study the Caution, and correct these errors:—*
1. Thou art sad, have you heard bad news? 2. You cannot always have thy way. 3. Bestow thou upon us your blessing. 4. Love thyself last, and others will love you.

Caution.—The pronoun *them* should not be used for the adjective *those,* or the pronoun *what* for the conjunction *that.*

Direction.—*Study the Caution, and correct these errors:-*
1. Hand me them things. 2. Who knows but what we may fail? 3. I cannot believe but what I shall see them men again. 4. We ought to have a great regard for them that are wise and good.

Caution.—The relative *who* should always represent persons; *which,* brute animals and inanimate things; *that,* persons, animals, and things; and *what,* things. The antecedent of *what* should not be expressed.

Direction.—*Study the Caution, and correct these errors:—*
1. Those which say so are mistaken. 2. He has some friends which I know. 3. He told that what he knew. 4. The dog who was called Fido went mad. 5. The lion whom they were exhibiting broke loose. 6. All what he saw he described. 7. The horse whom Alexander rode was named Bucephalus.

Direction.—*Write correct sentences illustrating every point in these five Cautions.*

LESSON 87.

CONSTRUCTION OF PRONOUNS—CONTINUED.

Caution.—Several connected relative clauses relating to the same antecedent require the same relative pronoun.

Direction.—*Study the Caution, and correct these errors :—*

1. It was Joseph that was sold into Egypt, who became governor of the land, and which saved his father and brothers from famine. 2. He who lives, that moves, and who has his being in God should not forget him. 3. This is the horse which started first, and that reached the stand last. 4. The man that fell overboard, and who was drowned was the first mate.

Caution.—When the relative clause is not restrictive, and could be introduced by *and he, and it, and they,* etc., *who* or *which,* and not *that,* is generally used.

Example.—Water, *which* (= *and it*) is composed of hydrogen and oxygen, covers three fourths of the earth's surface.

Direction.—*Study the Caution, and correct these errors :—*

1. The earth is enveloped by an ocean of air, that is a compound of oxygen and nitrogen. 2. Longfellow, that is the most popular American poet, has written beautiful prose. 3. Time, that is a precious gift, should not be wasted. 4. Man, that is born of woman, is of few days and full of trouble.

Caution.—The relative *that* * should be used instead of *who* or *which* (1) when the antecedent names both persons and things ; (2) when it would prevent ambiguity ; and (3) when it would sound better than *who* or *which, e. g.,* after

---

* Some grammarians claim that the relative *that* should *always* be used in restrictive clauses instead of *who* or *which ;* others say that *usually* it should be. But all admit that modern writers do not observe this distinction.

same, very, all, the interrogative *who,* the indefinite *it,* and adjectives expressing quality in the highest degree.

Example.—He lived near a *pond that* was a nuisance. (*That* relates to *pond*—the pond was a nuisance. *Which* might have, for its antecedent, *pond,* or the whole clause *He lived near a pond ;* and so its use here would be ambiguous.)

Direction.—*Study the Caution, and correct these errors :*—

1. The wisest men who ever lived made mistakes. 2. The chief material which is used now in building is brick. 3. Who who saw him did not pity him? 4. He is the very man whom we want. 5. He is the same who he has ever been. 6. He sent his boy to a school which did him good. 7. All who knew him respected him. 8. It was not I who did it.

Caution.—The relative clause should be placed as near as possible to the word which it modifies.

Direction.—*Correct these errors :*—

1. The pupil will receive a reward from his teacher who is diligent. 2. Her hair hung in ringlets, which was dark and glossy. 3. A dog was found in the street that wore a brass collar. 4. A purse was picked up by a boy that was made of leather. 5. Claudius was canonized among the gods, who scarcely deserved the name of man. 6. He should not keep a horse that cannot ride.

Caution.—When *this* and *that, these* and *those, the one* and *the other* refer to things previously mentioned, *this* and *these* refer to the last mentioned, and *that* and *those* to the first mentioned ; *the one* refers to the first mentioned, and *the other* to the last mentioned. (Obscurity is often prevented by a repetition of the words referred to.)

Examples.—*High* and *tall* are synonyms : *this* may be used in speaking of what grows—a tree ; *that* in speaking of what does not grow—a mountain. Homer was a genius, Virgil an artist ; in *the one* we most admire the man ; in *the other,* the work.

Construction of Pronouns—Continued.

Direction.—*Study the Caution, and correct these errors :—*

1. Talent speaks learnedly at the bar ; tact, triumphantly : this is complimented by the bench ; that gets the fees. 2. Charles XII. and Peter the Great were sovereigns : the one was loved by his people ; the other was hated. 3. The selfish and the benevolent are found in every community ; these are shunned, while those are sought after.

Direction.—*Write correct sentences illustrating every point in these five Cautions.*

LESSON 88.

CONSTRUCTION OF PRONOUNS—CONTINUED.

MISCELLANEOUS ERRORS.

Direction.—*Two of the sentences below are correct. Give the Cautions which the other sentences violate, and correct the errors :—*

1. He who does all which he can does enough. 2. John's father died before he was born. 3. Whales are the largest animals which swim. 4. Boys who study hard, and that study wisely make progress. 5. There are miners that live below ground, and who seldom see the light. 6. He did that what was right. 7. General Lee, that served under Washington, had been a British officer. 8. A man should sit down and count the cost who is about to build a house. 9. They need no spectacles that are blind. 10. They buy no books who are not able to read. 11. Cotton, that is a plant, is woven into cloth. 12. Cotton, which is a plant, is woven into cloth. 13. There is no book which, when we look through it sharply, we cannot find mistakes in it. 14. The reporter which said that was deceived. 15. The diamond, that is pure carbon, is a brilliant gem. 16. The brakemen and the cattle which were on the train were killed. 17. *Reputation* and *character* do not mean the same thing : the one denotes what we are ; the other, what we are thought to be. 18. Kosciusko, having come to this country, he aided us in our Revolutionary struggle. 19. What pleased me much, and which was spoken of by others, was the general appearance of the

class. 20. There are many boys whose fathers and mothers died when they were infants. 21. One does not know but that the future has these things in store for him. 22. Shall you be able to sell them boots? 23. I don't know but what I may. 24. Beer and wine are favorite drinks abroad: the one is made from grapes ; the other from barley. 25. There is one marked difference between shiners and trout ; these have scales, and those have not. 26. All the means that grace display which drew the wondrous plan. 27. Help thyself, and Heaven will help you.

LESSON 89.

CLASSES OF ADJECTIVES.

Introductory Hints.—You learned in Lesson 12 that, in the sentences *Ripe apples are healthful, Unripe apples are hurtful*, the adjectives *ripe* and *unripe* limit, or narrow, the application of *apples* by describing, or by expressing certain qualities of the fruit. You learned, also, that *the, this, an, no, some,* and *many* limit, or narrow, the application of any noun which they modify, as *apple* or *apples*, by pointing out the particular fruit, by numbering it, or by denoting the quantity of it.

Adjectives which limit by expressing quality are called **Descriptive Adjectives**; and those which limit by pointing out, numbering, or denoting quantity are called **Definitive Adjectives**.

Adjectives modifying a noun do *not* limit, or narrow, its application (1) when they denote qualities that always belong to the thing named; as, *yellow* gold, the *good* God, the *blue* sky; or (2) when they are attribute complements, denoting qualities *asserted* by the verb; as, The fields were *green*; The ground was *dry* and *hard*.

DEFINITIONS.

An *Adjective* is a word used to modify a noun or a pronoun.

A *Descriptive Adjective* is one that limits by expressing quality.

A *Definitive Adjective* is one that limits by pointing out, numbering, or denoting quantity.

The definitive adjectives *an* or *a* and *the* are commonly called *Articles*.

A noun may take the place of an adjective.

Examples.—*London* journals, the *New York* press, *silver* spoons, *diamond* pin, *state* papers, *gold* bracelet.

Direction.—*Point out the descriptive and the definitive adjectives below, and name such as do not limit :—*

Able statesmen, much rain, ten mice, brass kettle, small grains, Mansard roof, some feeling, all men, hundredth anniversary, the Pitt diamond, the patient Hannibal, little thread, crushing argument, moving spectacle, the martyr president, tin pans, eyes are bright, few people, less trouble, this toy, any book, brave Washington, Washington market, three cats, slender cord, that libel, happy children, the huge clouds were dark and threatening, the broad Atlantic.

Direction.—*Point out the descriptive and the definitive adjectives in Lessons 80 and 81, and tell whether they denote c o l o r , m o t i o n , s h a p e , p o s i t i o n , s i z e , or m o r a l q u a l i t i e s.*

LESSON 90.

CONSTRUCTION OF ADJECTIVES.

Caution.—*An* and *a* are different forms of *one*. *An* is used before vowel sounds. For the sake of euphony, *an* drops *n* and becomes *a* before consonant sounds.*

Examples.—*An* inkstand, *a* bag, *a* historian, *a* humble petition, *an* hour (*h* is silent), *a* unit (*unit* begins with the consonant sound of *y*), such *a* one (*one* begins with the consonant sound of *w*).

---

* Some writers still use *an* before such words as *historian, use, one ;* but present usage favors *a*

Direction.—*Study the Caution, and correct these errors :*—

A heir, a inheritance, an hook, an ewer, an usurper, a account, an uniform, an hundred, a umpire, an hard apple, an hero.

Caution.—*An* or *a* is used to limit a noun to *one* thing of a class—to *any* one. *The* is used to distinguish (1) one thing or several things from others, and (2) one class of things from other classes.

Explanation.—We can say a *horse*, meaning *any one horse;* but we cannot say *A gold* is heavy, This is a poor kind of *a gas*, William Pitt received the title of *an earl;* because *gold, gas,* and *earl* are here meant to denote each the *whole* of a class, and *a* limits its noun to *one* thing of a class.

The horse or *the horses* must be turned into *the lot*. Here *the* before *horse* distinguishes a certain animal, and *the* before *horses*, certain animals, from others of the same class; and *the* before *lot* distinguishes the field from the yard or the stable—things in *other* classes. *The horse* is a noble animal. Here *the* distinguishes *this class* of animals from other classes. But we cannot say, *The man* (meaning the *race*) is mortal, *The anger* is a short madness, *The truth* is eternal, *The poetry* and *the painting* are fine arts, because *man, anger, truth, poetry,* and *painting* are used in their widest sense, and name things that are sufficiently distinguished without *the*.

Direction.—*Study the Caution as explained, and correct these errors :*—

1. This is another kind of a sentence. 2. Churchill received the title of a duke. 3. A *hill* is from the same root as *column*. 4. Dog is a quadruped. 5. I expected some such an offer. 6. The woman is the equal of man. 7. The sculpture is a fine art. 8. Unicorn is kind of a rhinoceros. 9. Oak is harder than the maple.

Caution.—Use *an, a,* or *the* before *each* of two or more connected adjectives, when these adjectives modify different nouns, expressed or understood ; but, when they modify the same noun, the article should not be repeated.

Explanation.—*A cotton and a silk umbrella* means *two* umbrellas—

one cotton and the other silk; the word *umbrella* is understood after *cotton*. A *cotton and silk umbrella* means *one* umbrella partly cotton and partly silk; *cotton* and *silk* modify the same noun—*umbrella*. *The wise and the good* means two classes; *the wise and good* means one class.

Direction.—*Study the Caution as explained, and correct these errors :—*

1. The Northern and Southern Hemisphere. 2. The Northern and the Southern Hemispheres. 3. The right and left hand. 4. A Pullman and Wagner sleeping-coach. 5. The fourth and the fifth verses. 6. The fourth and fifth verse. 7. A Webster's and Worcester's dictionary.

Caution.—Repeat *an, a,* or *the* before connected nouns denoting things that are to be distinguished from each other or emphasized.

Direction.—*Study the Caution, and correct these errors :—*

1. There is a difference between the sin and sinner. 2. We criticise not the dress but address of the speaker. 3. A noun and pronoun are alike in office. 4. Distinguish carefully between an adjective and adverb. 5. The lion, as well as tiger, belongs to the cat tribe. 6. Neither the North Pole nor South Pole has yet been reached. 7. The secretary and treasurer were both absent. (*The secretary and treasurer was absent*—referring to one person—is correct.)

Caution.—*A few* and *a little* should be used when opposed to *none ; few* when opposed to *many ;* and *little* when opposed to *much.*

Examples.—He saved *a few* things and *a little* money from the wreck. *Few* shall part where many meet. *Little* was said or done about it.

Direction.—*Study the Caution, and correct these errors :—*

1. There are a few pleasant days in March, because it is a stormy month. 2. He saved a little from the fire, as it broke out in the

night. 3. Few men live to be a hundred years old, but not many. 4. Little can be done, but not much.

Direction.—*Write correct sentences illustrating every point in these Cautions.*

LESSON 91.

CONSTRUCTION OF ADJECTIVES—CONTINUED.

Caution.—Choose apt adjectives, but do not use them needlessly; avoid such as repeat the idea or exaggerate it.

Remark.—The following adjectives are obviously needless: *Good* virtues; *verdant* green; *painful* toothache; *umbrageous* shade.

Direction.—*Study the Caution carefully, and correct these errors:*—

1. It was splendid fun. 2. It was a tremendous dew. 3. He used less words than the other speaker. 4. The lad was neither docile nor teachable. 5. The belief in immortality is common and universal. 6. It was a gorgeous apple. 7. The arm-chair was roomy and capacious. 8. It was a lovely bunn, but I paid a frightful price for it.

Caution.—Place adjectives where there can be no doubt as to what you intend them to modify. If those forming a series are of different rank, place nearest the noun the one most closely modifying it. If they are of the same rank, place them where they will sound best—generally in the order of length—the shortest first.

Direction.—*Study the Caution, and correct these errors:*—

1. A new bottle of wine. 2. The house was comfortable and large. 3. A salt barrel of pork. 4. It was a blue soft beautiful sky. 5. A

fried dish of bacon. 6. We saw in the distance a precipitous, barren, towering mountain. 7. Two gray fiery little eyes. 8. A docile and mild pupil. 9. A pupil, docile and mild.

Direction.—*Write correct sentences illustrating every point in these two Cautions.*

Miscellaneous Errors.

Direction.—*Two of the expressions below are correct. Give the Cautions which the others violate and correct the errors:—*

1. I can bear the heat of summer, but not cold of winter. 2. The North and South Pole. 3. The eldest son of a duke is called "marquis." 4. He had deceived me, and so I had a little faith in him. 5. An old and young man. 6. A prodigious snow-ball hit my cheek. 7. The evil is intolerable and not to be borne. 8. The fat, two lazy men. 9. It was a fearful storm. 10. A white and red flag were flying. 11. His unusual, unexpected, and extraordinary success surprised him. 12. He wanted a apple, an hard apple. 13. A dried box of herrings. 14. He received a honor. 15. Such an use! 16. The day was delightful and warm. 17. Samuel Adams's habits were unostentatious, frugal, and simple. 18. The victory was complete, though a few of the enemy were killed or captured. 19. The truth is mighty and will prevail. 20. The scepter, the miter, and coronet seem to me poor things for great men to contend for. 21. A few can swim across the Straits of Dover, for the width is great and the current strong. 22. I have a contemptible opinion of you. 23. She has less friends than I.

LESSON 92.

CLASSES OF VERBS AND ADVERBS.

Introductory Hints.—You learned in Lesson 28 that in saying *Washington captured* we do not fully express the act performed. Adding *Cornwallis*, we complete the predicate by naming the one that receives the act that passes over from the doer. *Transitive* means *passing over*, and so all verbs that represent an action as passing over from a doer to a receiver are called **Transitive Verbs**. If we say *Cornwallis was captured by Washington*, the verb is still transitive; but the *object, Cornwallis*, which names the receiver, is here the *subject* of the sentence, and not, as before, the *object complement*. You see that the *object*, the word that names the receiver of the action, may be the subject, or it may be the object complement.

All verbs that, like *fall* in *Leaves fall*, do not represent the action as passing over to a receiver, and all that express mere being or state of being are called **Intransitive Verbs**.

A verb transitive in one sentence; as, He *writes* good English, may be intransitive in another; as, He *writes* well—meaning simply *He is a good writer*. A verb is transitive only when an object is expressed or obviously understood.

Washington captured Cornwallis. Here *captured* represents the action as having taken place in *past time*. *Tense* means *time*, and so this verb is in the *past tense*. *Cornwallis captured, the war speedily closed.* Here *captured* is, as you have learned, a participle; and, representing the action as past at the time indicated by *closed*, it is a *past participle*. Notice that *ed* is added to *capture* (final *e* is always dropped when *ed* is added) to form its past tense and its past participle. All verbs that form the past tense and the past participle by adding *ed* to the present are called **Regular Verbs**.

All verbs that do not form the past tense and the past participle by adding *ed* to the present; as, *fall, fell, fallen; go, went, gone*, are called **Irregular Verbs**.

Early, hereafter, now, often, soon, presently, etc., used to modify any verb—as *will go* in I *will go soon*—by expressing *time*, are called **Adverbs of Time**.

Away, back, elsewhere, hence, out, within, etc., used to modify any verb—as *will go* in I *will go away*—by expressing *direction* or *place*, are called **Adverbs of Place**.

Exceedingly, hardly, quite, sufficiently, too, very, etc., used to modify a word—as the adjective *hot* in The tea is *very hot*—by expressing *degree*, are called **Adverbs of Degree**.

Plainly, so, thus, well, no, yes,* etc., used to modify a word—as *spoke* in He *spoke plainly*—by expressing *manner*, are called **Adverbs of Manner.**

Hence, therefore, why, etc., used in making an inference or in expressing cause—as, It is dark, *hence,* or *therefore,* the sun is down ; *Why* is it dark ?—are called **Adverbs of Cause.**

Some adverbs fall into more than one class ; as, *as,* and *so.*

Some adverbs, as you have learned, connect clauses, and so are called **Conjunctive Adverbs.**

DEFINITIONS.

A *Verb* is a word that asserts action, being, or state of being.

An *Adverb* is a word used to modify a verb, an adjective, or an adverb.

CLASSES OF VERBS WITH RESPECT TO MEANING.

A *Transitive Verb* is one that requires an object.†

An *Intransitive Verb* is one that does not require an object.

CLASSES OF VERBS WITH RESPECT TO FORM.

A *Regular Verb* is one that forms its past tense and past participle by adding *ed* to the present.

An *Irregular Verb* is one that does not form its past tense and past participle by adding *ed* to the present.

---

* Many grammarians say that *no* and *yes* (*nay* and *yea*) are independent when they answer questions. But they seem rather to modify words omitted in the answer but contained in the question ; as, Did you see him ? *No* = I did *no* (*not*) see him. That the form *no* is not *now* used in an answer except when the modified words are omitted does not argue against the position taken. Compare *whether or no,* condemned by some, but good English nevertheless. *Other* words change their form when the modified words are omitted ; as, *My* book is new. *Mine* is new.

Yes (= *certainly*) may be explained in a similar way. Some make of these words a separate part of speech, and call them *responsives.*

† The *object* of a transitive verb, that is, the name of the receiver of the action, may be the *object complement,* or it may be the *subject ;* as, Brutus stabbed Cæsar, Cæsar was stabbed by Brutus. See p. 164.

CLASSES OF ADVERBS.

Adverbs of Time are those that generally answer the question, *When?*

Adverbs of Place are those that generally answer the question, *Where?*

Adverbs of Degree are those that generally answer the question, *To what extent?*

Adverbs of Manner are those that generally answer the question, *In what way?*

Adverbs of Cause are those that generally answer the question, *Why?*

Direction.—*Point out the transitive and the intransitive, the regular and the irregular verbs in Lesson 14, and classify the adverbs.*

LESSON 93.

CONSTRUCTION OF ADVERBS.

Caution.—Choose apt adverbs, but do not use them needlessly or instead of other forms of expression; avoid such as repeat the idea or exaggerate it.

Examples.—I could *ill* (not *illy*) afford the time. Do *as* (not *like*) I do. A diphthong is *the union of* two vowels (not *where* or *when* two vowels unite) in the same syllable. This (not this *here* or *'ere*) sentence is correct. He wrote that (not *how that*) he had been sick. The belief in immortality is *universally* held (not *universally* held *everywhere*). His nose was *very* (not *terribly* or *frightfully*) red.

Direction.—*Study the Caution and the Examples, and correct these errors:*—

1. I returned back here yesterday. 2. He had not hardly a minute to spare. 3. The affair was settled amicably, peaceably, and peacefully. 4. It was awfully amusing. 5. This 'ere knife is dull. 6. That

'ere horse has the heaves. 7. A direct quotation is when the exact words of another are copied. 8. I do not like too much sugar in my tea. 9. He seldom or ever went home sober. 10. The belief in immortality is universally held by all. 11. I am dreadfully glad to hear that. 12. This is a fearfully long lesson. 13. He said how that he would go.

Caution.—Place adverbs where there can be no doubt as to what you intend them to modify. Have regard to the sound also. They seldom stand between *to* and the *infinitive.*

Examples.—*I only* rowed across the river = *I only* (= *alone*, an adjective), and no one else, rowed, etc., or = I *only rowed*, etc., but did not *swim* or *wade*. I rowed *only across* the river = *across*, not *up* or *down*, etc. I rowed across the *river only* = the *river only*, not the *bay*, etc. *Merely to see* (not *to merely see*) her was sufficient. *Not every collegian* is a scholar (not *Every collegian* is *not* a scholar).

Direction.—*Study the Caution and the Examples, and correct these errors :—*

1. I have thought of marrying often. 2. We only eat three meals a day. 3. He hopes to rapidly recruit. 4. All is not gold that glitters. 5. He tries to distinctly speak. 6. He tries distinctly to speak. 7. All that glitters is not gold. 8. His sagacity almost appears miraculous.

Caution.—Unless you wish to *affirm*, do not use two negative words so that they shall contradict each other.

Examples.—No one *has* (not *hasn't*) yet reached the North Pole. *No unpleasant* circumstance happened (proper, because it is intended to affirm).

Direction.—*Study the Caution and the Examples, and correct these errors :—*

1. No other reason can never be given. 2. He doesn't do nothing. 3. He isn't improving much, I don't think. 4. There must be something wrong when children do not love neither father nor mother. 5. He isn't no sneak. 6. Charlie Ross can't nowhere be found.

Caution.—Do not use adverbs for adjectives or adjectives for adverbs.

Examples.—1. The moon looks *calm* and *peaceful* (not *calmly* and *peacefully*, as the words are intended *to describe the moon*). 2. The moon looks down *calmly* and *peacefully* on the battle field (not *calm* and *peaceful*, as the words are intended to tell *how* she *performs the act*). 3. These terms are *more nearly* (not *nearer*) related.

Direction.—*Study the Caution and the Examples, and correct these errors:—*

1. It was a softly blue sky. 2. The river runs rapid. 3. You must read more distinct. 4. It was an uncommon good harvest. 5. She is most sixteen. 6. The discussion waxed warmly. 7. The prima donna sings sweet. 8. She is miserable poor. 9. My head feels badly. 10. He spoke up prompt. 11. He went most there. 12. He behaved very bad. 13. This is a mighty cold day.

Direction.—*Write correct sentences illustrating every point in these four Cautions.*

LESSON 94.

CONSTRUCTION OF ADVERBS—CONTINUED.

Miscellaneous Errors.

Direction.—*Three of these sentences are correct. Give the Cautions which the others violate, and correct the errors:—*

1. Begin it over again. 2. This can be done easier. 3. The house is extra warm. 4. Most every one goes there. 5. The sparrow chirps constantly. 6. He hasn't his lesson, I don't believe. 7. A circle can't in no way be squared. 8. This is a remarkable cold winter. 9. The soldier died hard. 10. Feathers feel softly. 11. It is pretty near finished. 12. Verbosity is when too many words are used. 13. It is a wonderful fine day. 14. He is some better just now. 15. Generally every morning we went to the spring. 16. I wish to simply state this

point. 17. He tried to not only injure but to also ruin the man. 18. The lesson was prodigiously long. 19. The cars will not stop at this station only when the bell rings. 20. He can do it as good as any one can. 21. Most everybody talks so. 22. He hasn't yet gone, I don't believe. 23. He behaved thoughtlessly, recklessly, and carelessly. 24. That 'ere book is readable. 25. I will not go but once. 26. I can't find out neither where the lesson begins nor where it ends. 27. They were nearly dressed alike. 28. The tortured man begged that they would kill him again and again. 29. The fortune was lavishly, profusely, and prodigally spent. 30. He is not unjust. 31. We publish all the information, official and otherwise.

LESSON 95.

PREPOSITIONS.

DEFINITION.—A *Preposition* is a word that introduces a phrase modifier, and shows the relation, in sense, of its principal word to the word modified.

Composition.

Direction.— *We give, below, a list of the prepositions in common use. Make short sentences, in which each of these shall be aptly used. Use two or three of them in a single sentence, if you wish :—*

Aboard,	athwart,	ere,	till,
about,	before,	for,	to,
above,	behind,	from,	toward,
across,	below,	in,	towards,
after,	beneath,	into,	under,
against,	beside,	of,	underneath,
along,	besides,	on,	until,
amid,	between,	over,	unto,
amidst,	betwixt,	past,	up,
among,	beyond,	round,	upon,
amongst,	but,	since,	with,
around,	by,	through,	within,
at,	down,	throughout,	without.

Remark.—*Bating, concerning, during, excepting, notwithstanding, pending, regarding, respecting, saving,* and *touching* are still participles in form, and sometimes are such in use. But in most cases the participial meaning has faded out of them, and they express mere relations.

But, except, and *save,* in such a sentence as, All *but* or *except* or *save him* were lost, are usually classed with prepositions.

The phrases *aboard of, according to, along with, as to, because of* (by cause of), *from among, from between, from under,* etc., *instead of* (in stead of), *out of, over against,* and *round about* may be called compound prepositions. But *from* in these compounds; as, *He crawled from under the ruins,* really introduces a phrase, the principal term of which is the phrase that follows *from.*

Many prepositions become adverbs when the noun which ordinarily follows them is omitted; as, He rode *past,* He stands *above.*

LESSON 96.

COMPOSITION—PREPOSITIONS—CONTINUED.

To the Teacher.—Most prepositions express relations so diverse, and so delicate in their shades of distinction that a definition of them based upon etymology would mislead. A happy and discriminating use of prepositions can be acquired only by an extended study of good authors. We do, below, all that we think it prudent or profitable to do with them. He should be a man of wide and careful reading who assumes to teach pupils that such prepositions, and such *only,* should be used with certain words. Nowhere in grammar is dogmatism more dangerous than here. That grammarian exceeds his commission who marks out for the pupils' feet a path narrower than the highway which the usage of the best writers and speakers has cast up.*

---

* Take a single illustration : grammarians, in general, teach that *between* and *betwixt* "refer to two," are used "only when two things or sets of things are referred to." Ordinarily, and while clinging to their derivation, they are so used, but are they *always,* and *must* they be ? " A choice between two or more alternatives."—*Mulligan.* "There was a hunting match agreed upon betwixt a lion, an ass, and a fox."— *L'Estrange.* "Between two or more authors different readers will differ."—*Campbell.* "Read between the lines."—*Matthew Arnold.* " The Greeks left no spaces between

Direction.— *We give, below, a few words with the prepositions which usually accompany them. Form short sentences containing these words combined with each of the prepositions which follow them, and note carefully the different relations expressed by the different prepositions :—*

(Consult the dictionary for both the preposition and the accompanying word.)

Abide *at, by, with ;* accommodate *to, with ;* advantage *of, over ;* agree *to, with ;* angry *at, with ;* anxious *about, for ;* argue *against, with ;* arrive *at, in ;* attend *on,* or *upon, to ;* careless *about, in, of ;* communicate *to, with ;* compare *to, with ;* consists *in, of ;* defend *against, from ;* die *by, for, of ;* different *from ;* disappointed *in, of ;* distinguish *by, from ;* familiar *to, with ;* impatient *for, of ;* indulge *in, with ;* influence *on, over, with ;* insensible *of, to.*

LESSON 97.

CONSTRUCTION OF PREPOSITIONS.

Direction.—*Do with the following words as you were required to do above :—*

Inquire *after, for, into, of ;* intrude *into, upon ;* joined *to, with ;* liberal *of, to ;* live *at, in, on ;* look *after, for, on ;* need *of ;* obliged *for, to ;* part *from, with ;* placed *in, on ;* reconcile *to, with ;* regard *for, to ;* remonstrate *against, with ;* sank *beneath, in, into ;* share *in, of, with ;* sit *in, on,* or *upon ;* smile *at, on ;* solicitous *about, for ;* strive *for, with, against ;* taste *for, of ;* touch *at, on,* or *upon ;* useful *for, in, to ;* weary *of, in, with ;* yearn *for, towards.*

---

their words."—*Wilson.* "Betwixt the slender boughs came glimpses of her ivory neck."—*Bryant.* With what clumsy circumlocutions would our speech be filled if prepositions could never slip the leash of their etymology ! What simple and graceful substitute could be found for the last phrase in this sentence, for instance: There were forty desks in the room with ample space *between them ?*

LESSON 93.

CONSTRUCTION OF PREPOSITIONS—CONTINUED.

Caution.—Great care must be used in the choice of prepositions.

Direction.—*Correct these errors :*—

1. This book is different to that. 2. He stays to home. 3. They two quarreled among each other. 4. He is in want for money. 5. I was followed with a crowd. 6. He fell from the bridge in* the water. 7. He fought into* the Revolution. 8. He bears a close resemblance of his father. 9. He entered in the plot. 10. He lives at London. 11. He lives in the turn of the road. 12. I have need for a vacation. 13. The child died with the croup. 14. He took a walk, but was disappointed of it. 15. He did not take a walk; he was disappointed in it. 16. He was accused with felony. 17. School keeps upon Monday. 18. Place a mark between each leaf. 19. He is angry at his father. 20. He placed a letter into my hands. 21. She is angry with your conduct. 22. What is the matter of him? 23. I saw him over to the house. 24. These plants differ with each other. 25. He boards to the hotel. 26. I board in the hotel. 27. She stays at the North. 28. He was averse from the war. 29. You make no use with your talents. 30. He threw himself onto the bed. 31. They are hard to work. 32. He distributed the apples between his four brothers. 33. He went in the park. 34. You can confide on him. 35. He arrived to Toronto. 36. I agree with that plan. 37. The evening was spent by reading. 38. Can you accommodate me in one of those? 39. What a change a century has produced upon our country! 40. He stays to school late. 41. The year of the Restoration plunged Milton in bitter poverty. 42. The Colonies declared themselves independent from England. 43. I spent my Saturdays by going in the country, and enjoying myself by fishing.

---

* *In* denotes motion or rest in a condition or place ; *into*, change from one condition or place into another. "When one is outside of a place, he may be able to get *into* it; but he cannot do anything *in* it, until he has got *into* it."

LESSON 98.

CONSTRUCTION OF PREPOSITIONS—CONTINUED.

Caution.—Do not use prepositions needlessly.

Direction.—*Correct these errors :—*

1. I went there at about noon. 2. In what latitude is Boston in? 3. He came in for to have a talk. 4. I started a week ago from last Saturday. 5. He was born August 15, in 1834. 6. A good place to see a play is at Wallack's. 7. He went to home. 8. I was leading of a horse about (*leading* is transitive). 9. By what state is Kentucky bounded by? 10. His servants ye are to whom ye obey. 11. Where are you going to? 12. They admitted of the fact. 13. Raise your book off of the table. 14. He took the poker from out of the fire. 15. Of what is the air composed of? 16. You can tell by trying of it. 17. Where have you been to? 18. The boy is like to his father. 19. They offered to him a chair. 20. This is the subject of which I intend to write about. 21. Butter brings twenty cents for a pound. 22. Give to me a knife. 23. I have a brother of five years old. 24. To what may Italy be likened to? 25. In about April the farmer puts in his seed. 26. Jack's favorite sport was in robbing orchards. 27. Before answering of you, I must think. 28. He lives near to the river. 29. Keep off of the grass.

Caution.—Do not omit prepositions when they are needed.

Direction.—*Correct these errors :—*

1. There is no use going there. 2. He is worthy our help. 3. I was prevented going. 4. He was banished the country. 5. He is unworthy our charity. 6. What use is this to him? 7. He was born on the 15th August, 1834. 8. Adam and Eve were expelled the garden. 9. It was the size of a pea. 10. Egypt is the west side of the Red Sea. 11. His efforts were not for the great, but the lowly. 12. He received dispatches from England and Russia.

Direction.—*Point out the prepositions in Lessons 80 and 81, and name the words between which, in sense, they show the relation.*

LESSON 100.

CLASSES OF CONJUNCTIONS AND OTHER CONNECTIVES.

Introductory Hints.—The stars look down upon the roofs of the living *and* upon the graves of the dead, *but neither* the living *nor* the dead are conscious of their gaze. Here *and, but, neither,* and *nor* connect words, phrases, and clauses of *equal rank,* or *order,* and so are called **Co-ordinate Conjunctions.** Both clauses may be independent, or both dependent but of *equal* rank.

At the burning of Moscow, it seemed *as* [it would seem] *if* the heavens were lighted up *that* the nations might behold the scene. Here *as, if,* and *that* connect each a lower, or subordinate, clause to a clause of *higher* rank, and so are called **Subordinate Conjunctions.** One clause may be independent and the other dependent, or both dependent but of *unequal* rank.

DEFINITIONS.

A *Conjunction* is a word used to connect words, phrases, or clauses.*

Co-ordinate Conjunctions are such as connect words, phrases, or clauses of the same rank.

Subordinate Conjunctions are such as connect clauses of different rank.

Remark.—Some of the connectives below are conjunctions proper; some are relative pronouns; and some are adverbs or adverb phrases, which, in addition to their office as modifiers, may, in the absence of the conjunction, take its office upon themselves, and connect the clauses.

To the Teacher.—We do not advise the memorizing of these lists. The pupils should be able to name the different groups, and some of the most common connectives of each.

---

* Some of the co-ordinate conjunctions, as *and* and *but,* are used to connect, in thought, sentences separated by the period, and even to connect paragraphs. In analysis and parsing, we regard only the individual sentence and treat such connectives as introductory.

Classes of Conjunctions and other Connectives. 175

CO-ORDINATE CONNECTIVES.*

Copulative.—*And, both . . . and, as well as,*† are conjunctions proper. *Accordingly, also, besides, consequently, furthermore, hence, likewise, moreover, now, so, then,* and *therefore* are conjunctive adverbs.

Adversative.—*But* and *whereas* are conjunctions proper. *However, nevertheless, notwithstanding, on the contrary, on the other hand, still,* and *yet* are conjunctive adverbs.

Alternative.—*Neither, nor, or, either . . . or,* and *neither . . . nor* are conjunctions proper. *Else* and *otherwise* are conjunctive adverbs.

SUBORDINATE CONNECTIVES.

CONNECTIVES OF ADJECTIVE CLAUSES.

That, what, whatever, which, whichever, who, and *whoever* are relative pronouns. *When, where, whereby, wherein,* and *why* are conjunctive adverbs.

CONNECTIVES OF ADVERB CLAUSES.

Time.—*After, as, before, ere, since, till, until, when, whenever, while,* and *whilst* are conjunctive adverbs.

Place.—*Whence, where,* and *wherever* are conjunctive adverbs.

Degree.—*As, than, that,* and *the* are conjunctive adverbs, correlative with adjectives or adverbs.

Manner.—*As* is a conjunctive adverb, correlative, often, with an adjective or an adverb.

Real Cause.—*As, because, for, since,* and *whereas* are conjunctions proper.

Reason.—*Because, for,* and *since* are conjunctions proper.

Purpose.—*In order that, lest* (= *that not*), *that,* and *so that* are conjunctions proper.

Condition.—*Except, if, in case that, on condition that, provided, provided that,* and *unless* are conjunctions proper.

Concession.—*Although, if* (= *even if*), *notwithstanding, though,* and *whether* are conjunctions proper. *However* is a conjunctive adverb. *Whatever, whichever,* and *whoever* are relative pronouns used indefinitely.

---

* For explanations of *Copulative, Adversative,* and *Alternative,* see Lesson 76.
† The *as well as* in *He, as well as I, went;* and not that in *He is as well as I am.*

CONNECTIVES OF NOUN CLAUSES.

If, lest, that, and *whether* are conjunctions proper. *What, which,* and *who* are pronouns introducing questions; *how, when, whence, where,* and *why* are conjunctive adverbs.

Direction.—*Study the lists above, and point out all the connectives in Lessons* 80, *and* 81, *telling which are relative pronouns, which are conjunctions proper, and which are conjunctive adverbs.*

To the Teacher.—If the pupils lack maturity, or, if it is found necessary to abridge this work in order to conform to a prescribed course of study, the six following lessons may be omitted. The authors consider these exercises very profitable, but their omission will occasion no break in the course.

LESSON 101.

COMPOSITION—CONNECTIVES.

Direction.— *Write* 20 *compound sentences whose clauses shall be joined by connectives named in the three subdivisions of Co-ordinate connectives.*

LESSON 102.

COMPOSITION—CONNECTIVES—CONTINUED.

Direction.— *Write* 20 *complex sentences whose clauses shall be joined by connectives of adjective clauses, and by connectives of adverb clauses of time, place, degree, and manner.*

LESSON 103.

COMPOSITION—CONNECTIVES—CONTINUED.

Direction.— *Write* 20 *complex sentences whose clauses shall be joined by connectives of adverb clauses of real cause, reason, purpose, condition, and concession, and by connectives of noun clauses.*

LESSON 104.
CONNECTIVES.
ANALYSIS.

Direction.—*Tell what kinds of clauses follow the connectives below, and what are the u s u a l connectives of such clauses, and then analyze the sentences :—*

As may connect a clause expressing *manner, time, degree, cause,* or *reason.*

1. Mount Marcy is not so high as Mount Washington.
2. As I passed by, I found an altar with this inscription.
3. It must be raining, as men are carrying umbrellas.
4. Ice floats, as water expands in freezing.
5. Half-learned lessons slip from the memory, as an icicle from the hand.

If may connect a clause expressing *condition, time, concession,* or it may introduce a *noun* clause.

6. If a slave's lungs breathe our air, that moment he is free.
7. If wishes were horses, all beggars might ride.
8. Who knows if* one of the Pleiads is really missing.
9. If the flights of Dryden are higher, Pope continues longer on the wing.

Lest may connect a clause expressing *purpose* or it may introduce a *noun* clause.

10. England fears lest Russia may endanger British rule in India.
11. Watch and pray, lest ye enter into temptation.

Since may connect a clause expressing *time, cause,* or *reason.*

12. It must be raining, since men are carrying umbrellas.
13. Many thousand years have gone by since the Pyramids were built.
14. Since the Puritans could not be convinced, they were persecuted.

---
* Many grammarians say that *if* here is improperly used for *whether*. But this use of *if* is common with good authors in early and in modern English.

LESSON 105.

CONNECTIVES—CONTINUED.

ANALYSIS.

Direction.—*Tell what kinds of clauses follow the connectives below, and what are the u s u a l connectives of such clauses, and then analyze the sentences :—*

That may introduce a *noun clause* or an *adjective* clause, or connect a clause expressing *degree, cause,* or *purpose*.

1. The Pharisee thanked God that he was not like other men.
2. Vesuvius threw its lava so far that Herculaneum and Pompeii were buried.
3. The smith plunges his red-hot iron into water that he may harden it.
4. Socrates said that he who might be better employed was idle.
5. We never tell our secrets to people that pump for them.

When may connect a clause expressing *time, cause, condition,* an *adjective* clause, a *noun* clause, or it may connect *co-ordinate* clauses.

6. The Aztecs were astonished when they saw the Spanish horses.
7. November is the month when the deer sheds its horns.
8. When the future is uncertain, make the most of the present.
9. When the five great European races left Asia is a question.
10. When judges accept bribes, what may we expect from common people ?
11. The dial instituted a formal inquiry, when hands, wheels, and weights protested their innocence.

Where may connect a clause expressing *place,* an *adjective* clause, or a *noun* clause.

12. No one knows the place where Moses was buried.
13. Where Moses was buried is still a question.
14. No one has been where Moses was buried.

While may connect a clause expressing *time* or *concession*, or it may connect *co-ordinate* clauses.

15. Napoleon was a genius, while Wellington was a man of talents.
16. While we sleep, the body is rebuilt.
17. While Charles I. had many excellent traits, he was a bad king.

LESSON 106.

CONNECTIVES—CONTINUED.

ANALYSIS.

Direction.—*Use the appropriate connectives, and change these compound sentences to complex without changing the meaning, and then analyze them :—*

(Let one dependent clause be an adjective clause ; let three express cause ; five, condition ; and two, concession.)

1. Cæsar put the proffered crown aside, but he would fain have had it.
2. Take away honor and imagination and poetry from war, and it becomes carnage.
3. His crime has been discovered, and he must flee.
4. You must eat, or you will die.
5. Wisdom is the principal thing, therefore get wisdom.
6. Let but the commons hear this testament, and they would go and kiss dead Cæsar's wounds.
7. Men are carrying umbrellas; it is raining.
8. Have ye brave sons ? look in the next fierce brawl to see them die.
9. The Senate knows this, the Consul sees it, and yet the traitor lives.
10. Take away the grandeur of his cause, and Washington is a rebel instead of the purest of patriots.
11. The diamond is a sparkling gem, and it is pure carbon.

Direction.—*Two of the dependent clauses, below, express condition, and three concession. Place an appropriate conjunction before each, and then analyze the sentences :—*

12. Should we fail, it can be no worse for us.
13. Had the Plantagenets succeeded in France, there would never have been an England.
14. Were he my brother, I could do no more for him.
15. Were I so disposed, I could not gratify the reader.
16. " Were I [Admiral Nelson] to die this moment, *more frigates* would be found written on my heart."

LESSON 107.

CONSTRUCTION OF CONNECTIVES.

Caution.—Some conjunctions and conjunctive adverbs may stand in correlation with other words. *And* may be accompanied by *both ;* as by *as,* by *so,* or by *such ; but* (*but also* and *but likewise*) by *not only ; if* by *then ; nor* by *neither ; or* by *either* or by *whether ; that* by *so ; the* by *the; though* by *yet ; when* by *then ;* and *where* by *there.*

Be careful that the right words stand in correlation, and stand where they belong.

Examples.—Give me neither riches *nor* (not *or*) poverty. I cannot find either my book *or* (not *nor*) my hat. Dogs not only bark (not *not only dogs* bark) but also bite. Not only dogs (not *dogs not only*) bark but wolves also. He was neither (not *neither was*) rich nor poor.

Direction.—*Study the Caution, and correct these errors :—*

1. He not only gave me advice, but also money. 2. A theatrical part may either imply some peculiarity of gesture or a dissimulation of my real sentiments. 3. She not only dressed richly but tastefully. 4. Neither Massachusetts or Pennsylvania has the population of New York. 5. Thales was not only famous for his knowledge of nature,

Construction of Connectives.

but also for his moral wisdom. 6. Not only he is successful, but he deserves to succeed. 7. There was nothing either strange nor interesting.

Caution.—Choose apt connectives, but do not use them needlessly or instead of other parts of speech.

Examples.—Seldom, *if* (not *or*) ever, should an adverb stand between *to* and the infinitive. I will try *to* (not *and*) do better next time. No one can deny *that* (not *but*) he has money. A harrow is drawn over the ground, which (not *and which*) covers the seed. Who doubts *that* (not *but that* or *but what*) Napoleon lived? The doctor had scarcely left *when* (not *but*) a patient called. He has no love for his father *or* (not *nor*) for his mother (the negative *no* is felt throughout the sentence, and need not be repeated by *nor*). He was not well, nor (not *or*) was he sick (*not* is expended in the first clause; *nor* is needed to make the second clause negative).

Direction.—*Study the Caution and the Examples, and correct these errors :—*

1. The excellence of Virgil, and which he possesses beyond other poets, is tenderness. 2. Try and recite the lesson perfectly to-morrow. 3. Who can doubt but that there is a God? 4. No one can eat nor drink while he is talking. 5. He seldom or ever went to church. 6. No one can deny but that the summer is the hottest season. 7. I do not know as I shall like it. 8. You will not succeed without you are careful.

Caution.—*Else, other, otherwise, rather,* and adjectives and adverbs expressing a comparison are usually followed by *than.* But *else, other,* and *more,* implying something *additional,* but not different in kind, may be followed by *but* or *besides.*

Examples.—A diamond is nothing *else than* carbon. Junius was no *other than* Sir Philip Francis. The cripple cannot walk *otherwise than* on crutches. Americans would *rather* travel *than* stay at home. I rose *earlier than* I meant to. He can converse on *other* topics *besides* politics.

Direction.—*Study the Caution and the Examples, and correct these errors :—*

1. Battles are fought with other weapons besides pop-guns. 2. The moon is something else but green cheese. 3. Cornwallis could not do otherwise but surrender. 4. It was no other but the President. 5. He no sooner saw the enemy but he turned and ran.

Caution.—Two or more connected words or phrases referring to another word or phrase should each make good sense with it.

Examples.—I have always (add *said*) and still do say that labor is honorable. Shakespeare was greater than any other poet that has (add *lived*) or is now alive. The boy is stronger than his sister, but not so tall (not The boy is *stronger*, but not *so tall*, *as* his sister).

Direction.—*Study the Caution and the Examples, and correct these errors :—*

1. Gold is heavier, but not so useful, as iron. 2. Gold is not so useful, but heavier, than iron. 3. This is as valuable, if not more so, than that. 4. Faithful boys have always and always will learn the lessons. 5. Bread is more nutritious, but not so cheap, as potatoes. 6. This dedication may serve for almost any book that has, is, or shall be published.

LESSON 108.

MISCELLANEOUS ERRORS.

Direction.—*Correct these errors, telling what Caution each violates :—*

1. Carthage and Rome were rival powers: this city in Africa, and that in Europe; the one on the northern coast of the Mediterranean, the other on the southern. 2. The right and left lung were diseased. 3. The right and the left lungs were diseased. 4. My friend has sailed for Europe, who was here yesterday. 5. There are some men which

are always young. 6. I cannot think but what God is good. 7. Thimbles, that are worn on the finger, are used in pushing the needle. 8. A told B that he was his best friend. 9. Them scissors are very dull. 10. Ethan Allen, being a rash man, he tried to capture Canada. 11. The lady that was thrown from the carriage, and who was picked up insensible, died. 12. The eye and ear have different offices. 13. I only laugh when I feel like it. 14. This is the same man who called yesterday. 15. He was an humble man. 16. He was thrown forward onto his face. 17. A knows more, but does not talk so well, as B. 18. The book cost a dollar, and which is a great price. 19. At what wharf does the boat stop at? 20. The music sounded harshly. 21. He would neither go himself or send anybody. 22. It isn't but a short distance. 23. The butter is splendid. 24. The boy was graceful and tall. 25. He hasn't, I don't suppose, laid by much. 26. One would rather have few friends than a few friends. 27. He is outrageously proud. 28. Not only the boy skated, but he enjoyed it. 29. He has gone way out West. 30. Who doubts but what two and two are four? 31. Some people never have and never will bathe in salt water. 32. The problem was difficult to exactly understand. 33. It was the length of your finger. 34. He bought a condensed can of milk. 35. The fish breathes with other organs besides lungs. 36. The death is inevitable. 37. She wore a peculiar kind of a dress. 38. When shall we meet together? 39. He talks like you do.

LESSON 109.

VARIOUS USES OF WHAT, THAT, AND BUT.

What may be used as a *relative pronoun*, an *interrogative pronoun*, a *definitive adjective*, an *adverb*, and an *interjection*.

Examples.—He did *what* was right. *What* did he say? *What* man is happy with the toothache? *What* with confinement and *what* with bad diet, the prisoner found himself reduced to a skeleton (here *what* = *partly*, and modifies the phrase following it). *What!* you a lion?

That may be used as a *relative pronoun*, an *adjective pronoun*, a *definitive adjective*, a *conjunction*, and a *conjunctive adverb*.

Examples.—He *that* does a good deed is instantly ennobled. *That* is heroism. *That* man is a hero. We eat *that* we may live. It was so cold *that* the mercury froze.

But may be used as a *conjunction*, an *adverb*, an *adjective*, and a *preposition*.

Examples.—The ostrich is a bird, *but* (adversative conjunction) it cannot fly. Not a sparrow falls *but* (= *unless*—subordinate conjunction) God wills it. He was all *but* (conjunction or preposition) dead = He was all dead, *but* he was not dead, or He was all (anything in that line) *except* (the climax) dead. No man is so wicked *but* (conjunctive adverb) he loves virtue = No man is wicked *to that degree in which* he loves *not* virtue (*so = to that degree, but = in which not*). We meet *but* (adverb = *only*) to part. Life is *but* (adjective = *only*) a dream. All *but* (preposition = *except*) him had fled. The tears of love were hopeless *but* (preposition = *except*) for thee. I cannot *but* remember = I cannot *do anything but* (preposition = *except*) remember. There is no fireside *but* (preposition) has one vacant chair (*except the one which* has); or, regarding *but* as a negative relative = *that not*, the sentence = There is no fireside *that* has *not* one vacant chair.

Direction.—*Study the examples given above; point out the exact use of w h a t, t h a t, and b u t in these sentences, and then analyze the sentences :—*

1. He did nothing but laugh. 2. It was once supposed that crystal is ice frozen so hard that it cannot be thawed. 3. What love equals a mother's? 4. There is nobody here but me. 5. The fine arts were all but proscribed. 6. There's not a breeze but whispers of thy name. 7. The longest life is but a day. 8. What if the bee love not these barren boughs? 9. That life is long which answers life's great end. 10. What! I the weaker vessel? 11. Whom should I obey but thee? 12. What by industry and what by economy, he had amassed a fortune. 13. I long ago found that out. 14. One should not always eat what he

likes. 15. There's not a white hair on your face but should have its effect of gravity. 16. It was a look that, but for its quiet, would have seemed disdain. 17. He came but to return.

LESSON 110.

REVIEW QUESTIONS.

Lesson 85.—Define a noun. What is the distinction between a common and a proper noun? Why is *music* a common noun? What is a collective noun? An abstract noun? Define a pronoun. What are the classes of pronouns? Define them. What is an antecedent?

Lesson 86.—Give and illustrate the Cautions respecting *he, it,* and *they;* the needless use of pronouns; the two styles of the pronoun; the use of *them* for *those,* and of *what* for *that;* and the use of *who, which, that,* and *what.*

Lesson 87.—Give and illustrate the Cautions respecting connected relative clauses; the relative in clauses not restrictive; the use of *that* instead of *who* or *which;* the position of the relative clause; and the use of *this* and *that, the one* and *the other.*

Lesson 89.—Define an adjective. What two classes are there? Define them. What adjectives do not limit? Illustrate.

Lesson 90.—Give and illustrate the Cautions respecting the use of the adjectives *an, a,* and *the;* and the use of *a few* and *few, a little* and *little.*

Lesson 91.—Give and illustrate the Cautions respecting the *choice* and the *position* of adjectives.

Lesson 92.—Define a verb. What are transitive verbs? Intransitive? Illustrate. What distinction is made between the object and the object complement? What are regular verbs? Irregular? Illustrate. What are the several classes of adverbs? Define them. What is a conjunctive adverb?

Lesson 93.—Give and illustrate the Cautions respecting the *choice* and *position* of adverbs, the use of *double negatives,* and the use of *adverbs for adjectives* and *adjectives for adverbs.*

LESSON 111.

REVIEW QUESTIONS—CONTINUED.

Lesson 95.—Define a preposition. Name some of the common prepositions. What is said of some ending in *ing?* Of *but, except,* and *save?* Of certain compound prepositions? When do prepositions become adverbs?

Lesson 98.—Give and illustrate the Caution as to the choice of prepositions. What, in general, is the difference between *in* and *into?*

Lesson 99.—Give and illustrate the two Cautions relating to the use of prepositions.

Lesson 100.—Define a conjunction. What are the two great classes of conjunctions, and what is their difference? What other parts of speech besides conjunctions connect? What are adverbs that connect called? Into what three classes are co-ordinate connectives subdivided? Name some of the conjunctions and the conjunctive adverbs of each class. What three kinds of clauses are connected by subordinate connectives? The connectives of adverb clauses are subdivided into what classes? Give a leading connective of each class.

Lessons 104, 105.—Illustrate two or more offices of each of the connectives *as, if, lest, since, that, when, where,* and *while.*

Lesson 107.—Give and illustrate the four Cautions relating to the construction of connectives.

Lesson 109.—Illustrate the offices of *what, that,* and *but.*

GENERAL REVIEW.

Schemes for the Conj., Prep., and Int.

(The numbers refer to Lessons.)

THE CONJUNCTION. Classes. { Co-ordinate. Subordinate. } 100–107.

THE PREPOSITION. No Classes (95, 98, 99).

THE INTERJECTION. No Classes (20, 21).

MODIFICATIONS OF THE PARTS OF SPEECH.

LESSON 112.

Introductory Hints.—You have learned that two words may express a thought, and that the thought may be varied by adding modifying words. You are now to learn that the meaning or use of a word may be changed by simply changing its form. The English language has lost most of its inflections, or forms, so that many of the changes in the meaning and the use of words are not now marked by changes in form. These changes in the *form, meaning,* and *use* of the parts of speech we call their **Modifications**.*

---

* Those grammarians that attempt to restrict *number, case, mode,* etc.,—what we here call *Modifications*—to *form,* find themselves within bounds which they continually overleap. They define *number,* for instance, as a *form,* or *inflection,* and yet speak of nouns "plural in form but singular in sense," or "singular in form but plural in sense;" that is, if you construe them rigorously, plural or singular in form but *singular or plural form* in sense. They tell you that *case* is a *form,* and yet insist that nouns have three cases, though only two forms; and speak of the *nominative* and the *objective case* of the noun, "although in fact the two cases are always the same in form "—*the two forms always the same in form!*

On the other hand, those that make what we call *Modifications* denote only *relations* or *conditions of words* cannot cling to these abstract terms. For instance, they ask the pupil to "pronounce and write the possessive of nouns," hardly expecting, we suppose, that the "condition" of a noun will be sounded or written; and they speak of "a noun in the singular with a plural application," in which expression *singular* must be taken to mean *singular form* to save it from sheer nonsense.

We know no way to steer clear of Scylla and keep out of Charybdis but to do what by the common use of the word we are allowed; viz., to take *Modifications* with such breadth of signification that it will apply to *meaning* and to *use,* as well as to *form.* Primarily, of course, it meant *inflections,* used to mark changes in the *meaning* and *use* of words. But we shall use *Modifications* to indicate changes in meaning and use when the form in the particular instance is wanting, nowhere, however, recognizing that as a *modification* which is not *somewhere marked by form.*

Modifications of Nouns and Pronouns.

NUMBER.

The boy shouts. The boys shout. The form of the subject *boy* is changed by adding an *s* to it. The meaning has changed. *Boy* denotes one lad ; *boys* two or more lads. This change in the form and the meaning of nouns is called **Number** ; the word *boy*, denoting one thing, is in the **Singular Number** ; and *boys*, denoting more than one thing, is in the **Plural Number**. Number expresses only the distinction of one from more than one ; to express more precisely *how many*, we use adjectives, and say *two boys, four boys, many* or *several boys.*

DEFINITIONS.

Modifications of the Parts of Speech are changes in their form, meaning, and use.

Number is that modification of a noun or pronoun which denotes one thing or more than one.

The *Singular Number* denotes one thing.

The *Plural Number* denotes more than one thing.

NUMBER FORMS.

RULE.—The *plural* of nouns is regularly formed by adding *s* to the singular.

To this rule there are some exceptions.

When the singular ends in a sound that cannot unite with that of *s*, *es* is added to form another syllable.*

---

* In Anglo-Saxon, *as* was the plural termination for a certain class of nouns. In later English, *as* was changed to *es*, which became the regular plural ending ; as, *bird-es, cloud-es.* In modern English, *e* is dropped, and *s* is joined to the singular without increase of syllables. But, when the singular ends in an *s*-sound, the original syllable *es* is retained, as two hissing sounds will not unite.

Remark.—Such words as *horse, niche,* and *cage* drop the final *e* when *es* is added. See Rule 1, Lesson 127.

Direction.—*Form the plural of each of the following nouns, and note what letters represent sounds that cannot unite with the sound of s :—*

Ax *or* axe, arch, adz *or* adze, box, brush, cage, chaise, cross, ditch, face, gas, glass, hedge, horse, lash, lens, niche, prize, race, topaz.

Some nouns ending in *o* preceded by a consonant add *es* without increase of syllables.

Direction.—*Form the plural of each of the following nouns :—*
Buffalo, calico, cargo, echo, embargo, grotto, hero, innuendo, motto, mosquito, mulatto, negro, portico, potato, tornado, volcano.

Some nouns in *o* preceded by a consonant add *s* only.

Direction.—*Form the plural of each of the following nouns:—*
Canto, domino (*os* or *oes*), duodecimo, halo, junto, lasso, memento, octavo, piano, proviso, quarto, salvo, solo, two, tyro, zero (*os* or *oes*).

Nouns in *o* preceded by a vowel add *s*.
Bamboo, cameo, cuckoo, embryo, folio, portfolio, seraglio, trio.

Common nouns* in *y* after a consonant change *y* into *i* and add *es* without increase of syllables. Nouns in *y* after a vowel add *s*.

Direction.—*Form the plural of each of the following nouns :—*
Alley, ally, attorney, chimney, city, colloquy,† daisy, essay, fairy, fancy, kidney, lady, lily, money, monkey, mystery, soliloquy, turkey, valley, vanity.

---

* See Rule 2, Lesson 127. In old English such words as *lady, fancy,* etc., were spelled *ladie, fancie.* The modern plural simply retains the old spelling and adds *s*.
† *U* after *q* is a consonant.

Some nouns change *f* or *fe* into *ves*.

Direction.—*Form the plural of each of the following nouns:—*
Beef, calf, elf, half, knife, leaf, life, loaf, self, sheaf, shelf, staff,* thief, wharf,* wife, wolf.

Some nouns in *f* and *fe* are regular.

Direction.—*Form the plural of each of the following nouns:—*
Belief, brief, chief, dwarf, fife, grief, gulf, hoof, kerchief, proof, reef, roof, safe, scarf, strife, waif.

(Nouns in *ff*, except *staff*, are regular; as, *cuff*, *cuffs*.)

Some plurals are still more irregular.

Direction.—*Learn to form the following plurals:—*
Child, children; foot, feet; goose, geese; louse, lice; man, men; mouse, mice; Mr., Messrs.; ox, oxen; tooth, teeth; woman, women.

(For the plurals of pronouns, see Lesson 124.)

LESSON 113.

NUMBER FORMS—CONTINUED.

Some nouns adopted from foreign languages still retain their original plural forms. Some of these take the English plural also.

Direction.—*Learn to form the following plurals:—*
Analysis, analyses; antithesis, antitheses; appendix, appendices *or* appendixes; automaton, automata *or* automatons; axis, axes; bandit, banditti *or* bandits; basis, bases; beau, beaux *or* beaus; cherub,

---

* *Staff* (a stick or support), *staves* or *staffs*; *staff* (a body of officers), *staffs*. The compounds of *staff* are regular; as, *flag-staffs*. In England, generally *wharfs*.

cherubim *or* cherubs ; crisis, crises ; datum, data ; ellipsis, ellipses ; erratum, errata ; focus, foci ; fungus, fungi *or* funguses : genus, genera ; hypothesis, hypotheses ; ignis fatuus, ignes fatui ; madame, mesdames ; magus, magi : memorandum, memoranda *or* memorandums : monsieur, messieurs ; nebula, nebulæ ; oasis, oases; parenthesis, parentheses ; phenomenon, phenomena ; radius, radii *or* radiuses ; seraph, seraphim *or* seraphs ; stratum, strata ; synopsis, synopses ; terminus, termini ; vertebra, vertebræ ; vortex, vortices *or* vortexes.

Some compound nouns in which the principal word stands first vary the first word ; as, *sons*-in-law.

Direction.—*Form the plural of the following words :*—

Aid-de-camp, attorney-at-law, billet-doux, commander-in-chief, court-martial, cousin-german, father-in-law, hanger-on, knight-errant, man-of-war.

Most compounds vary the last word ; as, pailfuls,* gentlemen.

Direction.—*Form the plural of each of the following nouns :*—

Court-yard, dormouse, Englishman, fellow-servant, fisherman, Frenchman, forget-me-not, goose-quill, handful, maid-servant, man-trap, mouthful, piano-forte, porte-monnaie, spoonful, step-son, tête-à-tête, tooth-brush.

The following nouns are not treated as compounds of *man* —add *s*.

Brahman, German, Mussulman, Norman, Ottoman, talisman.

A few compounds vary both parts ; as, *man-singer*, *men-singers*.

Direction.—*Form the plural of each of the following nouns :*—

Man-child, man-servant, woman-servant, woman-singer.

---

* *Pails full* is not a compound. This expression denotes a number of pails, each full.

Compounds consisting of a proper name preceded by a title form the plural by varying *either* the *title* or the *name;* as, the Miss *Clarks* or the *Misses* Clark; but, when the title *Mrs.* is used, the *name* is usually varied; as, the Mrs. *Clarks.**

Direction.—*Form the plural of the following compounds:*—

Miss Jones, Mr. Jones, General Lee, Dr. Brown, Master Green.

A title used with two or more different names is made plural; as, *Drs.* Grimes and Steele, *Messrs.* Clark and Maynard.

Direction.—*Put each of the following expressions in its proper form:*—

General Lee and Jackson; Miss Mary, Julia, and Anna Scott; Mr. Green, Stacy, & Co.

Letters, figures, and other characters add the apostrophe and *s* to form the plural; † as, *a's; 2's,—'s.*

Direction.—*Form the plural of each of the following characters:*—

S, i, t, +, ×, *, †, 9, 1, ¼, ℥, ☉.

---

* Of the two forms, the *Miss Clarks* and the *Misses Clark,* we believe that the former is most used by classical authors. The latter is now quite popular; but, except in formal notes or when the title is to be emphasized, it is rather stiff, if not pedantic. Some claim that, when a numeral precedes the title, the *name* should *always* be varied; as, the *two Miss Clarks.*

The forms, the *Misses Clarks* and the *two Mrs. Clark,* have but little authority.

† Some good writers form the plural of words named merely as words, in the same way; as, the *if's* and *and's;* but the (') is here unnecessary.

LESSON 114.
NUMBER FORMS—CONTINUED.

Some nouns have two plurals differing in meaning.

Direction.—*Learn to form the following plurals; note the meaning of each, and be able to put each into a sentence :—*

Brother,
- brothers (by blood),
- brethren (of the same society).

Cannon,
- cannons (individuals),
- cannon (in a collective sense).

Die,
- dies (stamps for coining),
- dice (cubes for gaming).

Fish,*
- fishes (individuals),
- fish (collection).

Foot,
- feet (parts of the body),
- foot (foot-soldiers).

Genius,
- geniuses (men of genius),
- genii (spirits).

Head,
- heads (parts of the body),
- head (of cattle).

Horse,
- horses (animals),
- horse (horse-soldiers).

Index,
- indexes (tables of reference),
- indices (signs in algebra).

Penny,
- pennies (distinct coins),
- pence (quantity in value).

Sail,
- sails (pieces of canvas),
- sail (vessels).

Shot,
- shots (number of times fired),
- shot (number of balls).

Some nouns and pronouns have the same form in both numbers.

Direction.—*Study the following list :—*

Amends, bellows, corps,† deer, gross, grouse, hose, means, odds, pains (care), series, sheep, species, swine, vermin, wages, who, which, that (relative), what, any, none.

(The following have two forms in the plural.)

Apparatus, apparatus *or* apparatuses; heathen, heathen *or* heathens.

---

* The names of several sorts of fish, as *herring, shad, trout*, etc., are used in the same way. The *compounds* of *fish*, as *codfish*, have the same form in both numbers.
† The singular is pronounced kōr, the plural kōrz.

(The following nouns have the same form in both numbers when used with numerals; they add *s* in other cases; as, *one pair, two pair, in pairs, by scores*.)

Brace, couple, dozen, pair, score, yoke, hundred, thousand.

Some nouns have no plural.

(These are generally names of *materials, qualities,* or *sciences*.)

Names of materials when taken in their full or strict sense can have no plural, but they may be plural when *kinds* of the material or things made of it are referred to; as, *cottons, coffees, tins, coppers*.

Direction.—*Study the following list of words:*—

Bread, coffee, copper, flour, gold, goodness, grammar (science, not a book), grass, hay, honesty, iron, lead, marble, meekness, milk, molasses, music, peace, physiology, pride, tin, water, etc.

(The following were originally plural forms, but they are now more commonly treated as singular.)

Acoustics, ethics, mathematics, politics (and other names of sciences in *ics*), news.

Some words are always plural.

(They are generally names of things double or multiform in their character.)

Direction.—*Study the following list:*—

Aborigines, annals, ashes, assets, clothes, fireworks, hysterics. literati, measles, mumps, nippers, oats,* pincers, rickets, scissors, shears, snuffers, suds, thanks, tongs, tidings, trowsers, victuals, vitals.

(The following were originally singular forms, but they are now treated as plural.)

Alms (Anglo-Saxon, *ælmesse*), eaves (A. S., *efese*), riches (Norman French, *richesse*).

---

* *Oat* is sometimes used, but *a grain of oats* would be better.

(The following have no singular *corresponding in meaning*.)

Colors (flag), compasses (dividers), goods (property), grounds (dregs), letters (literature) manners (behavior), matins (morning service), morals (character), remains (dead body), spectacles (glasses), stays (corsets), vespers (evening service).

(The singular form is sometimes an adjective.)

Bitters, greens, narrows, sweets, valuables, etc.

Collective nouns are treated as plural when the individuals in the collection are thought of, and as singular when the collection as a whole is thought of.

Examples.—The *committee were* unable to agree, and *they* asked to be discharged. A *committee was* appointed, and *its* report will soon be made.

(Collective nouns have plural forms; as, *committees, armies.*)

LESSON 145.

REVIEW IN NUMBER.

Direction.—*Write the plural of the singular nouns and pronouns in the following list, and the singular of those that are plural; give the rule or the remark that applies to each; and note those that have no plural, and those that have no singular :*—

Hope, age, bench, bush, house, loss, tax, waltz, potato, shoe, colony, piano, kangaroo, pulley, wharf, staff, fife, loaf, flag-staff, handkerchief, Mr., child, ox, beaux, cherubim, mesdames, termini, genus, genius, bagnio, theory, galley, muff, mystery, colloquy, son-in-law, man-of-war, spoonful, maid-servant, Frenchman, German, man-servant, Dr. Smith, Messrs. Brown and Smith, ×, $\frac{1}{4}$, deer, series, bellows, molasses, pride, politics, news, wages, sun-fish, clothes, alms, goods, grounds, greens, who, that.

Direction.—*Give five words that have no plural, five that have no singular, and five that have the same form in both numbers.*

Direction.—*Correct the following plurals, and give the remark that applies to each :—*

Stagees, foxs, mosquitos, calicos, heros, soloes, babys, trioes, chimnies, storys, elfs, beefs, scarves, oxes, phenomenons, axises, terminuses, genuses, mother-in-laws, aldermans, Mussulmen, teethbrushes, mouthsful, attorney-at-laws, man-childs, geese-quills, 2s, ms, swines.

LESSON 116.

NUMBER FORMS IN CONSTRUCTION.

The number of a noun may be determined not only by its *form*, but also by the *verb*, the *adjective*, and the *pronoun* used in connection with it.

Remark.—*These scissors are* so dull that I cannot use *them.* The plurality of *scissors* is here made known in four ways. In the following sentence *this, is,* and *it* are incorrectly used: *This* scissors *is* so dull that I cannot use *it*.

Direction.—*Construct sentences in which the number of each of the following nouns shall be indicated by the form of the verb, the adjective, or the pronoun used in connection with it :—*

(With the singular nouns use the verbs *is, was,* and *has been ;* the adjectives *an, one, this,* and *that ;* the pronouns *he, his, him, she, her, it,* and *its.*)

(With the plural nouns use the verbs *are, were,* and *have been ;* the adjectives *these, those,* and *two ;* the pronouns *they, their,* and *them.*)

Bellows, deer, fish, gross, means, series, species, heathen, pair, trout, iron, irons, news, wages, eaves, riches, oats, gallows, vermin, molasses, Misses, brethren, dice, head (of cattle), pennies, child, parent, family, crowd, and meeting.

Direction.—*Compose sentences in which the first three of the following adjective pronouns shall be used as singular subjects, the fourth as a plural subject, and the remainder both as singular and as plural subjects :—*

Each, either, neither, both, former, none, all, any.

LESSON 117.

NOUNS AND PRONOUNS—GENDER.

Introductory Hints.—*The lion was caged. The lioness was caged.* In the first sentence something is said about a *male* lion, and in the second something is said about a *female* lion. The modification of the noun to denote the sex of the thing which it names is called **Gender**. *Lion*, denoting a male animal, is in the **Masculine Gender**; and *lioness*, denoting a female animal, is in the **Feminine Gender**. Names of things that are without sex are said to be in the **Neuter Gender**. Such nouns as *cousin, child, friend, neighbor*, naming things of whose sex you are ignorant, are either *masculine* or *feminine*.

Sex belongs to the *thing*, and *gender* to the *noun* that names the thing. Knowing the sex of the thing or its lack of sex, you know the gender of the noun in English that names it; for in our language gender follows the sex. But in such modern languages as the French and the German, and in Latin and Greek, the gender of nouns naming things without reference to sex is determined by the likeness of their endings in sound to the endings of words denoting things with sex. The German for table is a *masculine* noun, the French, *feminine*, and the English,* of course, *neuter*.

DEFINITIONS.

Gender is that modification of a noun or pronoun which denotes sex.

The *Masculine Gender* denotes the male sex.

The *Feminine Gender* denotes the female sex.

The *Neuter Gender* denotes want of sex.

---

* In Anglo-Saxon, the mother-tongue of our language, gender was grammatical, as in the French and German; but since the union of the Norman-French with it to form the English, gender has followed sex.

Gender Forms.

No English *nouns* have distinctive *neuter forms*, but a *few* have different forms to distinguish the *masculine* from the *feminine*.

The masculine is distinguished from the feminine in three ways :—

1st. By a difference in the ending of the words.
2d. By different words in the compound names.
3d. By using words wholly or radically different.

*Ess** is the most common ending for feminine nouns.

Direction.—*Form the feminine of each of the following masculine nouns by adding ess :—*

Author, baron, count, deacon, deacon, giant, god (see Rule 3, Lesson 127), heir, host, Jew, lion, patron, poet, prince (see Rule 1, Lesson 127), prior, prophet, shepherd, tailor, tutor.

(Drop the vowel *e* or *o* in the ending of the masculine, and add *ess*.)

Actor, ambassador, arbiter, benefactor, conductor, director, editor, enchanter, hunter, idolater, instructor, preceptor, tiger, waiter.

(Drop the masculine *er*, and add the feminine *ess*.)

Adventurer, caterer, governor, murderer, sorcerer.

(The following are somewhat irregular.)

Direction.—*Learn these forms :—*

Abbot, abbess ; duke, duchess ; emperor, empress ; lad, lass ; marquis, marchioness ; master, mistress ; negro, negress.

Ess was formerly more common than now. Such words as *editor* and *author* are now frequently used to denote persons of either sex.

---

* The suffix *ess* came into the English language from the Norman-French. It displaced the feminine termination of the mother-tongue (A. S. *estre*, old English *ster*). The original meaning of *ster* is preserved in *spinster*. *Er* (A. S. *ere*) was originally a masculine suffix ; but it now generally denotes an *agent* without reference to sex ; as, *read-er, speaker*.

Direction.—*Give five nouns ending in* e r *or* o r *that may be applied to either sex.*

Some words, mostly foreign, have various endings in the feminine.

Direction.—*Learn the following forms :—*

Administrator, administratrix ; Augustus, Augusta ; beau, belle ; Charles, Charlotte ; Cornelius, Cornelia ; czar, czarina ; don, donna ; equestrian, equestrienne ; executor, executrix ; Francis, Frances ; George, Georgiana ; Henry, Henrietta ; hero, heroine ; infante, infanta ; Jesse, Jessie ; Joseph, Josephine ; Julius, Julia *or* Juliet ; landgrave, landgravine ; Louis, Louisa *or* Louise ; Paul, Pauline ; signore *or* signor, signora ; sultan, sultana ; testator, testatrix ; widower, widow.

In some compounds distinguishing words are prefixed or affixed.

Direction.—*Learn the following forms :—*

Billy-goat, nanny-goat ; buck-rabbit, doe-rabbit ; cock-sparrow, hen-sparrow ; Englishman, Englishwoman ; gentleman, gentlewoman ; grand-father, grand-mother ; he-bear, she-bear ; landlord, landlady ; man-servant, maid-servant ; merman, mermaid ; Mr. Jones, Mrs. *or* Miss Jones ; peacock, peahen.

Words wholly or radically different are used to distinguish the masculine from the feminine.

(This is a matter pertaining to the meaning of words rather than to grammar.)

Direction.—*Learn the following forms :—*

Bachelor, maid ; buck, doe ; drake, duck ; earl, countess ; friar *or* monk, nun ; gander, goose ; hart, roe ; lord, lady ; nephew, niece ; sir, madam ; stag, hind ; steer, heifer ; wizard, witch ; youth, damsel *or* maiden.

The *pronoun* has *three* gender forms:—
Masculine *he*, feminine *she*, and neuter *it*.*

Direction.—*Give five examples of each of the three ways of distinguishing the masculine from the feminine.*

LESSON 118.

GENDER FORMS IN CONSTRUCTION.

Gender as a matter of orthography is of some importance, but in grammar it is chiefly important as involving the correct use of the pronouns *he, she,* and *it.*

When a singular noun is used so as to imply persons of both sexes, it is commonly represented by a masculine pronoun.†

Example.—Every *person* has *his* faults.

The names of animals are often considered as masculine or feminine without regard to the real sex.

Examples.—The *grizzly bear* is the most savage of *his* race. The *cat* steals upon *her* prey.

Remark.—The writer employs *he* or *she* according as he fancies the animal to possess masculine or feminine characteristics. *He* is more frequently employed than *she*.

The neuter pronoun *it* is often used with reference to animals and very young children, the sex being disregarded.

---

* *It*, although a neuter form, is used idiomatically to refer to a male or a female; as, *It* was *John*, *It* was *Mary*.

† When it is necessary to distinguish the sexes, both the masculine and the feminine pronouns should be used; as, Each person was required to name *his* or *her* favorite flower.

Examples.—When the *deer* is alarmed, *it* gives two or three graceful springs. The little *child* reached out *its* hand to catch the sunbeam.

Remark.—*It* is quite generally used instead of *he* or *she*, in referring to an animal, unless some masculine or feminine quality seems to predominate.

Inanimate things are often represented as living beings, that is, they are *personified,* and are referred to by the pronoun *he* or *she*.

Example.—The *oak* shall send *his* roots abroad and pierce thy mould.

Remark.—The names of objects distinguished for *size, power,* or *sublimity* are regarded as masculine; and the names of those distinguished for *grace, beauty, gentleness,* or *productiveness* are considered as feminine. Personification adds beauty and animation to style.

Direction.—*Study what is said above, and then fill each of the blanks in the following sentences with a masculine, a feminine, or a neuter pronoun, and in each case give the reason for your selection :*—

1. No one else is so much alone in the universe as —— who denies God. 2. A person's manners not unfrequently indicate —— morals. 3. Everybody should think for ——. 4. The forest's leaping panther shall yield —— spotted hide. 5. The catamount lies in the boughs to watch —— prey. 6. The mocking-bird shook from —— little throat floods of delirious music. 7. The wild beast from —— cavern sprang, the wild bird from —— grove. 8. The night-sparrow trills —— song. 9. The elephant is distinguished for —— strength and sagacity. 10. The bat is nocturnal in —— habits. 11. The dog is faithful to —— master. 12. The child was unconscious of —— danger. 13. The fox is noted for —— cunning. 14. Belgium's capital had gathered then —— beauty and —— chivalry. 15. Despair extends —— raven wing. 16. Life mocks the idle hate of —— arch-enemy, Death. 17. Spring comes forth —— work of gladness to contrive. 18. Truth is fearless, yet —— is meek and modest.

Direction.—*Write sentences in which the things named below shall be personified by means of masculine pronouns :*—

Death, time, winter, war, sun, river, wind.

Direction.— *Write sentences in which the things named below shall be personified by means of feminine pronouns :—*

Ship, moon, earth, spring, virtue, nature, night, England.

Caution.—Avoid changing the gender of the pronoun when referring to the same antecedent.

Direction.—*Correct these errors :—*

1. The polar bear is comparatively rare in menageries, as it suffers so much from the heat that he is not easily preserved in confinement. 2. The cat, when it comes to the light, contracts and elongates the pupil of her eye. 3. Summer clothes herself in green, and decks itself with flowers. 4. War leaves his victim on the field, and homes desolated by it mourn over her cruelty.

LESSON 119.

NOUNS AND PRONOUNS—PERSON AND CASE.

Introductory Hints.—*Number* and *gender*, as you have learned, are modifications affecting the *meaning* of nouns and pronouns—number being almost always indicated by *form*, or *inflection ;* gender sometimes. There are two other modifications which do not refer to changes in the *meaning* of nouns and pronouns, but to their different *uses* and *relations*, these uses and relations not often being indicated by *form*, or *inflection*.

I, Paul, have written. *Paul, thou* art beside thyself. *He* brought *Paul* before Agrippa. In these three sentences the word *Paul* has three different uses, though, as you see, its *form* is not changed. In the first it is used to name the *speaker ;* in the second to name the *one spoken to ;* in the third to name the *one spoken of.* These different uses of nouns and pronouns and the forms used to mark them constitute the modification called **Person**. *I, thou,* and *he* are *personal* pronouns, and, as you see, distinguish person by their *form*. *I*, denoting the speaker, is in the **First Person** ; *thou*, denoting the one spoken to, is in the **Second Person**; and *he*, denoting the one spoken of, is in the **Third Person**.

Instead of *I* a writer or speaker may use the plural *we;* and through courtesy it came to be customary, except among the Friends, or in the language of prayer and poetry, to use the plural *you* instead of *thou*.

The bear killed the man. The man killed the bear. The bear's grease was made into hair oil. In the first sentence the animal, bear, is represented as *performing* an action; in the second as *receiving* an action; in the third as *possessing* something. Consequently the word *bear* in these sentences has three different uses. These different uses of nouns and pronouns and the forms used to mark them constitute the modification called **Case**. A noun or pronoun used as subject is in the **Nominative Case**; used as object complement is in the **Objective Case**; and used to denote possession is in the **Possessive Case**.

Some of the *pronouns* have a special form for each case, but the *possessive case* of *nouns* is the only one that is now marked by a peculiar form. We inflect, below,* a noun from the Anglo-Saxon and one from the Latin, the parent of the Norman-French, in order that you may see how cases and the forms, or inflections, to mark them have been dropped in English. In English, prepositions have largely taken the place of case forms, and it is thought that by them our language can express the many relations of nouns to other words in the sentence better than other languages can by their cumbrous machinery of inflection.

---

* The Anglo-Saxon cases are *nominative, genitive, dative, accusative, vocative,* and *instrumental;* the Latin are *nominative, genitive, dative, accusative, vocative,* and *ablative;* the English are *nominative, possessive (genitive),* and *objective*.

ANGLO-SAXON.		LATIN.		ENGLISH.	
Hlaford, *lord.*		Dominus, *lord.*		Lord.	
Singular.	Plural.	Singular.	Plural.	Singular.	
Nom. hlaford,	hlaford-*as*.	Nom. domin-*us,*	domin-*i*.	Nom. lord,	
Gen. hlaford-*es,*	hlaford-*a*.	Gen. domin-*i,*	domin-*orum*.	Pos. lord-*'s,*	
Dat. hlaford-*e,*	hlaford-*um*.	Dat. domin-*o,*	domin-*is*.	Obj. lord.	
Acc. hlaford,	hlaford-*as*.	Acc. domin-*um,*	domin-*os*.	Plural.	
Voc. hlaford,	hlaford-*as*.	Voc. domin-*e,*	domin-*i*.	Nom. lord-*s,*	
Inst. hlaford-*e;*	hlaford-*um*.	Ab. domin-*o;*	domin-*is*.	Pos. lord-*s',*	
				Obj. lord-*s*.	

DEFINITIONS.

Person is that modification of a noun or pronoun which denotes the speaker, the one spoken to, or the one spoken of.

The *First Person* denotes the one speaking.

The *Second Person* denotes the one spoken to.

The *Third Person* denotes the one spoken of.

A *noun* is said to be of the *first* person when joined as an explanatory modifier to a pronoun of the first person; as, *I, John,* saw these things; *We Americans* are always in a hurry.*

A *noun* is of the *second* person when used as explanatory of a pronoun of the second person, or when used independently as a term of address; as, *Ye crags* and *peaks;* Idle time, *John,* is ruinous.

Direction.—*Compose sentences in which there shall be two examples of nouns and two of pronouns used in each of the three persons.*

Person Forms.

Personal pronouns and *verbs* are the only classes of words that have distinctive person forms.

Direction.—*From the forms of the pronouns given in Lesson* 124, *select and write in one list all the first person forms; in another list, all the second person forms; and in another, all the third person forms.*

Person is regarded in grammar, because the verb sometimes varies its form to agree with the person of its subject; as, *I see, Thou seest, He sees.*

---

* It is doubtful whether a *noun* is ever of the *first* person. It may be claimed with some propriety that, in the sentence *I, John, saw these things,* John speaks of his own name, the expression meaning, *I, and my name is John,* etc.

DEFINITIONS.

Case is that modification of a noun or pronoun which denotes its office in the sentence.

The *Nominative Case of a noun or pronoun* denotes its office as subject or as attribute complement.

The *Possessive Case of a noun or pronoun* denotes its office as possessive modifier.

The *Objective Case of a noun or pronoun* denotes its office as object complement, or as principal word in a prepositional phrase.

A noun or pronoun used independently is said to be in the nominative case.

Examples.—I am, *dear madam*, your friend. Alas, *poor Yorick! He being dead*, we shall live. *Liberty*, it has fled! (See Lesson 44.)

A noun or pronoun used as explanatory modifier is in the same case as the word explained—"is put by apposition in the same case."

Examples.—The first colonial *Congress*, *that* of 1774, addressed the *King, George III.* He buys his goods at *Stewart's*, the dry-goods merchant.

A noun or pronoun used as objective complement is in the objective case.

Example.—They made him *speaker*.

A noun or pronoun used as attribute complement of a participle or an infinitive is in the same case (*Nom.* or *Obj.*) as the word to which it relates as attribute.

Examples.—Being an *artist*, *he* appreciated it. I proved *it* to be *him*.

Remark.—When the assumed subject of the participle or the infinitive is a possessive, the attribute complement is said to be in the nominative case; as, Its *being he* * should make no difference. When the participle or the infinitive is used abstractly, without an assumed subject, its attribute complement is also said to be in the nominative case; as, *To be he* * is to be a scholar, *Being a scholar* is not *being an idler.*

Direction.—*Study carefully the definitions and the remarks, above, and then compose sentences in which a noun or a pronoun shall be put in the nominative case in f o u r ways; in the objective in f i v e ways; in the possessive in t w o ways.*

LESSON 120.

ANALYSIS AND PARSING.

Direction.—*Analyze the following sentences, and give the case of each noun and pronoun :—*

1. Not to know what happened before we were born is to be always a child.
2. His being a Roman saved him from being made a prisoner.
3. I am this day weak, though anointed king.

Explanation.—Nouns used adverbially are in the objective case, because equivalent to the principal word of a prepositional phrase. (See Lesson 35.)

---

* The case of *he* in these examples is rather doubtful. The nominative and the objective forms of the pronoun occur so rarely in such constructions that it seems impossible to determine the usage. It is, therefore, a matter of no great practical importance.

Some, reasoning from the analogy of the Latin, would put the attribute complement of the abstract infinitive in the objective, supposing *for*, with some word, to be understood; as, *For one to be him*, etc. Others, reasoning from the analogy of the German to which our language is closely allied, would put it in the nominative.

The assumed subject of the infinitive being omitted when it is the same as that of the principal subject, *him*, in the sentence *I wish* (*me* or *myself*) *to be him*—is the proper form, being in the same case as *me*. In the sentence *I have no doubt of his being a scholar*, *his* is used instead of *him* to prevent ambiguity; and some would put *scholar* in the same case as *him*. For a similar reason *scholar* would be nominative in the sentence *His* (*he*) *being a scholar is beyond doubt*.

4. What made Cromwell a great man was his unshaken reliance on God.

5. Amos, the herdsman of Tekoa, was not a prophet's son.

6. Arnold's success as teacher was remarkable.

Explanation.—*Teacher*, introduced by *as* and used without a possessive sign, is explanatory of *Arnold's*.

7. Worship thy Creator, God ; and obey his Son, the Master, King, and Saviour of men.

8. Bear ye one another's burdens.

Explanation.—The singular *one* is explanatory of the plural *ye*, or *one another's* may be treated as a compound.

9. What art thou, execrable shape, that darest advance ?
10. O you hard hearts ! you cruel men of Rome !
11. Everybody acknowledges Shakespeare to be the greatest of dramatists.
12. Think'st thou this heart could feel a moment's joy, thou being absent ?
13. Our great forefathers had left him naught to conquer but his country.

(For case of *him* see Explanation of (3), above.)

14. I will attend to it myself.

Explanation.—*Myself* may be treated as explanatory of *I*.

15. This news of papa's* puts me all in a flutter.
16. What means that hand upon that breast of thine ?*

LESSON 124.

PARSING.

To the Teacher.—We do not believe that the chief end of the study of grammar is to be able to parse well, or even to analyze well, though, without question, analysis reveals more clearly than parsing the structure of the sentence, and is immeasurably

---

* See foot-note, page 214.

superior to it as intellectual gymnastics. We would not do away with parsing altogether, but would give it a subordinate place.

But we must be allowed an emphatic protest against the needless and mechanical quoting, in parsing, of "Rules of Syntax." When a pupil has said that such a noun is in the nominative case, subject of such a verb, what is gained by a repetition of the definition in the Rule: "A noun or a pronoun which is the subject of a finite verb is in the nominative case"? Let the reasons for the disposition of words, when given at all, be specific.

Parsing a word is giving its classification, modifications, and syntax (*i. e.*, its relation to other words).

Direction.—*Select and parse in full all the nouns and pronouns found in the first ten sentences of Lesson* 120. *For the agreement of pronouns, see Less.* 142.

Model for Written Parsing.—*Elizabeth's favorite, Raleigh, was beheaded by James I.*

CLASSIFICATION.		MODIFICATIONS.				SYNTAX.
Nouns.	*Kind.*	*Person.*	*Number.*	*Gender.*	*Case.*	
Elizabeth's	Prop.	3d.	Sing.	Fem.	Pos.	Pos. Mod. of *favorite.*
favorite	Com.	"	"	Mas.	Nom.	Sub. of *was beheaded.*
Raleigh	Prop.	"	"	"	"	Exp. Mod. of *favorite.*
James I.	"	"	"	"	Obj.	Prin. word in Prep. phrase.

To the Teacher.—For exercises in parsing nouns and pronouns, see Lessons 28, 29, 30, 31, 33, 34, 35, 44, 46, 59, 60, 71, 73, 78, 80, and 81. Other exercises may be selected from examples previously given for analysis, and parsing continued as long as you think it profitable.

LESSON 122.

CASE FORMS—NOUNS

Nouns have two case forms, the *simple form,* common to the nominative and the objective case, and the *possessive form.*

RULE.—The *possessive case* of nouns is formed in the singular by adding to the nominative the apostrophe and the letter *s* ('s); in the plural, by adding (') only. If the plural does not end in s, ('s) are both added.*

Examples.—Boy's, boys', men's.

Remark.—To avoid an unpleasant succession of hissing sounds, the *s* in the possessive singular is sometimes omitted; as, *conscience' sake, goodness' sake, Achilles' sword, Archimedes' screw* (the *s* in the words following the possessive here has its influence). In prose this omission of the *s* should seldom occur. The weight of usage inclines to the *s* in such names as *Miss Rounds's, Mrs. Hemans's, King James's, witness's, prince's*. Without the *s* there would be no distinction, in spoken language, between *Miss Round's* and *Miss Rounds', Mrs. Heman's* and *Mrs. Hemans'*.

Remark.—Pronounce the ('s) as a separate syllable (= *es*), when the sound of *s* will not unite with the last sound of the nominative.

Remark.—When the singular and the plural are alike in the nominative, some place the apostrophe after the *s* in the plural to distinguish it from the possessive singular; as, singular, *sheep's;* plural, *sheeps'*.

Direction.—*Study the Rule and the Remarks given above, and then write the possessive singular and the possessive plural of each of the following nouns:—*

Actor, elephant, farmer, king, lion, genius, horse, princess, buffalo, hero, mosquito, negro, volcano, junto, tyro, cuckoo, ally, attorney, fairy, lady, monkey, calf, elf, thief, wife, wolf, chief, dwarf, waif, child, goose, mouse, ox, woman, beau, seraph, fish, deer, sheep, swine.

Compound names and groups of words that may be treated as compound names add the possessive sign to the last word; as, a *man-of-war's* rigging, the *queen of England's* palace,† *Frederick the Great's* verses.

---

* In Anglo Saxon, *es* was a genitive (possessive) ending of the singular; as, smith, *genitive*, smithes. In old English, *es* and *is* were both used. In modern English the vowel is dropped, and (') stands in its place. The use of the apostrophe has been extended to distinguish the possessive from other forms of the plural.

† In parsing the words *queen* and *England* separately, the ('s) must be regarded as belonging to *queen;* but the whole phrase *queen of England* may be treated as one noun in the possessive case.

Remark.—The *possessive plural* of such terms is not used.

The preposition *of* with the objective is often used instead of the possessive case form—*David's* Psalms = Psalms *of David* (*of* = *'s*).

Remark.—To denote the source from which a thing proceeds, or the idea of belonging to, *of* is used more frequently than (*'s*).

The possessive sign (*'s*) is confined *chiefly* to the names of persons, animals, and things personified. We do not say the *tree's* leaves, but the leaves *of the tree*.

The possessive sign, however, is often added to names of things which we frequently hear personified, or which we wish to dignify, and to names of periods of time; as, the *earth's* surface, *fortune's* smile, *eternity's* stillness, a *year's* interest, a *day's* work.

By the use of *of*, such expressions as *witness's statement, mothers-in-law's faults* may be avoided.

Direction.—*Study carefully the principles and remarks given above, and then make each of the following terms indicate possession, using either the possessive sign or the preposition of, as may seem most appropriate, and join an appropriate name denoting the thing possessed :—*

Father-in-law, William the Conqueror, king of Great Britain, aid-de-camp, Henry the Eighth, attorney-at-law, somebody else,* Jefferson, enemy, hero, eagle, elephant, gunpowder, book, house, chair, torrent, sun, ocean, mountain, summer, year, day, hour, princess, Socrates.

LESSON 123.

CONSTRUCTION OF POSSESSIVE FORMS.

As the possessive is the only case of nouns that has a distinctive form, or inflection, it is only with this case that mistakes can occur in construction.

---

* In such expressions as *everybody else's business*, the possessive sign is removed from the noun and attached to the adjective. The possessive sign should generally be placed immediately before the name of the thing possessed.

Caution.—When several possessive nouns modify the same word and imply common possession, the possessive sign is added to the last only. If they modify different words, expressed or understood, the sign is added to each.

Explanation.—*William* and *Henry's* boat, *William's* and *Henry's* coat. In the first example, William and Henry are represented as jointly owning a boat ; in the second, each is represented as owning a separate boat—*boat* is understood after *William's*.

Remark.—When the different possessors are thought of as separate or opposed, the sign may be repeated, although joint possession is implied ; as, He was his *father's*, *mother's*, and *sister's* favorite, He was the *king's*, as well as the *people's*, favorite.

Direction.—*Correct these errors, and give your reasons :*—

1. The Bank of England was established in William's and Mary's reign. 2. Messrs. Leggett's, Stacy's, Green's, & Co.'s business prospers. 3. This was James's, Charles's, and Robert's estate. 4. America was discovered during Ferdinand's and Isabella's reign. 5. We were comparing Cæsar and Napoleon's victories. 6. This was the sage and the poet's theme.

Explanation.—If an article precedes the possessive, the sign is repeated.

7. It was the king, not the people's, choice. 8. They are Thomas, as well as James's, books.

Caution.—When a possessive noun is followed by an explanatory word, the possessive sign is added to the explanatory word only. But, if the explanatory word has several modifiers, or, if there are more explanatory words than one, the principal word only takes the sign.

Remark.—When a common noun is explanatory of a proper noun, and the name of the thing possessed is omitted, the possessive sign may be added to either the modifying or the principal word ; as, We stopped at Tiffany, the *jeweler's*, or, We stopped at *Tiffany's*, the jeweler. (If the name of the thing possessed is *given*, the noun immediately before it takes the sign.)

Direction.—*Correct these errors :—*
1. This is Tennyson's, the poet's, home. 2. I took tea at Brown's, my old friend and schoolmate's. 3. This belongs to Victoria's, queen of England's, dominion. 4. This province is Victoria's, queen of England's. 5. That language is Homer's, the greatest poet of antiquity's. 6. This was Franklin's motto, the distinguished philosopher's and statesman's. 7. Wolsey's, the cardinal's, career ended in disgrace.

Direction.—*Tell which of the sentences, above, may be improved by using* other forms to denote possession. (See the following Caution.)

Caution.—The relation of possession may be expressed not only by ('s) and *of*, but by the use of such phrases as *belonging to, property of*, etc. In constructing sentences be careful to secure smoothness and clearness by taking advantage of these different forms.

Direction.—*Improve the following sentences :—*
1. This is my wife's father's opinion.

Correction.—This is the opinion *of my wife's father,* or *held by my wife's father.*

2. This is my wife's father's farm. 3. France's and England's interests differ widely. 4. Frederick the Great was the son of the daughter of George I., of England. 5. My brother's wife's sister's drawings have been much admired. 6. The drawings of the sister of the wife of my brother have been much admired.

Of is not always equivalent to the ('s).

Explanation.—The *president's reception* means the reception given *by* the president ; but *the reception of the president* means the reception given *to* the president.

Direction.—*Construct sentences illustrating the meaning of the following expressions :—*

A mother's love, the love of a mother ; a father's care, the care of a father ; my friend's picture, a picture of my friend.

Caution.—Often ambiguity may be prevented by changing the assumed subject of a participle from a nominative or an objective to a possessive.

Direction.—*Correct these errors :—*

1. The writer being a scholar is not doubted.

Correction.—This is ambiguous, as it may mean either that the writer is not doubted, because he is a scholar, or that the writer's scholarship is not doubted. It should be, *The writer's being a scholar is not doubted,* or *That the writer is a scholar is not doubted.*

2. I have no doubt of the writer being a scholar. 3. No one ever heard of that man running for office. 4. Brown being a politician prevented his election. 5. I do not doubt him being sincere. 6. Grouchy being behind time decided the fate of Waterloo.

LESSON 124.

NUMBER AND CASE FORMS.

DECLENSION.

DEFINITION.—*Declension* is the arrangement of the cases of nouns and pronouns in the two numbers.

Direction.—*Learn the following declensions :—*

Declension of Nouns.

	LADY.		BOY.		MAN.	
	Singular.	*Plural.*	*Singular.*	*Plural.*	*Sing.*	*Plural.*
Nom.	lady,	ladies,	boy,	boys,	man,	men,
Pos.	lady's,	ladies',	boy's,	boys',	man's,	men's,
Obj.	lady ;	ladies.	boy ;	boys.	man ;	men.

Declension of Pronouns.

Personal Pronouns.

	FIRST PERSON.		SECOND PERSON—*common form*.		SECOND PERSON—*old form*.	
	Singular.	*Plural.*	*Singular.*	*Plural.*	*Singular.*	*Plural.*
Nom.	I,	we,	you,	you,	thou,	ye *or* you,
Pos.	my *or* mine,*	our *or* ours,	your *or* yours,	your *or* yours,	thy *or* thine,	your *or* yours,
Obj.	me ;	us.	you ;	you.	thee ;	you.

	THIRD PERSON—*Mas.*		THIRD PERSON—*Fem.*		THIRD PERSON—*Neut.*	
	Singular.	*Plural.*	*Singular.*	*Plural.*	*Singular.*	*Plural.*
Nom.	he,	they,	she,	they,	it,	they,
Pos.	his,	their *or* theirs,	her *or* hers,	their *or* theirs,	its,	their *or* theirs,
Obj.	him ;	them.	her ;	them.	it ;	them.

Compound Personal Pronouns.

Singular. Nom. and Obj.	*Plural.* Nom. and Obj.	*Singular.* Nom. and Obj.	*Plural.* Nom. and Obj.	*Singular.* Nom. and Obj.	*Plural.* Nom. and Obj.
myself *or* ourself ;	ourselves.	thyself *or* yourself ;	yourselves.	himself ; herself ; itself ;	themselves.

Remark.—The possessive of these pronouns is wanting.

---

* The forms *mine, ours, yours, thine, hers,* and *theirs* are used only when the name of the thing possessed is omitted ; as, *Yours* is old, *mine* is new = Your *book* is old, etc. *Mine* and *thine* were formerly used before words beginning with a vowel sound; as, *thine enemy, mine honor.*

The expression *a friend of mine* presents a peculiar construction. The explanation generally given is, that *of* is partitive, and the expression equivalent to *one friend of my friends.* And it is claimed that this construction can be used only when more than one thing is possessed. But such expressions as *this heart of mine, that temper of yours* are good, idiomatic English. This sweet wee *wife of mine.*—*Burns.* This naughty *world of ours.*—*Byron.* This moral *life of mine.*—*Sher. Knowles.* Dim are those *heads of theirs.*—*Carlyle.* Some suggest that the word *possessing* or *owning* is understood after these possessives; as, *This temper of yours* (your possessing); others say that *of* simply marks identity ; as in *city of* (= viz.) *New York* (see Lesson 34). They would make the expression = *This temper, your temper.*

Ourself and *we* are used by rulers, editors, and others to hide their individuality, and give authority to what they say.

Relative Pronouns.

	Sing. and Plu.	Sing. and Plu.	Sing. and Plu.	Sing. and Plu.
Nom.	who,	which,	that,	what,
Pos.	whose,	whose,	——,	——.
Obj.	whom.	which.	that.	what.

Remark.—Instead of using *whose* as the possessive of *which*, some prefer the phrase *of which*.

Interrogative Pronouns.

The interrogative pronouns *who*, *which*, and *what* are declined like the relatives *who*, *which*, and *what*.

Compound Relative Pronouns.

	Singular and Plural.	Singular and Plural.
Nom.	whoever,	whosoever,
Pos.	whosever,	whosesoever,
Obj.	whomever.	whomsoever.

Whichever, *whichsoever*, *whatever*, and *whatsoever* do not change their form.

Adjective Pronouns.

This and *that* with their plurals, *these* and *those*, have no possessive form, and are alike in the nominative and the objective. *One* and *other* are declined like nouns; and *another*, declined like *other* in the singular, has no plural. *Each*, *either*, and *neither* are always singular;* *both* is al-

---

* Grammarians have taught that *each other*, *either*, and *neither* should always refer to two things, and *one another* to more than two; but good writers do not regard this restriction.

ways plural; and *all, any, former, latter, none, same, some,* and *such* are either singular or plural.

Descriptive adjectives used as nouns are plural, and are not declined. Such expressions as "the *wretched's* only plea" and "the *wicked's* den" are exceptional.

LESSON 125.

CASE FORMS—PRONOUNS.

The pronouns *I, thou, he, she,* and *who* are the only words in the language that have each three different case forms.

Direction.—*Study the Declensions, and correct these errors:*—
Our's, your's, hi's, her's, it's, their's, yourn, hisn, hern, theirn.

Construction of Case Forms—Pronouns.

Caution.—*I, we, thou, ye, he, she, they,* and *who* are *nominative* forms, and must not be used in the objective case. *Me, us, thee, him, her,* them,* and *whom* are *objective* forms, and must not be used in the nominative case.

Remark.—The eight nominative forms and the seven objective forms here given are the only distinctive nominative and objective forms in the language. All the rules of syntax given in the grammars to guide in the use of the nominative and the objective case apply, practically, only to these fifteen words.

Direction.—*Study carefully the definitions and principles given under the head of case, Lesson* 119, *and then correct these errors, giving your reasons in every instance:*—

---

* *Her* is also a possessive.

1. It is not me * you are in love with. 2. She was neither better bred nor wiser than you or me.* 3. Who* servest thou under ? 4. It was not them, it was her. 5. Its being me should make no difference. 6. Him and me are of the same age. 7. Them that study grammar talk no better than me. 8. I am not so old as her ; she is older than me by ten years. 9. He was angry, and me too. 10. Who will go ? Me. 11. It isn't for such as us to sit with the rulers of the land. 12. Not one in a thousand could have done it as well as him. 13. Him being a stranger, they easily misled him. 14. Oh, happy us ! surrounded thus with blessings. 15. It was Joseph, him whom Pharaoh promoted. 16. I referred to my old friend, he of whom I so often speak. 17. You have seen Cassio and she together. 18. Between you and I, I believe that he is losing his mind. 19. Who should I meet the other day but my old friend ? 20. Who did he refer to, he or I ? 21. Who did he choose ? Did he choose you and I ? 22. He that is idle and mischievous reprove. 23. We will refer it to whoever you may choose. 24. Whosoever the court favors is safe. 25. They that are diligent I will reward. 26. Scotland and thee did in each other live. 27. My hour is come, but not to render up my soul to such as thee. 28. I knew that it was him. 29. I knew it to be he. 30. Who did you suppose it to be ? 31. Whom did you suppose it was ? 32. I took that tall man to be he. 33. I thought that tall man was him.

---

* Dr. Latham defends *It is me*, but condemns *It is him* and *It is her*. Dean Alford regards as correct the forms condemned by Latham, and asserts that *thee* and *me* are correct in " The nations not so blest as *thee*," "Such weak minister as *me* may the oppressor bruise." Prof. Bain justifies *If I were him, It was her, He is better than me*, and even defends the use of *who* as an objective form by quoting from Shakespeare, " Who servest thou under ?" and from Steele, " Who should I meet ?"

They justify such expressions as *It is me* from the analogy of the French *c'est moi*, and on the ground that they are " more frequently heard than the prescribed form." But such analogy would justify *It are them* (*ce sont eux*); and, if the argument from the speech of the uneducated is to have weight, we have good authority for " *Her ain't a calling we ; us don't belong to she.*" A course of reading will satisfy any one that the best writers and speakers in England are not in the habit of using such expressions as *It is me*, and that they are almost, if not quite, unknown in American literature. No one has so freed himself from the influence of early associations that in a careless moment some *vicious* colloquialism may not creep into his discourse. A violation of every principle of grammar may be defended, if such inadvertencies are to be erected into authority. To whatever is the *prevailing*, the *habitual*, usage of a majority of the best writers and speakers the grammarian bows without question ; but not to the accidental slips of even the greatest, or to the common usage of the unreflecting and the uncultivated.

LESSON 126.

CONSTRUCTION OF CASE FORMS.

Miscellaneous—Review.

Direction.—*Correct these errors, and give your reasons :—*

1. Who was Joseph's and Benjamin's mother ? 2. It did not occur during Washington, Jefferson, or Adams's administration. 3. I consulted Webster, Worcester, and Walker's dictionary. 4. This state was south of Mason's and Dixon's line. 5. These are neither George nor Fanny's books. 6. Howard's, the philanthropist's, life was a noble one. 7. It is Othello's pleasure, our noble and valiant general's. 8. He visited his sons-in-law's homes.

Explanation.—If the possessive plural of such nouns were used, this would be correct ; but it is better to avoid these awkward forms.

9. A valuable horse of my friend William's father's was killed. 10. For Herodias's sake, his brother Philip's wife. 11. For the queen's sake, his sister's. 12. Peter's, John's, and Andrew's occupation was that of fishermen. 13. He spoke of you studying Latin. 14. It being difficult did not deter him. 15. What need is there of the man swearing ? 16. I am opposed to the gentleman speaking again. 17. He thought it was us. 18. We shall shortly see which is the fittest object of scorn, you or me. 19. I shall not learn my duty from such as thee. 20. A lady entered, whom I afterwards found was Miss B. 21. A lady entered, who I afterwards found to be Miss B. 22. Ask somebody's else opinion. 23. Let him be whom he may. 24. I am sure it could not have been them. 25. I understood it to be they. 26. It is not him whom you thought it was. 27. Let you and I try it. 28. All enjoyed themselves, us excepted. 29. Us boys enjoy the holidays. 30. It was Virgil, him who wrote the Æneid.

GENERAL REVIEW.

To the Teacher.—These schemes and questions under the head of General Review are especially designed to aid in securing an outline of technical grammar.

The questions given below may be made to call for minute details or only for outlines. In some cases a single question may suffice for a whole lesson.

Scheme for the Noun.
(The numbers refer to Lessons.)

NOUN.
- **Uses.**
  - Subject (4, 8).
  - Object Complement (28).
  - Attribute Complement (29, 30).
  - Objective Complement (31).
  - Adjective Modifier (33).
  - Adverb Modifier (35).
  - Principal word in Prep. Phrase (17).
  - Independent (44).
- **Classes.**
  - Common (85).
  - (*Abstract and Collective.*)
  - Proper (85).
- **Modifications.**
  - Number.
    - Singular (112-116).
    - Plural (112-116).
  - Gender.
    - Masculine (117, 118).
    - Feminine (117, 118).
    - Neuter (117, 118).
  - Person.
    - First (119).
    - Second (119).
    - Third (119).
  - Case.
    - Nominative (119).
    - Possessive (119, 122, 123).
    - Objective (119).

Questions on the Noun.

1. Define the noun and its classes.—Lesson 85.
2. Name and define the modifications of the noun.—Less. 112, 117, 119.
3. Name and define the several numbers, genders, persons, and cases.—Less. 112, 117, 119.
4. Give and illustrate the several ways of forming the plural.—Less. 112, 113, 114.

5. Give and illustrate the several ways of distinguishing the genders.—Less. 117.

6. How is the possessive case formed ?—Less. 122.

7. Give and illustrate the principles which guide in use of the possessive forms.—Less. 123.

Scheme for the Pronoun.

PRONOUN.
- **Uses.**—Same as those of the Noun.
- **Classes.**
  - Personal (85, 86, 87).
  - Relative (85, 86, 87).
  - Interrogative (85).
  - Adjective (85, 87).
- **Modifications.**—Same as those of the Noun (112, 117, 118, 119, 124, 125, 142).

Questions on the Pronoun.

1. Define the pronoun and its classes, and give the lists.—Less. 85.
2. Decline the several pronouns.—Less. 124.
3. Give and illustrate the principles which guide in the use of the different pronouns.—Less. 86, 87.
4. Give and illustrate the principles which guide in the use of the number forms, the gender forms, and the case forms.—Less. 142, 118, 125.

LESSON 127.

COMPARISON.

Introductory Hints.—*That apple is sweet, that other is sweeter, but this one is the sweetest.* The adjective *sweet*, expressing a quality of the three apples, is, as you see, inflected by adding *er* and *est*.

Adjectives, then, have one modification, and this is marked by *form*, or *inflection*. This modification is called **Comparison**, because it is used when things are *compared* with one another in respect to some quality common to them all, but possessed by them in different degrees. The form of the adjective which expresses the simple quality, as *sweet*, is of the **Positive Degree**; that which expresses the quality in a greater or a less degree, as *sweeter, less sweet,* is of the **Comparative Degree**; and that which expresses the quality in the greatest or the least degree, as *sweetest, least sweet,* is of the **Superlative Degree**.

But even the positive *implies* a comparison; we should not say, *This apple is sweet,* unless this particular fruit had more of the quality than ordinary apples possess.

Notice, too, that the adjective in the comparative and superlative degrees always expresses the quality *relatively*. When we say, *This apple is sweeter than that,* or, *This apple is the sweetest of the three,* we do not mean that any of the apples is really or in the highest degree sweet; but only that one apple is sweeter than the other, or the sweetest of those compared.

The several degrees of the quality expressed by the adjective may be increased or diminished by adverbs modifying the adjective—we can say *very, exceedingly, rather,* or *somewhat* sweet; *far, still,* or *much* sweeter; *by far* or *much* the sweetest.

Some *adverbs,* as well as adjectives, are compared.

Adjectives have one modification; viz., *Comparison.**

DEFINITIONS.

Comparison is a modification of the adjective (or the adverb) to express the relative degree of the quality † in the things compared.

The *Positive Degree* expresses the simple quality.

The *Comparative Degree* expresses a greater or a less degree of the quality.

The *Superlative Degree* expresses the greatest or the least degree of the quality.

RULE.—Adjectives are regularly compared by adding *er* to the positive to form the comparative, and *est* to the positive to form the superlative.

---

* *Two* adjectives, *this* and *that,* have number forms—*this, these; that, those.* In Anglo-Saxon and Latin, adjectives have forms to indicate *gender, number,* and *case.*

† Different degrees of *quantity,* also, may sometimes be expressed by comparison.

RULES FOR SPELLING.

RULE I.—Final *e* is dropped before a suffix beginning with a vowel; as, *fine, finer; love, loving.*

Exceptions.—The *e* is retained (1) after *c* and *g*, when the suffix begins with *a* or *o*; as, *peaceable, changeable;* (2) after *o*; as, *hoeing;* and (3) when it is needed to preserve the identity of the word; as, *singeing, dyeing.*

RULE II.—Final *y* preceded by a consonant changes to *i* when a suffix is added not beginning with *i*; as, *witty, wittier; dry, dried.*

RULE III.—Those monosyllables and words accented on the last syllable that end in a single consonant following a single vowel double this consonant before a suffix beginning with a vowel; as, *hot, hotter; begin, beginning.*

Exceptions.—*X, k,* and *v* are never doubled, and *gas* has *gases* in the plural.

Adjectives of more than two syllables are generally compared by prefixing *more* and *most*. This method is often used with adjectives of two syllables and sometimes with those of one.

Remark.—*More beautiful, most beautiful,* etc., can hardly be called degree forms of the adjective. The adverbs *more* and *most* have the degree forms, and in parsing they may be regarded as separate words. The adjective, however, is varied in sense the same as when the inflections *er* and *est* are added.

Degrees of diminution are expressed by prefixing *less* and *least;* as, *valuable, less valuable, least valuable.*

Most definitive and many descriptive adjectives cannot be compared, as their meaning will not admit of different degrees.

Direction.—*From this list of adjectives select those that cannot be compared, and compare those that remain:—*

Observe the Rules for Spelling given above.

Wooden, English, unwelcome, physical, one, that, common, handsome, happy, able, polite, hot, sweet, vertical, two-wheeled, infinite, witty, humble, any, thin, intemperate, undeviating, nimble, holy, lunar, superior.

Of the two forms of comparison, that which is more easily pronounced and more agreeable to the ear is to be preferred.

Direction.—*Correct the following:—*

Famousest, virtuousest, eloquenter, comfortabler, amusingest.

Some *adverbs* are compared by adding *er* and *est*, and some by prefixing *more* and *most*.

Direction.—*Compare the following:—*

Early, easily, fast, firmly, foolishly, late, long, often, soon, wisely.

Some adjectives and adverbs are irregular in their comparison.

Direction.—*Learn to compare the following adjectives and adverbs:—*

Adjectives Irregularly Compared.

Pos.	Comp.	Superlative.	Pos.	Comp.	Superlative.
(Aft),*	after,	aftmost or aftermost.	Far,	farther,	farthest or farthermost.
Bad, Evil, Ill,	worse,	worst.	Fore,	former,	foremost or first.
			(Forth),	further,	furthest or furthermost.

* The words enclosed in curves are adverbs—the adjectives following having no positive form.

Pos.	Comp.	Superlative.	Pos.	Comp.	Superlative.
Good,	better,	best.	Near,	nearer,	nearest *or* next.
Hind,	hinder,	hindmost *or* hindermost.	Old,	older *or* elder,	oldest *or* eldest.
(In),	inner,	inmost *or* innermost.	(Out),	outer *or* utter,	outmost *or* outermost; utmost *or* uttermost.
Late,	later *or* latter,	latest *or* last.	Under,	——	undermost.
Little,*	less *or* lesser,	least.	(Up),	upper,	upmost *or* uppermost.
Many *or* Much,	more,	most.	Top,	——	topmost.

Adverbs Irregularly Compared.

Pos.	Comp.	Superlative.	Pos.	Comp.	Superlative.
Badly, Ill,	worse,	worst.	Little,	less,	least.
			Much,	more,	most.
Far,	farther,	farthest.	Well,	better,	best.
Forth,	further,	furthest.			

To the Teacher.—We give, below, a model for writing the parsing of adjectives. A similar form may be used for adverbs.

Exercises for the parsing of adjectives and adverbs may be selected from Lessons 12, 14, 29, 30, 31, 44, 46, 47, 48, 60, 63, 64, 65.

Model for Written Parsing.—*All the dewy glades are still.*

CLASSIFICATION.		MODIFICATION.	SYNTAX.
Adjectives.	*Kind.*	*Deg. of Comp.*	
All	Def.	——	Modifier of *glades*.
the	"	——	" " "
dewy	Des.	Pos.	" " "
still	"	"	Completes *are* and modifies *glades*.

* For the comparative and the superlative of *little*, in the sense of small in size, *smaller* and *smallest* are substituted; as, *little* boy, *smaller* boy, *smallest* boy.

LESSON 128.

CONSTRUCTION OF COMPARATIVES AND SUPERLATIVES.

Caution.—In stating a comparison avoid comparing a thing with itself.*

Remark.—The comparative degree refers to two things (or sets of things) as distinct from each other, and implies that one has more of the quality than the other. The comparative degree is generally followed by *than*.†

Direction.—*Study the Caution and the Remark, and correct these errors :—*

1. London is larger than any city in Europe.

Correction.—The second term of comparison, *any city in Europe*, includes London, and so London is represented as being larger than itself. It should be, *London is larger than any other city in Europe*, or, *London is the largest city in Europe.*

2. China has a greater population than any nation on the globe. 3. I like this book better than any book I have seen. 4. There is no metal so useful as iron.

(A comparison is here stated, although no degree form is employed.)

5. All the metals are less useful than iron. 6. Time ought, above all kinds of property, to be free from invasion.

Caution.—In using the superlative degree be careful to make the latter term of the comparison, or the term introduced by *of*, include the former.

Remark.—The superlative degree refers to one thing (or set of things)

---

* A thing may, of course, be compared with itself as existing under different conditions; as, *The star is brighter to-night, The grass is greener to-day.*
† The comparative is *generally* used with reference to *two things* only, but it may be used to compare one thing with a number of things taken separately or together; as, *He is no better than other men, It contains more than all the others combined.*

15

as belonging to a group or class, and as having more of the quality than any of the rest. The superlative is generally followed by *of*.*

Direction.—*Study the Caution and the Remark, and correct these errors:*—

1. Solomon was the wisest of all the other Hebrew kings.

Correction.—*Of* (= *belonging to*) represents Solomon as belonging to a group of kings, and *other* excludes him from this group—a contradiction in terms. It should be, *Solomon was the wisest of Hebrew kings,* or, *Solomon was wiser than any other Hebrew king.*

2. Of all the other books I have examined, this is the most satisfactory. 3. Profane swearing is, of all other vices, the most inexcusable. 4. He was the most active of all his companions.

(He was not one of his own companions.)

5. This was the most satisfactory of any preceding effort.

Caution.—Avoid double comparatives and double superlatives, and the comparison of adjectives whose meaning will not admit of different degrees.†

Direction.—*Correct these errors:*—

1. A more healthier location cannot be found. 2. He took the longest, but the most pleasantest, route. 3. Draw that line more perpendicular.

---

* The superlative is generally used with reference to more than two things, but it is sometimes used to compare two; as, *Which is the best of the two?* Many grammarians claim that the comparative should *always* be used in such constructions; but the superlative can hardly be condemned, for (1) it is supported by good usage, (2) it is sometimes less stiff and formal than the comparative, and (3) *the* precedes the adjective, *of* follows it, and the latter term of the comparison includes the former—the construction peculiar to the superlative.

† Double comparatives and double superlatives were formerly used by good writers for the sake of emphasis; as, Our *worser* thoughts Heaven mend!—*Shakespeare.* The *most straitest* sect.—*Bible.*

Many words which grammarians have considered incapable of comparison are used in a sense short of their literal meaning, and are compared by good writers; as, My *chiefest* entertainment.—*Sheridan.* The *chiefest* prize.—*Byron. Divinest* Melancholy. —*Milton. Extremest* hell.—*Whittier. Most perfect* harmony.—*Longfellow. Less perfect* imitations.—*Macaulay.* These exceptional forms should not be encouraged.

Construction of Comparatives and Superlatives.

Correction.—Draw that line *perpendicular,* or *more nearly perpendicular.*

4. The opinion is becoming more universal. 5. A worser evil awaits us. 6. The most principal point was entirely overlooked. 7. That form of expression is more preferable.

Caution.—When an adjective denoting one or more than one is joined to a noun, the adjective and the noun must agree in number.

Remark.—A numeral denoting more than one may be prefixed to a singular noun to form a compound adjective ; as, a *ten-foot* pole (not a *ten-feet* pole), a *three-cent* stamp.

Direction.—*Study the Caution and the Remark, and correct these errors :—*

1. These kind of people will never be satisfied. 2. The room is fifteen foot square ; I measured it with a two-feet rule. 3. The farmer exchanged five barrel of potatoes for fifty pound of sugar. 4. These sort of expressions should be avoided. 5. We were traveling at the rate of forty mile an hour. 6. Remove this ashes and put away that tongs.

Miscellaneous.

(Two of these examples are correct.)

1. He was more active than any other of his companions.

Correction.—As he is not one of his companions, *other* is unnecessary.

2. He did more to accomplish this result than any other man that preceded or followed him. 3. The younger of the three sisters is the prettier.

(This is the construction which requires the superlative. See the second Remark in this Lesson.)

4. This result, of all others, is most to be dreaded. 5. She was willing to take a more humbler part. 6. Solomon was wiser than any of the ancient kings. 7. Which of these two books is the best ? 8. A farmer sold two span of horses, five yoke of oxen, twenty head of cattle, and fifty pair of ducks. 9. This is the more preferable form.

10. Which are the two more important ranges of mountains in North America?

GENERAL REVIEW.

To the Teacher.—See suggestions to the teacher page 219.

Scheme for the Adjective.
(The numbers refer to Lessons.)

ADJECTIVE.
- Uses.
  - Modifier (12).
  - Attribute Complement (29, 30).
  - Objective Complement (31).
- Classes.
  - Descriptive (89-91).
  - Definitive (89-91).
- Modification.—Comparison.
  - Pos. Degree
  - Comp. "
  - Sup. "
  — 127, 128.

Questions on the Adjective.

1. Define the adjective and its classes.—Less. 89.
2. Define comparison and the degrees of comparison.—Less. 127.
3. Give and illustrate the regular method and the irregular methods of comparison.—Less. 127.
4. Give and illustrate the principles which guide in the use of adjectives.—Less. 90, 91.
5. Give and illustrate the principles which guide in the use of comparative and superlative forms.—Less. 128.

Scheme for the Adverb.

ADVERB.
- Classes.
  - Time.
  - Place.
  - Degree.
  - Manner.
  - Cause.
  — 92-94.
- Modification.—Comparison.
  - Pos. Deg.
  - Comp. "
  - Sup. "
  — 127, 128.

Questions on the Adverb.

1. Define the adverb and its classes.—Less. 92.

2. Illustrate the regular method and the irregular methods of comparison.—Less. 127.

3. Give and illustrate the principles which guide in the use of adverbs.—Less. 93.

LESSON 129.

MODIFICATIONS OF THE VERB.

VOICE.

Introductory Hints.—*He picked a rose. A rose was picked by him.* The same thing is here told in two ways. The first verb, *picked*, shows that the subject names the actor; the second verb, *was picked*, shows that the subject names the thing acted upon. These different forms and uses of the verb constitute the modification called **Voice**. The first form is in the **Active Voice**; the second is in the **Passive Voice**.

The active voice is used when the *agent*, or *actor*, is to be made prominent; the passive, when the *thing acted upon* is to be made prominent. The passive voice may be used when the agent is unknown, or when, for any reason, we do not care to name it; as, *The ship was wrecked, Money is coined.*

DEFINITIONS.

Voice is that modification of the transitive verb which shows whether the subject names the *actor* or the *thing acted upon*.

The *Active Voice* shows that the subject names the actor.

The *Passive Voice* shows that the subject names the thing acted upon.

The passive form is compound, and may be resolved into

an asserting word (some form of the verb *be*), and an attribute complement (a past participle of a transitive verb).

An expression consisting of an asserting word followed by an adjective complement or by a participle used adjectively may be mistaken for a verb in the passive voice.

Examples.—The coat *was* sometimes *worn* by Joseph (*was worn*—passive voice). The coat *was* badly *worn* (*was*—incomplete predicate, *worn*—adjective complement).

Remark.—To test the passive voice note whether the one named by the subject is acted upon, and whether the verb may be followed by *by* before the name of the agent.

Direction.—*Tell which of the following completed predicates may be treated as single verbs, and which should be resolved into incomplete predicates and attribute complements :—*

1. The lady is accomplished. 2. This task was not accomplished in a day. 3. Are you prepared to recite? 4. Dinner was soon prepared. 5. A shadow was mistaken for a foot-bridge. 6. You are mistaken. 7. The man was drunk before the wine was drunk. 8. The house is situated on the bank of the river. 9. I am obliged to you. 10. I am obliged to do this. 11. The horse is tired. 12. A fool and his money are soon parted. 13. The tower is inclined. 14. My body is inclined by years.

Direction.—*Name all the transitive verbs in Lesson 78, and give their voice.*

LESSON 130.

COMPOSITION—VOICE.

The *objec' complement* of a verb in the *active voice* becomes the *subject* when the verb is changed to the *passive voice.*

Example.—The Danes invaded *England* = *England* was invaded by the Danes.

Remark.—You will notice that in the first sentence the *agent* is made prominent; in the second sentence the *receiver*.

Direction.—*In each of these sentences change the v o i c e of the transitive verb without altering the meaning of the sentence, and note the other changes that occur :—*

1. Mercury, the messenger of the gods, wore a winged cap and winged shoes. 2. When the Saxons subdued the Britons, they introduced into England their own language, which was a dialect of the Teutonic, or Gothic. 3. My wife was chosen as her wedding dress was chosen, not for a fine, glossy surface, but for such qualities as would wear well. 4. Bacchus, the god of wine, was worshiped in many parts of Greece and Rome. 5. The minds of children are dressed by their parents as their bodies are dressed—in the prevailing fashion. 6. Harvey, an English physician, discovered that blood circulates. 7. The luxury of Capua, more powerful than the Roman legions, vanquished the victorious Carthaginians. 8. His eloquence had struck them dumb.

Remark.—Notice that the *objective* complement becomes the *attribute* complement when the verb is changed from the active to the passive voice.

9. That tribunal pronounced Charles a tyrant. 10. The town had nicknamed him Beau Seymour. 11. Even silent night proclaims my soul immortal. 12. We saw the storm approaching.

(Notice that the objective complement is here a participle.)

13. He kept his mother waiting. 14. We found him lying dead on the field. 15. We all believe him to be an honest man.

(Notice that the objective complement is here an infinitive phrase.)

16. Some, sunk to beasts, find pleasure end in pain. 17. Everybody acknowledged him to be a genius.

The so-called *indirect*, or *dative, object* is sometimes made the *subject* of a verb in the passive voice, while the object complement is retained after the verb.*

Example.—The porter refused *him* admittance = *He* was refused *admittance* by the porter.

(Some would treat *admittance* as adverbial modifier of *was refused*.)

Direction.—*Change the voice of the transitive verbs in these sentences, and note the other changes that occur :—*

18. They were refused the protection of the law. 19. He was offered a pension by the government. 20. I was asked that question yesterday. 21. He told me to leave the room.

Explanation.—Here the infinitive phrase is the object complement, and (*to*) *me* is used adverbially. *To leave the room* = *that I should leave the room.*

22. I taught the child to read. 23. I taught the child reading. 24. They told me that your name was Fontibell.

Direction.—*Change the following transitive verbs to the passive form, using first the regular and then the idiomatic construction :—*

Model.—*He promised me a present* = *A present was promised me* (regular) = *I was promised a present* (idiomatic).

25. They must allow us the privilege of thinking for ourselves. 26. He offered them their lives if they would abjure their religion.

An intransitive verb is sometimes made transitive by the aid of a preposition.

Example.—All his friends *laughed* at him = He *was laughed* at (ridiculed) by all his friends.

Remark.—*Was laughed at* may be treated as one verb. Some grammarians, however, would call *at* an adverb. The intransitive verb and

---

* Some grammarians condemn this construction. It is true that it is a violation of the general analogies, or laws, of language; but that it is an idiom of our language, established by good usage, is beyond controversy.

preposition are together equivalent to a transitive verb in the passive voice.

Direction.—*Change the voice of the following verbs:*—

27. This artful fellow has imposed upon us all. 28. The speaker did not even touch upon this topic. 29. He dropped the matter there, and did not refer to it afterward.

Remark.—The following sentences present a peculiar idiomatic construction. A transitive verb which, in the active voice, is followed by an object complement and a prepositional phrase, takes, in the passive, the principal word of the phrase for its subject, retaining the complement and the preposition to complete its meaning; as, They *took care of it, It was taken care of.*

Direction.—*Put the following sentences into several different forms, and determine which is the best:*—

30. His original purpose was lost sight of * (forgotten). 31. Such talents should be made much of. 32. He was taken care of by his friends. 33. Some of his characters have been found fault with as insipid.

LESSON 131.

MODIFICATIONS OF THE VERB—CONTINUED

Mode, Tense, Number, and Person.

Introductory Hints.—*James walks.* Here the walking is asserted as an *actual* fact. *James may walk.* Here the walking is asserted not

---

* Some would parse *of* as an adverb relating to *was lost*, and *sight* as a noun used adverbially to modify *was lost;* others would treat *sight* as an object [complement] of *was lost;* others would call *was lost sight of* a compound verb; and others, claiming that the logical relation of these words is not lost by a change of position, analyze it as if arranged thus: *Sight of his original purpose was lost.*

It seems to us that any separate disposition of these words is unsatisfactory.

Mr. Goo'd Brown pronounces this construction "an unparsable synchysis, a vile snarl, which no grammarian should hesitate to condemn."

as an actual, but as a *possible* fact. *If James walk out, he will improve.* Here the walking is asserted only as *thought of*, without regard to its being or becoming either an actual or a possible fact. *James, walk out.* Here the walking is not asserted as a fact, but only as a *command*—James is ordered to make it a fact. These different uses and forms of the verb constitute the modification which we call **Mode**. The first verb is in the **Indicative Mode**; the second in the **Potential Mode**; the third in the **Subjunctive Mode**; the fourth in the **Imperative Mode**.

For the two forms of the verb called the **Participle** and the **Infinitive**, see Lessons 37 and 40.

I walk. I walked. I shall walk. In these three sentences the *manner* of asserting the action is the same, but the *time* in which the action takes place is different. *Walk* asserts the action as going on in present time, and, as **Tense** means time, is in the **Present Tense**. *Walked* asserts the action as *past*, and is in the **Past Tense**. *Shall walk* asserts the action as future, and is in the **Future Tense**.

I have walked out to-day. I had walked out when he called. I shall have walked out by to-morrow. Have walked asserts the action as *completed* at the present, and is in the **Present Perfect Tense**. *Had walked* asserts the action as *completed* in the past, and is in the **Past Perfect Tense**. *Shall have walked* asserts the action as *completed* in the future, and is in the **Future Perfect Tense**.

I walk. Thou walkest. He walks. They walk. In the second sentence *walk* is changed by adding *est*; in the third sentence by adding *s*. Verbs are said to agree in **Person** and **Number** with their subjects. But this agreement is not often, as here, marked by changes in the form of the verb.

DEFINITIONS.

Mode is that modification of the verb which denotes the manner of asserting the action or being.

The *Indicative Mode* asserts the action or being as a fact.

The *Potential Mode* asserts the power, liberty, possibility, or necessity of acting or being.

The *Subjunctive Mode* asserts the action or being as a mere condition, supposition, or wish.

The *Imperative Mode* asserts the action or being as a command or an entreaty.

The *Infinitive* is a form of the verb which names the action or being in a general way, without asserting it of anything.

The *Participle* is a form of the verb partaking of the nature of an adjective or of a noun, and expressing the action or being as assumed.

The *Present Participle* denotes action or being as continuing at the time indicated by the predicate.

The *Past Participle* denotes action or being as past or completed at the time indicated by the predicate.

The *Past Perfect Participle* denotes action or being as completed at a time previous to that indicated by the predicate.

Tense is that modification of the verb which expresses the time of the action or being.

The *Present Tense* expresses action or being as present.

The *Past Tense* expresses action or being as past.

The *Future Tense* expresses action or being as yet to come.

The *Present Perfect Tense* expresses action or being as completed at the present time.

The *Past Perfect Tense* expresses action or being as completed at some past time.

The *Future Perfect Tense* expresses action or being to be completed at some future time.

Number and *Person* of a verb are those modifications that show its agreement with the number and person of its subject.

LESSON 132.

FORMS OF THE VERB.
CONJUGATION.
DEFINITIONS.

Conjugation is the regular arrangement of all the forms of the verb.

Synopsis is the regular arrangement of the forms of one number and person in all the modes and tenses.

Auxiliary Verbs are those that help in the conjugation of other verbs.

The auxiliaries are *do, did, be* (with all its variations, see Lesson 135), *have, had, shall, should, will, would, may, might, can, could,* and *must.*

The *Principal Parts* of a verb, or those from which the other parts are derived, are the present indicative or the present infinitive, the past indicative, and the past participle.

List of Irregular Verbs.

To the Teacher.—It would be well to require the pupils, in studying and in reciting these lists of irregular verbs, to frame short sentences illustrating the proper use of the *past tense* and the *past participle, e. g.*, I *began* yesterday, He has *begun* to do better. In this way the pupils will be saved the mechanical labor of memorizing forms which they already know how to use, and they will be led to correct what has been faulty in their use of other forms.

Remark.—Verbs that have both a regular and an irregular form are called **Redundant**.

Verbs that are wanting in any of their parts, as *can* and *may*, are called **Defective**.

The present participle is not here given as a principal part. It may always be formed from the present tense by adding *ing*.

In adding *ing* and other terminations, the Rules for Spelling (see Lesson 127) should be observed.

Remark.—The forms, below, in Italics are *regular;* and those in smaller type are *obsolete*, and need not be committed to memory.

Forms of the Verb.

Present.	Past.	Past Par.	Present.	Past.	Past Par.
Abide,	abode,	abode.	Chide,	chid,	chidden, chid.
Awake,	awoke, awaked,	awaked.	Choose,	chose,	chosen.
Be, or am,	was,	been.	Cleave,	cleaved,	cleaved.
Bear, (bring forth)	bore, bare,	born, borne.	(adhere)	clave,	
Bear, (carry)	bore, bare,	borne.	Cleave, (split)	clove, cleft, clave,	cloven, cleft.
Beat,	beat,	beaten.	Cling,	clung,	clung.
Begin,	began,	begun.	Clothe,	clad, clothed,	clad. clothed.
Bend,	bent, bended,	bent. bended.	(Be) Come,	came,	come.
Bereave,	bereft, bereaved,	bereft. bereaved.	Cost,	cost,	cost.
Beseech,	besought,	besought.	Creep,	crept,	crept.
Bet,	bet, betted,	bet. betted.	Crow,	crew, crowed,	crowed.
Bid,	bade, bid,	bidden, bid.	Cut,	cut,	cut.
Bind,	bound,	bound.	Dare, (venture)	durst, dared,	dared.
Bite,	bit,	bitten, bit.	Deal,	dealt,	dealt.
Bleed,	bled,	bled.	Dig,	dug, digged,	dug. digged.
Blend,	blent, blended,	blent. blended.	Do,	did,	done.
Bless,	blest, blessed,	blest. blessed.	Draw,	drew,	drawn.
Blow,	blew,	blown.	Dream,	dreamt, dreamed	dreamt. dreamed.
Break,	broke, brake,	broken.	Dress,	drest, dressed,	drest. dressed.
Breed,	bred,	bred.	Drink,	drank,	drunk.
Bring,	brought,	brought.	Drive,	drove,	driven.
Build,	built, builded,	built. builded.	Dwell,	dwelt, dwelled,	dwelt. dwelled.
Burn,	burnt, burned,	burnt. burned.	Eat,	ate,	eaten.
Burst,	burst,	burst.	(Be) Fall,	fell,	fallen.
Buy,	bought,	bought.	Feed,	fed,	fed.
Can,	could,	——.	Feel,	felt,	felt.
Cast,	cast,	cast.	Fight,	fought,	fought.
Catch,	caught,	caught.	Find,	found,	found.

Present.	Past.	Past Par.	Present.	Past.	Past Par.
Flee,	fled,	fled.	Knit,	knit,	knit.
Fling,	flung,	flung.		*knitted*,	*knitted*.
Fly,	flew,	flown.	Know,	knew,	known.
Forsake,	forsook,	forsaken.	Lade,	*laded*,	*laded*.
Forbear,	forbore,	forborne.	(load)		laden.
Freeze,	froze,	frozen.	Lay,	laid,	laid.
(For) Get,	got,	got, gotten.*	Lead,	led,	led.
Gild,	gilt, *gilded*,	gilt. *gilded*.	Lean,	leant, *leaned*,	leant. *leaned*.
Gird,	girt, *girded*,	girt. *girded*.	Leap,	leapt, *leaped*,	leapt. *leaped*.
(For) Give,	gave,	given.	Learn,	learnt, *learned*,	learnt. *learned*.
Go,	went,	gone.	Leave,	left,	left.
(En)Grave,	*graved*,	*graved*. graven.	Lend,	lent,	lent.
Grind,	ground,	ground.	Let,	let,	let.
Grow,	grew,	grown.	Lie, (*recline*)	lay,	lain.
Hang,	hung, *hanged*,	hung. *hanged*.†	Light,	lit, *lighted*,	lit.§ *lighted*.
Have,	had,	had.	Lose,	lost,	lost.
Hear,	heard,	heard.	Make,	made,	made.
Heave,	hove, *heaved*,	hove.‡ *heaved*.	May,	might,	—
Hew,	*hewed*,	*hewed*. hewn.	Mean,	meant,	meant.
			Meet,	met,	met.
Hide,	hid,	hidden, hid.	Mow,	*mowed*,	*mowed*. mown.
Hit,	hit,	hit.	Must,	—	—.
(Be) Hold,	held,	held, holden.	Ought,	—	—.
Hurt,	hurt,	hurt.	Pay,	paid,	paid.
Keep,	kept,	kept.	Pen, (*enclose*)	pent, *penned*,	pent. *penned*.
Kneel,	knelt, *kneeled*,	knelt. *kneeled*.	Put,	put,	put.

* *Gotten* is obsolescent except in *forgotten*.
† *Hang*, to execute by hanging, is regular.
‡ *Hove* is used in sea language.
§ *Lighted* is preferred to *lit*.

LESSON 133.

LIST OF IRREGULAR VERBS—CONTINUED.

Present.	Past.	Past Par.	Present.	Past.	Past Par.
Quit,	quit, *quitted,* quoth,	quit. *quitted.* —.	Shed,	shed,	shed.
			Shine,	shone, *shined,*	shone. *shined.*
Rap,	rapt, *rapped,*	rapt. *rapped.*	Shoe,	shod,	shod.
			Shoot,	shot,	shot.
Read,	read,	read.	Show,	*showed,*	shown. *showed.*
Rend,	rent,	rent.			
Rid,	rid,	rid.	Shred,	shred,	shred.
Ride,	rode,	ridden.	Shrink,	shrank, shrunk,	shrunk, shrunken.
Ring,	rang, rung,	rung.	Shut,	shut,	shut.
(A)Rise,	rose,	risen.	Sing,	sang, sung,	sung.
Rive,	*rived,*	riven. *rived.*	Sink,	sank, sunk,	sunk, sunken.
Run,	ran,	run.	Sit,	sat,	sat.
Saw,	*sawed,*	*sawed.* sawn.	Slay,	slew,	slain.
			Sleep,	slept,	slept.
Say,	said,	said.	Slide,	slid,	slidden, slid.
See,	saw,	seen.			
Seek,	sought,	sought.	Sling,	slung, slang,	slung.
Seethe,	*seethed,* sod,	*seethed.* sodden.	Slink,	slunk,	slunk.
Sell,	sold,	sold.	Slit,	slit, *slitted,*	slit. *slitted.*
Send,	sent,	sent.			
(Be)Set,	set,	set.	Smell,	smelt, *smelled,*	smelt. *smelled.*
Shake,	shook,	shaken.			
Shall,	should,	—.	Smite,	smote,	smitten, smit.
Shape,	*shaped,*	*shaped.* *shapen.*	Sow,	*sowed,*	sown. *sowed.*
Shave,	*shaved,*	*shaved.* *shaven.*	Speak,	spoke, spake,	spoken.
Shear,	*sheared,* shore,	*sheared.* shorn.	Speed,	sped,	sped.

Present.	Past.	Past Par.	Present.	Past.	Past Par.
Spell,	spelt, *spelled,*	spelt. *spelled.*	Sweep,	swept,	swept.
Spend,	spent,	spent.	Swell,	swelled,	swelled. swollen.
Spill,	spilt, *spilled,*	spilt. *spilled.*	Swim,	swam, swum,	swum.
Spin,	spun, span,	spun.	Swing,	swung,	swung.
			Take,	took,	taken.
Spit,	spit, spat,	spit, spitten.	Teach,	taught,	taught.
Split,	split,	split.	Tear,	tore, tare,	torn.
Spoil,	spoilt, *spoiled,*	spoilt. *spoiled.*	Tell,	told,	told.
Spread,	spread,	spread.	Think,	thought,	thought.
Spring,	sprang, sprung,	sprung.	Thrive,	throve, *thrived,*	thriven. *thrived.*
Stand,	stood,	stood.	Throw,	threw,	thrown.
Stave,	stove, *staved,*	stove. *staved.*	Thrust,	thrust,	thrust.
			Tread,	trod,	trodden, trod.
Stay,	staid, *stayed,*	staid. *stayed.*	Wake,	*waked,* woke.	*waked.*
Steal,	stole,	stolen.			
Stick,	stuck,	stuck.	Wax,	*waxed,*	waxen. *waxed.*
Sting,	stung,	stung.	Wear,	wore,	worn.
Stink,	stunk, stank,	stunk.	Weave,	wove,	woven.
Strew,	*strewed,*	strewn. *strewed.*	Weep,	wept,	wept.
Stride,	strode,	stridden.	Wet,	wet, *wetted,*	wet. *wetted.*
Strike,	struck,	struck, stricken.	Will,	would,	———.
String,	strung,	strung.	Win,	won,	won.
Strive,	strove,	striven.	Wind,	wound,	wound.
Strow,	*strowed,*	strown. *strowed.*	Work,	wrought, *worked,*	wrought. *worked.*
Swear,	swore, sware,	sworn.	(to)wit, wot,	wist,	———.
Sweat,	sweat, *sweated,*	sweat. *sweated.*	Wring,	wrung,	wrung.
			Write,	wrote,	written.

LESSON 134.

FORMS OF THE VERB—CONTINUED.

CONJUGATION—SIMPLEST FORM.

Remark.—English verbs have few inflections compared with those of other languages. Some irregular verbs have seven forms—see, saw, seeing, seen, sees, seest, sawest; regular verbs have six—walk, walked, walking, walks, walkest, walkedst. As a substitute for other inflections we prefix auxiliary verbs, and make what are called *compound*, or *periphrastic*, forms.

Direction.—*Fill out the following forms, using the principal parts of the verb walk. Present, walk; past, walked; past participle, walked.*

INDICATIVE MODE.

PRESENT TENSE.

Singular.   *Plural.*
1. (I) ___Pres.___   1. (We) ___Pres.___,
2. {(You) ___Pres.___   2. (You) ___Pres.___
   {(Thou) ___Pres.___ est,*
3. (He) ___Pres.___ s;*   3. (They) ___Pres.___

PAST TENSE.

1. (I) ___Past.___,   1. (We) ___Past.___,
2. {(You) ___Past.___   2. (You) ___Past.___,
   {(Thou) ___Past.___ st,
3. (He) ___Past.___;   3. (They) ___Past.___.

FUTURE TENSE.

1. (I) *shall* ___Pres.___   1. (We) *shall* ___Pres.___,
2. {(You) *will* ___Pres.___   2. (You) *will* ___Pres.___,
   {(Thou) *wil-t* ___Pres.___
3. (He) *will* ___Pres.___;   3. (They) *will* ___Pres.___

---

* In the indicative, present, second, singular, old style, *st* is sometimes added instead of *est*; and in the third person, common style, *es* is added, when *s* will not unite. In the third person, old style, *eth* is added.

Present Perfect Tense.

Singular.		Plural.	
1. (I) *have*	*Past Par.*,	1. (We) *have*	*Past Par.*,
2. { (You) *have*	*Past Par.*,	2. (You) *have*	*Past Par.*,
{ (Thou) *ha-st*	*Past Par.*		
3. (He) *ha-s*	*Past Par.*;	3. (They) *have*	*Past Par.*

Past Perfect Tense.

1. (I) *had*	*Past Par.*,	1. (We) *had*	*Past Par.*,
2. { (You) *had*	*Past Par.*,	2. (You) *had*	*Past Par.*,
{ (Thou) *had-st*	*Past Par.*,		
3. (He) *had*	*Past Par.*;	3. (They) *had*	*Past Par.*

Future Perfect Tense.

1. (I) *shall have*	*Past Par.*,	1. (We) *shall have*	*Past Par.*,
2. { (You) *will have*	*Past Par.*,	2. (You) *will have*	*Past Par.*,
{ (Thou) *wil-t have*	*Past Par.*,		
3. (He) *will have*	*Past Par.*;	3. (They) *will have*	*Past Par.*

POTENTIAL MODE.

Present Tense.

Singular.		Plural.	
1. (I) *may*	*Pres.*,	1. (We) *may*	*Pres.*,
2. { (You) *may*	*Pres.*,	2. (You) *may*	*Pres.*,
{ (Thou) *may-st*	*Pres.*,		
3. (He) *may*	*Pres.*;	3. (They) *may*	*Pres.*

Past Tense.

1. (I) *might*	*Pres.*,	1. (We) *might*	*Pres.*,
2. { (You) *might*	*Pres.*,	2. (You) *might*	*Pres.*,
{ (Thou) *might-st*	*Pres.*,		
3. (He) *might*	*Pres.*;	3. (They) *might*	*Pres.*

Present Perfect Tense.

1. (I) *may have*	*Past Par.*,	1. (We) *may have*	*Past Par.*,
2. { (You) *may have*	*Past Par.*,	2. (You) *may have*	*Past Par.*,
{ (Thou) *may-st have*	*Past Par.*,		
3. (He) *may have*	*Past Par.*;	3. (They) *may have*	*Past Par.*

Conjugation.

Past Perfect Tense.

Singular.
1. (I) *might have* <u>Past Par.</u>,
2. {(You) *might have* <u>Past Par.</u>,
   {(Thou) *might-st have* <u>Past Par.</u>,
3. (He) *might have* <u>Past Par.</u>;

Plural.
1. (We) *might have* <u>Past Par.</u>,
2. (You) *might have* <u>Past Par.</u>,
3. (They) *might have* <u>Past Par.</u>.

SUBJUNCTIVE MODE.

Present Tense.

Singular.

2. (If thou) <u>Pres.</u>, 3. (If he)* <u>Pres.</u>.

IMPERATIVE MODE.

Present Tense.

Singular.
2. <u>Pres.</u> (you *or* thou);

Plural.
2. <u>Pres.</u> (you *or* ye).

INFINITIVES.

Present Tense.
† (To) <u>Pres.</u>

Present Perfect Tense.
(To) *have* <u>Past Par.</u>.

---

* The subjunctive as a form of the verb is fading out of the language. The only distinctive forms remaining (except for the verb *be*) are the second and the third person singular of the present, and even these are giving way to the indicative. Such forms as If he *have* loved, etc., are exceptional. It is true that other forms ; as, *If he had known, Had he been, Should he fall,* may be used in a true subjunctive sense, to assert what is a mere *conception of the mind, i. e.,* what is merely thought of, without regard to its being or becoming a fact ; but in these cases it is not the *form of the verb,* but the connective or something in the construction of the sentence that determines the manner of assertion. In parsing, the verbs in such constructions may be treated as indicative or potential, with a subjunctive meaning.

The offices of the different mode and tense forms are constantly interchanging ; a classification based strictly on meaning would be very difficult, and would confuse the learner.

† *To,* as indicated by the ( ), is not treated as a part of the verb. Writers on language are generally agreed that when *to* introduces an infinitive phrase used as an adjective or an adverb, it performs its proper function as a preposition, meaning *toward, for,* etc. ; as, I am inclined *to* believe, I came *to* hear. When the infinitive phrase is used as a noun, the *to* expresses no relation ; it seems merely to introduce the phrase. When a word loses its proper function without taking on the function of some other part of speech, we do not see why it should change its name. In the expressions, *For* me to do this would be wrong, *Over* the fence is out of danger, few

PARTICIPLES.

PRESENT.	PAST.	PAST PERFECT.
Pres. *ing*.	Past Par.	Having Past Par.

May, can, and *must* are potential auxiliaries in the present and the present perfect tense; *might, could, would,* and *should,* in the past and the past perfect.

The *emphatic* form of the present and the past tense indicative is made by prefixing *do* and *did* to the present. *Do* is prefixed to the imperative also.

To the Teacher.—Require the pupils to fill out these forms with other verbs, regular and irregular, using the auxiliaries named above.

LESSON 135.

FORMS OF THE VERB—CONTINUED.
CONJUGATION OF THE VERB BE.

Direction.—*Learn the following forms, paying no attention to the line at the right of each verb* :—

INDICATIVE MODE.
PRESENT TENSE.

Singular.
1. (I) am ——,
2. {(You) are ——, *or* (Thou) art ——,
3. (He) is —— ;

Plural.
1. (We) are ——,
2. (You) are ——,
3. (They) are ——.

---

grammarians would hesitate to call *for* and *over* prepositions, although they have no antecedent term of *relation*.

We cannot see that *to* is a part of the verb, for it in no way affects the meaning, as does an auxiliary, or as does the *to* in He *was spoken to*. Those who call it a part of the verb confuse the learner by speaking of it as the "preposition *to*" (which, as they have said, is not a preposition) "placed before the infinitive," *i. e.*, placed before that of which it forms a part—placed before itself.

In the Anglo-Saxon, *to* was used with the infinitive only in the dative case, where it had its proper function as a preposition ; as, nominative, *etan* (to eat) ; dative, *to etanne;* accusative, *etan*. When the dative ending *ne* was dropped, making the three forms alike, the *to* came to be used before the nominative and the accusative, but without expressing relation.

Forms of the Verb—Continued.

Past Tense.

Singular.
1. (I) was ——,
2. { (You) were ——, *or*
   { (Thou) wast ——,
3. (He) was —— ;

Plural.
1. (We) were ——,
2. (You) were ——,
3. (They) were ——.

Future Tense.

1. (I) shall be ——,
2. { (You) will be ——, *or*
   { (Thou) wilt be ——,
3. (He) will be —— ;

1. (We) shall be ——,
2. (You) will be ——,
3. (They) will be ——.

Present Perfect Tense.

1. (I) have been ——,
2. { (You) have been ——, *or*
   { (Thou) hast been ——,
3. (He) has been —— ;

1. (We) have been ——,
2. (You) have been ——,
3. (They) have been ——.

Past Perfect Tense.

1. (I) had been ——,
2. { (You) had been ——, *or*
   { (Thou) hadst been ——,
3. (He) had been —— ;

1. (We) had been ——,
2. (You) had been ——,
3. (They) had been ——.

Future Perfect Tense.

1. (I) shall have been ——,
2. { (You) will have been ——, *or*
   { (Thou) wilt have been ——,
3. (He) will have been —— ;

1. (We) shall have been ——,
2. (You) will have been ——,
3. (They) will have been ——.

POTENTIAL MODE.

Present Tense.

Singular.
1. (I) may be ——,
2. { (You) may be —— *or*
   { (Thou) mayst be ——,
3. (He) may be —— ;

Plural.
1. (We) may be ——.
2. (You) may be ——,
3. (They) may be ——.

Past Tense.

Singular.
1. (I) might be ———,
2. { (You) might be ———, *or*
   { (Thou) mightst be ———,
3. (He) might be ——— ;

Plural.
1. (We) might be ———,
2. (You) might be ———,
3. (They) might be ———.

Present Perfect Tense.

1. (I) may have been ———,
2. { (You) may have been ———, *or*
   { (Thou) mayst have been ———,
3. (He) may have been ——— ;

1. (We) may have been ———,
2. (You) may have been ———,
3. (They) may have been ———.

Past Perfect Tense.

1. (I) might have been ———,
2. { (You) might have been ———, *or*
   { (Thou) mightst have been ———,
3. (He) might have been ——— ;

1. (We) might have been ———,
2. (You) might have been ———,
3. (They) might have been ———.

SUBJUNCTIVE MODE.

Present Tense.

Singular.
1. (If I) be ———,
2. { (If you) be ———, *or*
   { (If thou) be ———,
3. (If he) be ——— ;

Plural.
1. (If we) be ———,
2. (If you) be ———.
3. (If they) be ———.

Past Tense.

Singular.
1. (If I) were ———,
2. { (If you) were ———, *or*
   { (If thou) wert ———,
3. (If he) were ———.

IMPERATIVE MODE.

Present Tense.

Singular.
2. Be (you *or* thou) ——— :

Plural.
2. Be (you *or* ye) ———.

INFINITIVES.

PRESENT TENSE. PRESENT PERFECT TENSE.
(To) be ———. (To) have been ———.

PARTICIPLES.

PRESENT. PAST. PAST PERFECT.
Being ———. Been. Having been ———.

LESSON 136.

FORMS OF THE VERB—CONTINUED.

CONJUGATION—PROGRESSIVE AND PASSIVE FORMS.

A verb is conjugated in the *progressive form* by joining its *present participle* to the different forms of the verb *be*.

A transitive verb is conjugated in the *passive voice* by joining its *past participle* to the different forms of the verb *be*.

Remark.—The progressive form denotes a continuance of the action or being; as, The birds *are singing*.

Verbs that in their simple form denote continuance—such as *love, respect, know*—should not be conjugated in the progressive form. We say, I *love* the child—not, I *am loving* the child.

Remark.—The *progressive form* is sometimes used with a *passive* meaning; as, The house *is building*. In such cases the word in *ing* was once a verbal noun preceded by the preposition *a*, a contraction from *on* or *in*; as, While the ark *was a preparing*. While the flesh *was in seething*. In modern language the preposition is dropped, and the word in *ing* is treated adjectively.

Another *passive progressive form*, consisting of the verb *be* completed by the *present passive participle*, has recently appeared in our language—The house *is being built*. Although it has been condemned by many of our ablest linguists as awkward and otherwise objectionable, yet it has grown rapidly into good use, especially in England. Such a form seems to be needed when the simpler form would be ambiguous, *i. e.*, when its subject might be taken to name either the actor or the receiver; as, The child *is whipping*, The prisoner *is trying*.

Direction.—*Conjugate the verb c h o o s e in the progressive form by filling all the blanks left after the different forms of the verb b e, in the preceding Lesson, with the present participle c h o o s i n g; and then in the passive form by filling these blanks with the past participle c h o s e n.*

Notice that after the past participle of the verb *be* no blank is left. The past participle of the passive is not formed by the aid of *be*, but is the same in form as the simple active participle. In the progressive, the past participle is wanting. All the participles of the verb *choose* are arranged in order below.

	Present.	*Past.*	*Past Perfect.*
Simplest form.	Choosing,	chosen,	having chosen.
Progressive form.	Being choosing,	——	having been choosing.
Passive form.	Being chosen,	chosen,	having been chosen.

Direction.—*Write and arrange, as above, all the participles of the verbs b r e a k, d r i v e, r e a d, l i f t.*

To the Teacher.—Select other verbs, and require the pupils to conjugate them in the progressive and the passive form. Require them to give synopses of all the forms. Require them in some of their synopses to use *it* or some *noun* for the subject in the third person.

LESSON 137.

CONJUGATION—CONTINUED.

INTERROGATIVE AND NEGATIVE FORMS.

A verb may be conjugated *interrogatively* in the indicative and potential modes by placing the subject after the first auxiliary; as, *Does he sing?*

A verb may be conjugated *negatively* by placing *not* after the first auxiliary; as, He *does not sing*. *Not* is placed before the infinitives and the participles; as, *not to sing, not singing.*

A *question with negation* is expressed in the indicative and potential modes by placing the subject and *not* after the first auxiliary ; as, *Does he not sing?*

Remark.—Formerly, it was common to use the simple form of the present and past tenses interrogatively and negatively thus: *Loves he? I know not.* Such forms are still common in poetry, but in prose they are now scarcely used. We say, *Does he love? I do not know.* The verbs *be* and *have* are exceptions, as they do not regularly take the auxiliary *do*. We say, *Have you another? Is it right?*

Direction.—*Write a synopsis in the third person, singular, of the verb walk conjugated* (1) *interrogatively,* (2) *negatively, and* (3) *so as to express a question with negation. Remember that the indicative and the potential are the only modes that can be used interrogatively.*

To the Teacher.—Select other verbs, and require the pupils to conjugate them negatively and interrogatively in the progressive and the passive form. Require the pupils to give synopses of all the forms.

LESSON 138.

MODE AND TENSE FORMS.

COMPOUND FORMS—ANALYSIS.

The **compound**, or **periphrastic**, forms of the verb may each be resolved into an asserting word, and a participle or an infinitive used as a *complement*.

If we look at the original meaning of the forms I do write, I shall write, I will write, we shall find that the so-called auxiliary is the real verb, and that *write* is an infinitive used as object complement. I do write = I do or perform the action (*to*) write. I shall write = I owe (*to*) write. I will write = I determine (*to*) write.

May write, can write, must write, might write, could write, would write, and should write may each be resolved into an asserting word in the indicative mode and an infinitive complement.

The forms **is writing, was written**, etc., consist each of an asserting word (the verb *be*) and a participle, used as attribute complement.

The forms **have written, had written** are so far removed from their original meaning that their analysis cannot be made to correspond with their history. They originated from such expressions as *I have a letter written*, in which *have* (= *possess*) is a transitive verb, taking *letter* for its object complement, and *written* is a passive participle modifying *letter*. The idea of possession has faded out of *have*, and the participle, having lost its passive meaning, has become a complement of *have*. The use of this form has been extended to intransitive verbs—Spring *has come*, Birds *have flown*, etc., being now regularly used instead of Spring *is come*, Birds *are flown*. (*Is come, are flown*, etc., must not be mistaken for transitive verbs in the passive voice.)

Compounds of more than two words may be analyzed thus : **May have been written** is composed of the compound auxiliary **may have been** and the participle complement **written**; **may have been** is composed of the compound auxiliary **may have** and the participle complement **been**; and **may have** is composed of the auxiliary **may** and the infinitive complement **have**. *May* is the asserting word—the first auxiliary is always the asserting word.

Direction.—*Study what has been said above and analyze the following verbal forms, distinguishing carefully between participles that may be considered as part of the verb, and words that must be treated as attribute complements:—*

1. I may be mistaken. 2. The farm was sold. 3. I shall be contented. 4. Has it been decided? 5. You should have been working. 6. The danger might have been avoided. 7. He may have been tired and sleepy. 8. She is singing. 9. I shall be satisfied. 10. The rule has not been observed. 11. Stars have disappeared. 12. Times will surely change.

TENSE FORMS—MEANING.

The *Present Tense* is used to express (1) what is actually present, (2) what is true at all times, (3) what frequently or habitually takes place, (4) what is to take place in the future, and (5) it is used in describing past or future events as if occurring at the time of the speaking.

Examples.—I *hear* a voice (action as present). The sun *gives* light (true at all times). He *writes* for the newspapers (habitual). Phillips *speaks* in Boston to-morrow night (future). He *mounts* the scaffold ; the executioners *approach* to bind him ; he *struggles, resists,* etc. (past events pictured to the imagination as present). The clans of Culloden *are* scattered in fight ; they *rally,* they *bleed,* etc. (future events now seen in vision).

The *Past Tense* may express (1) simply past action or being, (2) a past habit or custom, (3) a future event, and (4) it may refer to present time.

Examples.—The birds *sang* (simply past action). He *wrote* for the newspapers (past habit). If I *should go,* you *would miss* me (future events). If he *were* here, he *would enjoy* this (refers to present time).

The *Future Tense* may express (1) simply future action or being, (2) a habit or custom as future or as indefinite in time.

Examples.—I *shall write* soon (simply future action). He *will sit* there by the hour (indefinite in time).

The *Present Perfect Tense* expresses (1) action or being as *completed* in present time (*i.e.,* a *period* of time—an *hour,* a *year,* an *age*—of which the present forms a part), and (2) action or being to be completed in a future period.

Examples.—Homer *has written* poems (the period of time affected by this completed action embraces the present). The cock shall not crow till thou *hast denied* me thrice (action completed in a future period).

The *Past Perfect Tense* expresses (1) action or being as completed at some specified past time, and (2) in a conditional or hypothetical clause it may express past time.

Examples.—I *had seen* him when I met you (action completed at a specified past time). If I *had had* time, I *should have written* (I *had* not time—I *did* not *write*).

The *Future Perfect Tense* expresses an action as completed at some specified future time.

Example.—I *shall have seen* him by to-morrow noon.

Direction.—*Study what has been said above about the meaning of the tense forms, and describe carefully the time expressed by each of the following verbs :—*

1. I go to the city to-morrow. 2. The village master taught his little school. 3. Plato reasons well. 4. A triangle has three sides. 5. To-morrow is the day appointed. 6. Moses has told many important facts. 7. The ship sails next week. 8. She sings well. 9. Cicero has written orations. 10. He would sit for hours and watch the smoke curl from his pipe. 11. You may hear when the next mail arrives. 12. Had I known this before, I could have saved you much trouble. 13. He will occasionally lose his temper. 14. At the end of this week I shall have been in school four years. 15. If I were you, I would try that. 16. He will become discouraged before he has thoroughly tried it. 17. She starts, she moves, she seems to feel the thrill of life along her keel.

LESSON 139.

PARSING.

Direction.—*Select and parse, according to the Model below, the verbs in the sentences of Lesson 42. For the agreement of verbs, see Less.* 142.

Model for Written Parsing—Verbs.—*The Yankee, selling his farm, wanders away to seek new lands.*

CLASSIFICATION.		MODIFICATIONS.					SYNTAX.
Verbs.	Kind.	Voice.	Mode.	Tense.	Num.	Per.	
*selling	Pr. Par., Ir., Tr.	Ac.	—	—	—	—	Mod. of *Yankee.*
wanders	Reg., Int.	—	Ind.	Pres.	Sing.	3d.	Pred. of "
*seek	Inf., Ir., Tr.	Ac.	—	"	—	—	Prin. word in phrase Mod. of *wanders.*

* Participles and infinitives have no subject, and, consequently, no *person or number.*

Model for Written Parsing adapted to all Parts of Speech.—Oh! it has a voice for those who on their sick beds lie and waste away.

Sentence.	CLASSIFICATION.		MODIFICATIONS.							SYNTAX.
	Class.	Sub-C.	Voice.	Mode.	Tense.	Per.	Num.	Gen.	Case.	Deg. of Comp.	
Oh!	Int.										Independent.
It	Pro.	Per.				3d.	Sing.	Neut.	Nom.		Sub. of *has*
has	Vb.	Ir., Tr.	Act.	Ind.	Pres.	"	"				Pred. of *it*.
a	Adj.	Def.								—	Mod. of *voice*.
voice	N.	Com.				"	"	"	Obj.		Obj. Com. of *has*.
for	Prep.										Shows Rel. of *has* to *those*.
those	Pro.	Adj.				"	Pln.	M. or F.	"		Prin. word in Prep. phrase.
who	Pro.	Rel.				"	"	"	Nom.		Sub. of *lie* and *waste*.
on	Prep.										Shows Rel. of *lie* to *beds*.
their	Pro.	Per.				"	"	"	Pos.		Pos. Mod. of *beds*.
sick	Adj.	Des.								Pos.	Mod. of *beds*.
beds	N.	Com.				"	"	Neut.	Obj.		Prin. word in Prep. phrase.
lie	Vb.	Ir., Int.		Ind.	Pres.	"	"				Pred. of *who*.
and	Conj.	Co-or.									Con. *lie* and *waste*.
waste	Vb.	Reg., Int.		"	"	"	"				Pred. of *who*.
away.	Adv.	Place.								—	Mod. of *waste*.

To the Teacher.—For further exercises in parsing the verb and for exercises in general parsing, select from the preceding Lessons on Analysis.

LESSON 140.

CONSTRUCTION OF MODE AND TENSE FORMS.

Caution.—Be careful to give every verb its proper form and meaning.

Direction.—*Correct the following errors, and give your reasons :—*

1. I done it myself. 2. He throwed it into the river, for I seen him him when he done it. 3. She sets by the open window enjoying the scene that lays before her.

Explanation.—*Lay* (to place) is transitive, *lie* (to rest) is intransitive; *set* (to place) is transitive, *sit* (to rest) is intransitive. *Set* in some of its meanings is intransitive.

4. The tide sits in. 5. Go and lay down. 6. The sun sits in the west. 7. I remember when the corner stone was lain. 8. Sit the plates on the table. 9. He sat out for London yesterday. 10. Your dress sets well. 11. The bird is setting on its eggs. 12. I laid there an hour. 13. Set down and talk a little while. 14. He has laid there an hour. 15. I am setting by the river. 16. He has went and done it without my permission. 17. He flew from justice. 18. Some valuable land was overflown. 19. She come just after you left. 20. They sung a new tune which they had not sang before. 21. The water I drunk there was better than any that I had drank before. 22. The leaves had fell. 23. I had rode a short distance when the storm begun to gather. 24. I found the water froze. 25. He raised up. 26. He run till he became so weary that he was forced to lay down. 27. I knowed that it was so, for I seen him when he done it. 28. I had began to think that you had forsook us. 29. I am afraid that I cannot learn him to do it. 30. I guess that I will stop. 31. Tell me where you live, and I will come to your house to-morrow. 32. I expect that he has gone to Boston. 33. There ain't any use of trying. 34. I have got no mother. 35. Can I speak to you ? 36. He had ought to see him.

Explanation.—As *ought* is never a participle, it cannot be used after *had* to form a compound tense.

Caution. — A conditional or a concessive clause requires a verb in the indicative mode when the action or being is assumed as a fact, or when the uncertainty lies merely in the speaker's knowledge of the fact. But when the action or being is merely thought of as a future contingency, the subjunctive present is preferred. The subjunctive past of the verb *be* is used chiefly to express a wish, or a mere supposition contrary to the fact.

Examples. — 1. If (= since) it *rains*, why do you go?
2. If it *rains* (now), I cannot go out.
3. If it *rain*, the work will be delayed.
4. If my friend *were* here, he would enjoy this.

Explanation. — In (1) the raining is assumed as a fact. In (2) there is a mere uncertainty of knowledge. It either rains or it does not rain — the speaker is uncertain which is the fact. In (3) no existing fact is referred to; the raining is merely thought of as a future contingency. In (4) a mere supposition, contrary to the fact, is made. My friend's not being here is clearly implied.

Remarks. — When there is doubt as to whether the indicative or the subjunctive mode is required, use the indicative.

The present subjunctive forms may be treated as infinitives used to complete omitted auxiliaries; as, If it (should) rain, the work will be delayed, Till one greater man (shall) restore us, etc. This will often serve as a guide in distinguishing the indicative from the subjunctive mode.

If, though, lest, unless, etc., are usually spoken of as signs of the subjunctive mode, but they are now more frequently followed by the indicative than by the subjunctive mode.

Direction. — *Justify the mode of the italicized verbs in the following sentences:* —

1. If this *were* so, the difficulty would vanish. 2. If he *was* there, I did not see him. 3. If to-morrow *be* fine, I will walk with you. 4. Though this *seems* improbable, it is true. 5. If my friend *is* in town, he will call this evening. 6. If he ever *comes*, we shall know it.

Explanation.—In (6) and (7) the coming is referred to as a fact to be decided in future time.

7. If he *comes* by noon, let me know. 8. The ship leaps, as it *were*, from billow to billow. 9. Take heed that thou *speak* not to Jacob. 10. If a pendulum *is drawn* to one side, it will swing to the other.

Explanation.—*Be* is often employed in making scientific statements like the preceding, and may therefore be allowed; but there is nothing in the nature of the case to justify such usage. *If a pendulum is drawn = Whenever a pendulum is drawn.*

11. I wish that I *were* a musician. 12. *Were* I disposed, I could not gratify you. 13. This sword shall end thee unless thou *yield*. 14. Govern well thy appetite, lest sin *surprise* thee. 15. I know not whether it *is* so or not.

Direction.—*Supply in each of the following sentences a verb in the indicative or the subjunctive mode, and give a reason for your choice:*—

1. I wish it —— in my power to help you. 2. I tremble lest he ——. 3. If he —— guilty, the evidence does not show it. 4. He deserves our pity, unless his tale —— a false one. 5. Though he —— there, I did not see him. 6. If he —— but discreet, he will succeed. 7. If I —— he, I would do differently. 8. If ye —— men, fight.

LESSON 141.

CONSTRUCTION OF MODE AND TENSE FORMS—CONTINUED.

Caution.—Be careful to employ the tense forms of the different modes in accordance with their meaning, and in such a way as to preserve the proper order of time.

Direction.—*Correct the following errors, and give your reasons:*—

1. That custom has been formerly quite popular. 2. Neither will they be persuaded, though one rose from the dead. 3. He that was dead sat up and began to speak. 4. A man bought a horse for one

Construction of Mode and Tense Forms—Cont.

hundred dollars; and, after keeping it three months, at an expense of ten dollars a month, he sells it for two hundred dollars. What per cent. does he gain? 5. I should say that it was an hour's ride. 6. If I had have seen him, I should have known him. 7. I wish I was in Dixie. 8. We should be obliged if you will favor us with a song. 9. I intended to have called.

Explanation.—This is incorrect; it should be, *I intended to call.* One does not *intend* to do what is already *completed*.

Remark.—Verbs of *commanding, desiring, expecting, hoping, intending, permitting,* etc., are followed by verbs denoting *present* or *future* time.

The *present infinitive* expresses an action as *present* or *future*, and the *present perfect* as *completed*, at the time indicated by the principal verb. I *am glad to have met* you is correct, because the *meeting* took place *before* the time of *being glad*.

I *ought to have gone* is exceptional. *Ought* has no past tense form, and so the present perfect infinitive is used to make the expression refer to past time.

10. We hoped to have seen you before. 11. I should not have let you eaten it. 12. I should have liked to have seen it. 13. He would not have dared done that. 14. You ought to have helped me to have done it. 15. We expected that he would have arrived last night. 16. The experiment proved that air had weight.

Remark.—What is true or false at all times is generally expressed in the present tense, whatever tense precedes.

There seems to be danger of applying this rule too rigidly. When a speaker does not wish to vouch for the truth of the general proposition, he may use the past tense, giving it the appearance of an indirect quotation; as, He said that iron *was* the most valuable of metals. The tense of the dependent verb is sometimes attracted into that of the principal verb; as, I *knew* where the place *was*.

17. I had never known before how short life really was. 18. We then fell into a discussion whether there is any beauty independent of utility. The General maintained that there was not; Dr. Johnson maintained that there was. 19. I have already told you that I was a gentleman. 20. Our fathers held that all men were created equal.

Caution.—Use *will* and *would* whenever the subject names the one whose will controls the action, and *shall* and *should* whenever the one named by the subject is under the control of external influence.

Remark.—The original meaning of *shall* (*to owe, to be obliged*) and *will* (*to determine*) gives us the real key to their proper use.

The only case in which some trace of the original meaning of these auxiliaries cannot be found is, when the subject of *will* names something incapable of volition; as, The *wind will* blow. Even this may be a kind of personification.

Examples.—I *shall go*, You *will go*, He *will go*. These are the proper forms to express mere futurity, but even here we can trace the original meaning of *shall* and *will*. In the first person the speaker avoids egotism by referring to the act as an obligation or duty rather than as something under the control of his own will. In the second and third persons it is more courteous to refer to the will of others than to their duty.

I *will go*. Here the action is under the control of the speaker's will. He either promises or determines to go.

You *shall go*, He *shall go*. Here the speaker either promises the going or determines to compel these persons to go; in either case the actor is under some external influence.

Shall I *go?* Here the speaker puts himself under the control of some external influence—the will of another.

Will I *go?*—i. e., Is it my will to go?—is not used except to repeat another's question. It would be absurd for one to ask what his own will is.

Shall you go? Ans. I *shall*. *Will* you go? Ans. I *will*. *Shall* he go? Ans. He *shall*. *Will* he go? Ans. He *will*. The same auxiliary is used in the question that is used in the answer.

No difficulty *shall hinder* me. The difficulty that might do the hindering is not to be left to itself, but is to be kept under the control of the speaker.

He says that he *shall go*, He says that he *will go*. Change the indirect quotations introduced by *that* to direct quotations, and the application of the Caution will be apparent.

You *will see* that my horse is at the door by nine o'clock. This is only an apparent exception to the rule. A superior may courteously avoid the appearance of compulsion, and refer to his subordinate's willingness to obey.

They knew that I *should be* there, and that he *would be* there. The same principles apply to *should* and *would* that apply to *shall* and *will*. In this example the events are future as to past time; making them future as to present time, we have, They know that I *shall be* there, and that he *will be* there.

My friend said that he *should* not set out to-morrow. Change the indirect to a direct quotation, and the force of *should* will be seen.

Direction.—*Assign a reason for the use of s h a l l or w i l l in each of the following sentences :—*

1. Hear me, for I will speak. 2. If you will call, I shall be happy to accompany you. 3. Shall you be at liberty to-day ? 4. I shall never see him again. 5. I will never see him again. 6. I said that he should be rewarded. 7. Thou shalt surely die. 8. Truth, crushed to earth, shall rise again. 9. Though I should die, yet will I not deny thee. 10. Though I should receive a thousand shekels of silver in mine hand, yet would I not put forth my hand against the king's son.

Direction.—*Fill each of the following blanks with s h a l l, w i l l, s h o u l d, or w o u l d, and give the reasons for your choice :—*

1. He knew who —— betray him. 2. I —— be fatigued if I had walked so far. 3. You did better than I —— have done. 4. If he —— come by noon, —— you be ready ? 5. They do me wrong, and I —— not endure it. 6. I —— be greatly obliged if you —— do me the favor. 7. If I —— say so, I —— be guilty of falsehood. 8. You —— be disappointed if you —— see it. 9. —— he be allowed to go on ? 10. —— you be unhappy, if I do not come ?

Direction.—*Correct the following errors, and give your reasons :—*

1. Where will I leave you ? 2. Will I be in time ? 3. It was requested that no person would leave his seat. 4. They requested that the appointment would be given to a man who should be known to his party. 5. When will we get through this tedious controversy ? 6. I think we will have rain.

LESSON 142.

CONSTRUCTION OF NUMBER AND PERSON FORMS.

AGREEMENT.—VERBS—PRONOUNS.

Caution.—A verb must agree with its subject in number and person.

Remark.—Practically, this rule applies to but few *forms*. **Are** and **were** are the only plural forms retained by the English verb. In the common style, most verbs have one person form, made by adding **s** or **es** (*has*, in the present perfect tense, is a contraction of the indicative present—*ha(ve)s*). The verb *be* has **am** (first person) and **is** (third person).

In the solemn style, the second person singular takes the ending **est, st,** or **t,** and, in the indicative present, the third person singular adds **eth.** (See Lessons 134 and 135.)

Caution.—A collective noun requires a verb in the plural when the individuals in the collection are thought of; but, when the collection as a whole is thought of, the verb should be singular.

Examples.—1. The *multitude were* of one mind. 2. The *multitude was* too large to number. 3. A *number were* inclined to turn back. 4. The *number* present *was* not ascertained.

Caution.—When a verb has two or more subjects connected by *and*, it must agree with them in the plural.

Exceptions.—1. When the connected subjects are different names of the same thing, or when they name several things taken as one whole, the verb must be singular; as, My old *friend and schoolmate is* in town. *Bread and milk is* excellent food.

2. When singular subjects are preceded by *each, every,* or *no,* they

are taken separately and require a singular verb; as, *Every man, woman, and child was* lost.

3. When the subjects are emphatically distinguished, the verb agrees with the first and is understood with the second; as, *Time, and patience also, is* needed. (The same is true of subjects connected by *as well as;* as, *Time, as well as patience, is* needed.)

4. When one of the subjects is affirmative and the other negative, the verb agrees with the affirmative; as, *Books, and not pleasure, occupy* his time.

5. When several subjects follow the verb, each subject may be emphasized by making the verb agree with that which stands nearest; as, Thine *is* the *kingdom and* the *power and* the *glory*.

Caution.—When a verb has two or more singular subjects connected by *or* or *nor*, it must agree with them in the singular; as, Neither *poverty nor wealth was* desired.

Remark.—When the subjects are of different numbers or persons, the verb agrees with the nearest; as, Neither *he* nor *they* were satisfied.

When a singular and a plural subject are used, the plural subject is generally placed next to the verb.

In using pronouns of different persons, it is generally more polite for the speaker to mention the one addressed first, and himself last, except when he confesses a fault, or when, by using the pronoun *we*, he associates others with him.

When the subjects require different forms of the verb, it is generally better to express the verb with each subject or to recast the sentence.

Caution.—A pronoun must agree with its antecedent in number, gender, and person; as, *Thou who writest, he who writes, they who write*, etc.

The three special Cautions given above for the agreement of the verb apply also to the agreement of the pronoun.

Remark.—These special directions for agreement may be summed up in this: Let the *meaning* rather than the *form* control the agreement of the verb and of the pronoun.

The pronoun *you*, however, even when singular in meaning, requires a verb and a pronoun of the plural form.

Direction—*Justify the use of the following italicized verbs and pronouns:*—

1. *Books is* a noun. 2. The good *are* great. 3. The committee *were* unable to agree, and *they* asked to be discharged. 4. The House *has* decided not to allow *its* members the privilege. 5. Three times four *is* twelve.* 6. Five dollars *is* not too much. 7. Twice as much *is* too much. 8. Two hours *is* a long time to wait. 9. To relieve the wretched *was* his pride. 10. To profess and to possess *are* two different things. 11. Talking and eloquence *are* not the same. 12. The tongs *are* not in *their* place. 13. Every one *is* accountable for *his* own acts. 14. Every book and every paper *was* found in *its* place. 15. Not a loud voice, but strong proofs *bring* conviction. 16. This orator and statesman *has* gone to *his* rest. 17. Young's "Night Thoughts" *is his* most celebrated poetical work. 18. Flesh and blood *hath* not revealed it. 19. The hue and cry of the country *pursues* him. 20. The second and the third Epistle of John *contain* each a single chapter. 21. *Man is* masculine because *it* denotes a male. 22. Therein *consists* the force and use and nature of language. 23. Neither wealth nor wisdom *is* the chief thing. 24. Either you or I *am* right. 25. Neither you nor he *is* to blame. 26. John, and his sister also, *is* going. 27. The lowest mechanic, as well as the richest citizen, *is* here protected in *his* right. 28. There *are* one or two reasons.† 29. Nine o'clock and forty-five minutes *is* fifteen minutes of ten. 30. Mexican figures, or picture-writing, *represent* things, not words.‡

Direction.—*Correct the following errors, and give your reasons:*—

1. *Victuals* are always plural. 2. Plutarch's "Parallel Lives" are

---

* "Three times four *is* twelve," and "Three times four *are* twelve" are both used, and both may be defended. The question is (see Caution for collective nouns), Is the number four thought of as a whole, or are the individual units composing it thought of? The expression = Four *taken* three times is twelve. *Times* is a noun used adverbially without a preposition (see Lesson 35).

† When two adjectives differing in number are connected without a repetition of the noun, the tendency is to make the verb agree with the noun expressed.

‡ The verb here agrees with *figures*, as *picture-writing* is logically explanatory of *figures* (see Lesson 33).

his great work. 3. What sounds have each of the vowels? 4. "No, no," says I. 5. "We agree," says they. 6. Where was you? 7. Every one of these are good in their place. 8. Neither of them have recited their lesson. 9. There comes the boys. 10. Each of these expressions denote action. 11. One of you are mistaken. 12. There is several reasons for this. 13. The assembly was divided in its opinion. 14. The public is invited to attend. 15. The committee were full when this point was decided. 16. The nation are prosperous. 17. Money, as well as men, were needed. 18. Now, boys, I want every one of you to decide for themselves. 19. Neither the intellect nor the heart are capable of being driven. 20. She fell to laughing like one out of their right mind. 21. Five years' interest are due. 22. Three quarters of the men was discharged. 23. Nine tenths of every man's happiness depend upon this. 24. No time, no money, no labor, were spared. 25. One or the other have erred in their statement. 26. Why are dust and ashes proud? 27. Either the master or his servants is to blame. 28. Neither the servants nor their master are to blame. 29. Our welfare and security consists in unity. 30. The mind, and not the body, sin. 31. He don't like it.

To the Teacher.—These exercises may profitably be continued by requiring the pupils to compose sentences illustrating those constructions in which mistakes are liable to be made.

Remark.—The following exceptional forms are worthy of note :—

Need and *dare*, when followed by an infinitive, are often used instead of *needs* and *dares;* as, He *need* not do it; He *dare* not do it.

The pronoun and the verb of an adjective clause relating to the indefinite subject *it* take, by attraction, the *person* and *number* of the complement when this complement immediately precedes the adjective clause ; as, It is I *that am* in the wrong ; It is thou *that liftest* me up ; It is the dews and showers *that make* the grass grow.

GENERAL REVIEW.

To the Teacher.—See suggestions to the teacher, page 219.

Scheme for the Verb.

(The numbers refer to Lessons.)

VERB.

- **Uses.**
  - To *assert* action, being, or state.—Predicate (4, 11).
  - To *assume* action, being, or state.
    - Participles (37).
    - Infinitives (40).

- **Classes.**
  - Form.
    - Regular (92).
    - Irregular (92, 132, 133).
    - (*Redundant and Defective.*)
  - Meaning.
    - Transitive (92).
    - Intransitive (92).

- **Modifications.**
  - Voice.
    - Active (129, 130).
    - Passive (129, 130).
  - Mode.
    - Indicative (131, 134-137).
    - Potential (131, 134-137).
    - Subjunctive (131, 134-137, 140).
    - Imperative (131, 134-137).
  - Tense.
    - Present.
    - Past.
    - Future.
    - Present Perfect.
    - Past Perfect.
    - Future Perfect.
    - } 131, 134-138, 140, 141.
  - Number.
    - Singular.
    - Plural.
    - } 131, 134, 135.
  - Person.
    - First.
    - Second.
    - Third.
    - } 131, 134, 135.

- **Participles.**— Classes.
  - Present.
  - Past.
  - Past Perfect.
  - } 131, 134-136.

- **Infinitives.**—
  - Present.
  - Present Perfect.
  - } 131, 134, 135.

Questions on the Verb.

1. Define the verb and its classes.—Less. 92, 132.
2. Name and define the modifications of the verb.—Less. 129, 131.
3. Name and define the several voices. modes, and tenses.—Less. 129, 131.
4. Define the participle and its classes.—Less. 131.
5. Define the infinitive.—Less. 131.
6. Give a synopsis of a regular and of an irregular verb in all the different forms.—Less. 134, 135, 136, 137.
7. Analyze the different mode and tense forms, and give the functions of the different tenses.—Less. 138.
8. Give and illustrate the principles which guide in the use of the mode and tense forms, and of the person and number forms.—Less. 140, 141, 142.

LESSON 143.

REVIEW QUESTIONS.

Lesson 112.—What are *Modifications ?* Have English words many inflections ? Have they lost any ? What is *Number ?* Define the singular and the plural number. How is the plural of nouns *regularly* formed ? In what ways may the plural be formed *irregularly ?* Illustrate.

Lesson 113.—Give the plural of some nouns adopted from other languages. How do compounds form the plural ? Illustrate the several ways. How do letters, figures, etc., form the plural ? Illustrate.

Lesson 114.—Give examples of nouns having each two forms differing in meaning. Some which have the same form in both numbers. Some which have no plural. Some which are always plural. What is said of the number of collective nouns ?

Lesson 116.—In what four ways may the number of nouns be determined ? Illustrate.

Lesson 117.—What is *Gender ?* Define the different genders. What is the difference between *sex* and *gender ?* The gender of English nouns follows what ? Have English nouns a *neuter form ?* Have all English nouns a *masculine* and a *feminine form ?* In what three ways may the masculine of nouns be distinguished from the feminine ? Illustrate. Give the three gender forms of the pronoun.

Lesson 118.—How is gender in grammar important ? When is the pronoun of the masculine gender used ? When is the neuter pronoun *it* used ? By what pronouns are inanimate things personified ? In personification, when is the masculine pronoun used, and when the feminine ? Illustrate. What is the Caution relating to gender ?

Lesson 119.—What is *Person?* Is the person of nouns marked by form ? Define the three persons. When is a noun in the first person ? In the second person ? What classes of words have distinctive person forms ? Why is person regarded in grammar ? What is *Case?* Define the three cases. What is the case of a noun used independently ? Of an explanatory modifier ? Of an objective complement ? Of a noun or pronoun used as attribute complement ? Illustrate all these.

Lesson 121.—What is *Parsing?* Illustrate the parsing of nouns.

LESSON 144.

REVIEW QUESTIONS.

Lesson 122.—How many case forms have nouns, and what are they ? How is the possessive of nouns in the singular formed ? Of nouns in the plural ? Illustrate. What is the possessive sign ? To which word of compound names or of groups of words treated as such is the sign added ? Illustrate. Instead of the possessive form, what may be used ? Illustrate.

Lesson 123.—In what case only, can mistakes in the construction of nouns occur ? Illustrate the Cautions relating to possessive forms.

Lesson 124.—What i. *Declension?* Decline *girl* and *tooth*. Decline the several personal pronouns, the relative and the interrogative. What adjective pronouns are declined wholly or in part ? Illustrate.

Lesson 125.—What words in the language have each three different case forms? What are the nominative, and what the objective, forms of the pronouns?

Lesson 127.—What one modification have adjectives? What is *Comparison?* Define the three degrees. How are adjectives *regularly* compared? What are the Rules for Spelling? Illustrate them. How are adjectives of more than one syllable generally compared? How are degrees of diminution expressed? Can all adjectives be compared? How are some adverbs compared? Illustrate the irregular comparison of adjectives and adverbs.

Lesson 128.—To how many things does the comparative degree refer? What does it imply? Explain the office of the superlative. What word usually follows the comparative, and what the superlative? Give the Cautions relating to the use of comparatives and superlatives, and illustrate them fully.

Lesson 129.—What is *Voice?* Of what class of verbs is it a modification? Name and define the two voices. When is the one voice used, and when the other? Into what may the passive form be resolved? Illustrate. What may be mistaken for a verb in the passive voice? Illustrate.

Lesson 130.—In changing a verb from the active to the passive, what does the object complement become? How may an intransitive verb sometimes be made transitive? Illustrate.

LESSON 145.

REVIEW QUESTIONS.

Lesson 131.—What is *Mode?* Define the four modes. What is *Tense?* Define the six tenses. Define the infinitive. Define the participle. Define the classes of participles. What are the number and person of a verb?

Lesson 132.—What is *Conjugation? Synopsis?* What are auxiliary verbs? Name them. What are the principal parts of a verb? What are redundant and what are defective verbs?

Lesson 134.—How many forms have irregular verbs? How many have regular verbs? What is said of the subjunctive mode? Of *to* with the infinitive? How is a verb conjugated in the *emphatic* form?

Lesson 136.—How is a verb conjugated in the *progressive* form? How is a transitive verb conjugated in the *passive* voice? Give an example of a verb in the progressive form with a passive meaning. What does the progressive form denote? Can all verbs be conjugated in this form? Give all the participles of the verbs *choose, break, drive, read, lift*.

Lesson 137.—How may a verb be conjugated interrogatively? Negatively? Illustrate. How may a question with negation be expressed in the indicative and potential modes?

Lesson 138.—Into what may the compound, or periphrastic, forms of the verb be resolved? Illustrate fully. What is said of the participle in *have written, had written*, etc.? Analyze *may have been written*. Give and illustrate the several uses of the six tenses.

Lesson 140.—Give and correct the more prominent errors under the first Caution. When does a conditional or a concessive clause require the verb to be in the indicative? Illustrate. When is the subjunctive preferred? Illustrate. How is the subjunctive past of the verb *be* used?

Lesson 141.—Give and illustrate the General Caution relating to mode and tense forms. Give the Caution in regard to *will* and *would, shall* and *should*. Illustrate the Caution.

Lesson 142.—Give and illustrate the Cautions relating to the agreement of verbs and pronouns. Illustrate the exceptions and the Remarks.

ADDITIONAL EXAMPLES FOR ANALYSIS.

It is thought by some people that all those stars which you see glittering so restlessly on a keen, frosty night in a high latitude, and which seem to have been sown broadcast with as much carelessness as grain lies on a threshing-floor, here showing vast zaarahs of desert blue sky, there again lying close, and to some eyes presenting

"The beauteous semblance of a flock at rest,"

are, in fact, gathered into zones or *strata;* that our own wicked little earth, with the whole of our peculiar solar system, is a part of such a zone; and that all this perfect geometry of the heavens, these radii in the mighty wheel, would become apparent, if we, the spectators, could but survey it from the true center; which center may be far too distant for any vision of man, naked or armed, to reach.—*De Quincey.*

On this question of principle, while actual suffering was yet afar off, they [our fathers] raised their flag against a power to which, for purposes of foreign conquest and subjugation, Rome, in the height of her glory, is not to be compared—a power which has dotted over the surface of the whole globe with her possessions and military posts; whose morning drum-beat, following the sun and keeping company with the hours, circles the earth daily with one continuous and unbroken strain of the martial airs of England.—*Webster.*

In some far-away and yet undreamt-of hour, I can even imagine that England may cast all thoughts of possessive wealth back to the barbaric nations among whom they first arose; and that, while the sands of the Indus and adamant of Golconda may yet stiffen the housings of the charger and flash from the turban of the slave, she, as a Christian mother, may at last attain to the virtues and the treasures of a Heathen one, and be able to lead forth her Sons, saying,—"These are my Jewels."—*Ruskin.*

And, when those who have rivaled her [Athens's] greatness shall have shared her fate; when civilization and knowledge shall have fixed their abode in distant continents; when the scepter shall have passed away from England; when, perhaps, travelers from distant regions shall in vain labor to decipher on some mouldering pedestal the name of our proudest chief, shall hear savage hymns chanted to some misshapen idol over the ruined dome of our proudest temple, and shall see a single naked fisherman wash his nets in the river of the ten thousand masts, —her influence and her glory will still survive, fresh in eternal youth, exempt from mutability and decay, immortal as the intellectual principle from which they derived their origin, and over which they exercise their control.—*Macaulay.*

> To him who in the love of Nature holds
> Communion with her visible forms, she speaks
> A various language ; for his gayer hours
> She has a voice of gladness and a smile
> And eloquence of beauty, and she glides
> Into his darker musings with a mild
> And healing sympathy, that steals away
> Their sharpness ere he is aware. When thoughts
> Of the last, bitter hour come like a blight
> Over thy spirit, and sad images
> Of the stern agony and shroud and pall
> And breathless darkness and the narrow house
> Make thee to shudder and grow sick at heart,—
> Go forth under the open sky, and list
> To Nature's teachings, while from all around—
> Earth and her waters and the depths of air—
> Comes a still voice.—*Bryant.*

> Pleasant it was, when woods were green,
>   And winds were soft and low,
> To lie amid some sylvan scene,
> Where, the long drooping boughs between,
> Shadows dark and sunlight sheen
>   Alternate come and go ;
> Or where the denser grove receives
>   No sunlight from above,
> But the dark foliage interweaves
> In one unbroken roof of leaves,
> Underneath whose sloping eaves
>   The shadows hardly move.—*Longfellow.*

I like the lad who, when his father thought
To clip his morning nap by hackneyed praise
Of vagrant worm by early songster caught,
Cried, "Served him right ! 'tis not at all surprising ;
The worm was punished, sir, for early rising."—*Saxe.*

There were communities, scarce known by name
In these degenerate days, but once far-famed,
Where liberty and justice, hand in hand,
Ordered the common weal ; where great men grew
Up to their natural eminence, and none
Saving the wise, just, eloquent, were great ;
Where power was of God's gift to whom he gave
Supremacy of merit—the sole means
And broad highway to power, that ever then
Was meritoriously administered;
Whilst all its instruments, from first to last,
The tools of state for service high or low,
Were chosen for their aptness to those ends
Which virtue meditates.—*Henry Taylor.*

      Stranger, these gloomy boughs
Had charms for him ; and here he loved to sit,
His only visitants a straggling sheep,
The stone-chat, or the glancing sand-piper ;
And on these barren rocks, with fern and heath
And juniper and thistle sprinkled o'er,
Fixing his downcast eye, he many an hour
A morbid pleasure nourished, tracing here
An emblem of his own unfruitful life ;
And, lifting up his head, he then would gaze
On the more distant scene,—how lovely 'tis
Thou seest,—and he would gaze till it became
Far lovelier, and his heart could not sustain
The beauty, still more beauteous.—*Wordsworth.*

But, when the next sun brake from underground,
Then, those two brethren slowly with bent brows
Accompanying, the sad chariot-bier

Past like a shadow thro' the field, that shone
Full-summer, to that stream whereon the barge,
Pall'd all its length in blackest samite, lay.
There sat the life-long creature of the house,
Loyal, the dumb old servitor, on deck,
Winking his eyes, and twisted all his face.
So those two brethren from the chariot took
And on the black decks laid her in her bed,
Set in her hand a lily, o'er her hung
The silken case with braided blazonings,
And kiss'd her quiet brows, and, saying to her,
"Sister, farewell forever," and again,
"Farewell, sweet sister," parted all in tears.—*Tennyson.*

Good name in man and woman, dear my lord,
Is the immediate jewel of their souls.
Who steals my purse steals trash ; 'tis something, nothing;
'Twas mine, 'tis his, and has been slave to thousands
But he that filches from me my good name
Robs me of that which not enriches him,
And makes me poor indeed.—*Shakespeare.*

When I consider how my light is spent
Ere half my days, in this dark world and wide,
And that one talent, which is death to hide,
Lodged with me useless, though my soul more bent
To serve therewith my Maker, and present
My true account, lest he, returning, chide,—
"Doth God exact day-labor, light denied ?"
I fondly ask : but Patience, to prevent
That murmur, soon replies, "God doth not need
Either man's work or his own gifts ; who best
Bear his mild yoke, they serve him best : his state
Is kingly ; thousands at his bidding speed,
And post o'er land and ocean without rest ;
They also serve who only stand and wait."
—*Milton.—Sonnet on his Blindness.*

Ah ! on Thanksgiving Day, when from East and from West,
From North and from South come the pilgrim and guest ;
When the gray-haired New-Englander sees round his board
The old broken links of affection restored ;
When the care-wearied man seeks his mother once more,
And the worn matron smiles where the girl smiled before,—
What moistens the lip, and what brightens the eye ?
What calls back the past like the rich pumpkin-pie ?
— *Whittier.*

   That orbéd maiden with white fire laden,
     Whom mortals call the moon,
   Glides glimmering o'er my fleece-like floor,
     By the midnight breezes strewn ;
   And wherever the beat of her unseen feet,
     Which only the angels hear,
   May have broken the woof of my tent's thin roof,
     The stars peep behind her and peer ;
   And I laugh to see them whirl and flee
     Like a swarm of golden bees,
   When I widen the rent in my wind-built tent,
     Till the calm river, lakes, and seas,
   Like strips of the sky fallen through me on high,
     Are each paved with the moon and these.
—*Shelley.—The Cloud.*

Sweet was the sound, when oft, at evening's close,
Up yonder hill the village murmur rose.
There, as I passed with careless steps and slow,
The mingling notes came softened from below ;
The swain responsive as the milk-maid sung,
The sober herd that lowed to meet their young,
The noisy geese that gabbled o'er the pool,
The playful children just let loose from school,
The watch-dog's voice that bayed the whispering wind,
And the loud laugh that spoke the vacant mind,—
These all in sweet confusion sought the shade,
And filled each pause the nightingale had made.
—*Goldsmith.*

To sit on rocks, to muse o'er flood and fell,
To slowly trace the forest's shady scene,
Where things that own not man's dominion dwell,
And mortal foot hath ne'er or rarely been;
To climb the trackless mountain all unseen,
With the wild flock that never needs a fold;
Alone o'er steeps and foaming falls to lean:—
This is not solitude; 'tis but to hold
Converse with nature's charms, and view her stores unrolled.
—*Byron.*

The drawbridge dropped with a surly clang,
And through the dark arch a charger sprang,
Bearing Sir Launfal, the maiden knight,
In his gilded mail, that flamed so bright
It seemed the dark castle had gathered all
Those shafts the fierce sun had shot over its wall
In his siege of three hundred summers long,
And, binding them all in one blazing sheaf,
Had cast them forth; so, young and strong,
And lightsome as a locust leaf,
Sir Launfal flashed forth in his unscarred mail
To seek in all climes for the Holy Grail.—*Lowell.*

Be it a weakness, it deserves some praise,—
We love the play-place of our early days;
The scene is touching, and the heart is stone
That feels not at the sight, and feels at none.
The wall on which we tried our graving skill,
The very name we carved subsisting still;
The bench on which we sat while deep employed,
Tho' mangled, hacked, and hewed, not yet destroyed;
The little ones, unbuttoned, glowing hot,
Playing our games, and on the very spot,
As happy as we once, to kneel and draw
The chalky ring and knuckle down at taw,
To pitch the ball into the grounded hat,
Or drive it devious with a dexterous pat;—

> The pleasing spectacle at once excites
> Such recollection of our own delights
> That, viewing it, we seem almost t' obtain
> Our innocent, sweet, simple years again.—*Cowper.*

To the Teacher.—Require the pupils to change the poetry, above, into prose.

Considering our present advanced state of culture, and how the torch of science has now been brandished and borne about, with more or less effect, for five thousand years and upwards; how, in these times especially, not only the torch still burns, and perhaps more fiercely than ever, but innumerable rush-lights and sulphur-matches, kindled thereat, are also glancing in every direction, so that not the smallest cranny or doghole in nature or art can remain unilluminated,—it might strike the reflective mind with some surprise that hitherto little or nothing of a fundamental character, whether in the way of philosophy or history, has been written on the subject of Clothes.—*Carlyle.*

When we see one word of a frail man on the throne of France tearing a hundred thousand sons from their homes, breaking asunder the sacred ties of domestic life, sentencing myriads of the young to make murder their calling, and rapacity their means of support, and extorting from nations their treasures to extend this ruinous sway, we are ready to ask ourselves, Is not this a dream? and, when the sad reality comes home to us, we blush for a race which can stoop to such an abject lot. At length, indeed, we see the tyrant humbled, stripped of power, but stripped by those who, in the main, are not unwilling to play the despot on a narrower scale, and to break down the spirit of nations under the same iron sway.—*Channing.*

There are days which occur in this climate, at almost any season of the year, wherein the world reaches its perfection; when the air, the heavenly bodies, and the earth make a harmony, as if Nature would indulge her offspring; when, in these bleak upper sides of the planet, nothing is to desire that we have heard of the happiest latitudes, and we bask in the shining hours of Florida and Cuba; when everything that has life gives sign of satisfaction, and the cattle that lie on the ground seem to have great and tranquil thoughts.—*Emerson.*

Did you never, in walking in the fields, come across a large flat stone, which had lain, nobody knows how long, just where you found it, with the grass forming a little hedge, as it were, all round it, close to its edges; and have you not, in obedience to a kind feeling that told you it had been lying there long enough, insinuated your stick or your foot or your fingers under its edge, and turned it over as a housewife turns a cake, when she says to herself, "It's done brown enough by this time"? But no sooner is the stone turned and the wholesome light of day let upon this compressed and blinded community of creeping things than all of them which enjoy the luxury of legs—and some of them have a good many—rush round wildly, butting each other and everything in their way, and end in a general stampede for underground retreats from the region poisoned by sunshine. *Next year* you will find the grass growing tall and green where the stone lay; the ground-bird builds her nest where the beetle had his hole; the dandelion and the buttercup are growing there, and the broad fans of insect-angels open and shut over their golden disks, as the rhythmic waves of blissful consciousness pulsate through their glorified being.—*Holmes.*

There is a different and sterner path;—I know not whether there be any now qualified to tread it; I am not sure that even one has ever followed it implicitly, in view of the certain meagerness of its temporal rewards, and the haste wherewith any fame acquired in a sphere so thoroughly ephemeral as the Editor's must be shrouded by the dark waters of oblivion. This path demands an ear ever open to the plaints of the wronged and the suffering, though they can never repay advocacy, and those who mainly support newspapers will be annoyed and often exposed by it; a heart as sensitive to oppression and degradation in the next street as if they were practiced in Brazil or Japan; a pen as ready to expose and reprove the crimes whereby wealth is amassed and luxury enjoyed in our own country at this hour as if they had been committed only by Turks or Pagans in Asia some centuries ago.—*Greeley.*

To sweeten the beverage, a lump of sugar was laid beside each cup, and the company alternately nibbled and sipped with great decorum, until an improvement was introduced by a shrewd and economical old lady, which was to suspend a large lump directly over the tea-table, by a string from the ceiling, so that it could be swung from mouth to mouth—an ingenious expedient, which is still kept up by some families in Albany, but which prevails without exception in Communipaw, Bergen, Flatbush, and all our uncontaminated Dutch villages.—*Irving.*

COMPOSITION.

LESSON 146.

SUMMARY OF RULES FOR CAPITAL LETTERS AND PUNCTUATION.

CAPITAL LETTERS, TERMINAL MARKS, AND THE COMMA.

Capital Letters.—The first word of (1) a sentence, (2) a line of poetry, (3) a direct quotation making complete sense or a direct question introduced into a sentence, and (4) phrases or clauses separately numbered or paragraphed should begin with a capital letter. Begin with a capital letter (5) proper names (including all names of the Deity), and words derived from them, (6) names of things personified, and (7) most abbreviations. Write in capital letters (8) the words I and O, and (9) numbers in the Roman notation.*

Period.—Place a period after (1) a declarative or an imperative sentence, (2) an abbreviation, (3) a number written in the Roman notation, and (4) Arabic figures used to enumerate.

Interrogation Point.—Every direct interrogative sentence or clause should be followed by an interrogation point.

Exclamation Point.—All exclamatory expressions must be followed by the exclamation point.

Comma.—Set off by the comma (1) a phrase out of its natural order or not closely connected with the word it modifies; (2) an explanatory modifier which does not re-

---

* Small letters are preferred where numerous references to chapters, etc., are made.

strict the modified term or combine closely with it ; (3) a participle used as an adjective modifier, with the words belonging to it, unless restrictive ; (4) the adjective clause, when not restrictive ; (5) the adverb clause, unless it closely follows and restricts the word it modifies ; (6) a word or phrase independent or nearly so ; (7) a direct quotation introduced into a sentence, unless *formally* introduced ; (8) a noun clause used as an attribute complement ; and (9) a term connected to another by *or* and having the same meaning. Separate by the comma (10) connected words and phrases, unless all the conjunctions are expressed ; (11) co-ordinate clauses, when short and closely connected ; and (12) the parts of a compound predicate, and other phrases, when long or differently modified. Use the comma (13) to denote an omission of words ; (14) after *as, namely,* etc., introducing illustrations ; and (15) when it is needed to prevent ambiguity.

Direction.—*Give the Rule for each capital letter and each mark of punctuation in these sentences, except the colon, the semicolon, and the quotation marks :—*

1. Francis II., Charles IX., and Henry III., three sons of Catherine de Medici and Henry II., sat upon the French throne. 2. The pupil asked, " When shall I use *O*, and when shall I use *oh ?* " 3. Purity of style forbids us to use : 1. Foreign words ; 2. Obsolete words ; 3. Low words, or slang. 4. It is easy, Mistress Dial, for you, who have always, as everybody knows, set yourself up above me, to accuse one of laziness. 5. He rushed into the field, and, foremost fighting, fell. 6. The Holy Land was, indeed, among the early conquests of the Saracens, Caliph Omar having, in 637 A. D., taken Jerusalem. 7. The first maxim among philosophers, and men of sense everywhere is, that merit only, should make distinctions. 8. San Salvador, Oct. 12, 1492. 9. Some letters are superfluous ; as, *c* and *q*.

10 No sleep till morn, when Youth and Pleasure meet
To chase the glowing hours with flying feet !

Direction.—*Use capital letters and the proper marks of punctuation in these sentences, and give your reasons :*—

1. and lo from the assembled crowd
   there rose a shout prolonged and loud
   that to the ocean seemed to say
   take her o bridegroom old and gray
2. a large rough mantle of sheepskin fastened around the loins by a girdle or belt of hide was the only covering of that strange solitary man elijah the tishbite 3. the result however of the three years' reign or tyranny of jas ii was that wm of orange came over from holland and without shedding a drop of blood became a d 1688 wm iii of england 4. o has three sounds : 1. that in *not ;* 2. that in *note ;* 3. that in *more* 5. lowell asks and what is so rare as a day in june 6. spring is a fickle mistress but summer is more staid 7. if i may judge by his gorgeous colors and the exquisite sweetness and variety of his music autumn is i should say the poet of the family 8. new york apr 30 1789 9. some letters stand each for many sounds; as *a* and *o.*

LESSON 147.

SUMMARY OF RULES—CONTINUED

SEMICOLON AND COLON.

Semicolon.—Co-ordinate clauses, (1) when slightly connected, or (2) when themselves divided by the comma, must be separated by the semicolon. Use the semicolon (3) between serial phrases or clauses having a common dependence on something which precedes or follows; and (4) before *as, to wit, namely, i. e.,* and *that is,* when they introduce examples or illustrations.

Direction.—*Justify each capital letter and each mark of punctuation (except the colon) in these sentences :*—

1. It may cost treasure, and it may cost blood ; but it will stand, and it will richly compensate for both. 2. Some words are delightful to the ear; as, *Ontario, golden, oriole.* 3. The shouts of revelry had

died away; the roar of the lion had ceased; the last loiterer had retired from the banquet; and the lights in the palace of the victor were extinguished. 4. Send it to the public halls; proclaim it there; let them hear it who heard the first roar of the enemy's cannon; let them see it who saw their brothers and their sons fall on the field of Bunker Hill; and the very walls will cry out in its support.

Direction.—*Use capital letters and the proper marks of punctuation in these sentences, and give your reasons:*—

1. all parts of a plant reduce to three namely root stem and leaf 2. when the world is dark with tempests when thunder rolls and lightning flies thou lookest in thy beauty from the clouds and laughest at the storm 3. the oaks of the mountains fall the mountains themselves decay with years the ocean shrinks and grows again the moon herself is lost in heaven 4. kennedy taking from her a handkerchief edged with gold pinned it over her eyes the executioners holding her by the arms led her to the block and the queen kneeling down said repeatedly with a firm voice into thy hands o lord i commend my spirit

Colon.—Use the colon (1) between the parts of a sentence when these parts are themselves divided by the semicolon, and (2) before a quotation or an enumeration of particulars when *formally* introduced.

Direction.—*Justify each capital letter and each mark of punctuation in these sentences:*—

1. You may swell every expense, and strain every effort, still more extravagantly; accumulate every assistance you can beg and borrow, traffic and barter with every little, pitiful German prince that sells and sends his subjects to the shambles of a foreign country: your efforts are forever vain and impotent. 2. This is a precept of Socrates: "Know thyself."

Direction.—*Use capital letters and the proper marks of punctuation in these sentences, and give your reasons:*—

1. the advice given ran thus take care of the minutes and the hours will take care of themselves 2. we may abound in meetings and move-

ments enthusiastic gatherings in the field and forest may kindle all minds with a common sentiment but it is all in vain if men do not retire from the tumult to the silent culture of every right disposition

Direction.—*Write sentences illustrating the several uses of the semicolon, the colon, and the comma.*

LESSON 148.

SUMMARY OF RULES—CONTINUED.

THE DASH, MARKS OF PARENTHESIS, APOSTROPHE, HYPHEN, QUOTATION MARKS, AND BRACKETS.

Dash.—Use the dash where there is an omission (1) of letters or figures, and (2) of such words as *as, namely,* or *that is,* introducing illustrations or equivalent expressions. Use the dash (3) where the sentence breaks off abruptly, and the same thought is resumed after a slight suspension, or another takes its place; and (4) before a word or phrase repeated at intervals for emphasis. The dash may be used (5) instead of marks of parenthesis, and may (6) follow other marks, adding to their force.

Direction.—*Justify each capital letter and each mark of punctuation in these sentences:—*

1. The most noted kings of Israel were the first three—Saul, David, and Solomon. 2. In E——s xx. 1—18, you may find the ten commandments. 3. And—"This to me?" he said. 4. Assyria, Greece, Rome, Carthage—what are they? 5. I do not rise to supplicate you to be merciful toward the nation to which I belong,—toward a nation which, though subject to England, yet is distinct from it. 6. We know the uses—and sweet they are—of adversity.

Direction.—*Use capital letters and the proper marks of punctuation in these sentences, and give your reasons:—*

1. the human species is composed of two distinct races those who borrow and those who lend 2. this bill this infamous bill the way it

has been received by the house the manner in which its opponents have been treated the personalities to which they have been subjected all these things dissipate my doubts 3. during the winter of 1775 6 gen w n was besieging b n 4. lord marmion turned well was his need and dashed the rowels in his steed

Marks of Parenthesis.—Marks of parenthesis may be used to enclose what has no essential connection with the rest of the sentence.

Apostrophe.—Use the apostrophe (1) to mark the omission of letters, (2) in the pluralizing of letters, figures, and characters, and (3) to distinguish the possessive from other cases.

Hyphen.—Use the hyphen (-) (1) to join the parts of compound words, and (2) between syllables when a word is divided.

Quotation Marks.—Use quotation marks to enclose a copied word or passage. If the quotation contains a quotation, the latter is enclosed within single marks. (See Less. 74.)

Brackets.—Use brackets [ ] to enclose what, in quoting another's words, you insert by way of explanation or correction.

Direction.—*Justify the the marks of punctuation used in these sentences:*—

1. Luke says, Acts xxi. 15, "We took up our carriages [luggage], and went up to Jerusalem." 2. The last sentence of the composition was, "I close in the words of Patrick Henry, 'Give me liberty, or give me death.'" 3. *Telegraph-pole* is a recent compound ; *telegraph* is divided thus : *tel-e-graph.* 4. The profound learning of Sir William Jones (he was master of twenty-eight languages) was the wonder of his contemporaries. 5. By means of the apostrophe you know that *love* in *mothers' love* is a noun, and that *i's* isn't a verb.

Direction.—*Use capital letters and the proper marks of punctuation in these sentences, and give your reasons :—*

1. next to a conscience void of offense without which by the bye life isnt worth the living is the enjoyment of the social feelings 2. man the life boat 3. dont neglect in writing to dot your *is* cross your *ts* and make your 7*s* unlike your 9*s* and dont in speaking omit the *hs* from such words as *which when* and *why* or insert *rs* in *law saw* and *raw* 4. the scriptures tell us take no thought anxiety for the morrow 5. The speaker said american oratory rose to its high water mark in that great speech ending liberty and union now and forever one and inseparable.

LESSON 149.

CAPITAL LETTERS AND PUNCTUATION—REVIEW.

Direction.—*Give the reason for each capital letter and each mark of punctuation in these sentences :—*

1. A bigot's mind is like the pupil of the eye ; the more light you pour upon it, the more it contracts. 2. This is the motto of the University of Oxford : "The Lord is my light." 3. The only fault ever found with him is, that he sometimes fights ahead of his orders. 4. The land flowing with "milk and honey" (see N——s xiv. 8.) was a long, narrow strip, lying along the eastern edge, or coast, of the Mediterranean, and consisted of three divisions ; namely, 1. On the north, Galilee ; 2. On the south, Judea ; 3. In the middle, Samaria. 5 "What a lesson," Trench well says, "the word 'diligence' contains !"

6. An honest man, my neighbor,—there he stands—
   Was struck,—struck like a dog. by one who wore
   The badge of Ursini.
7. Thou, too, sail on, O Ship of State ;
   Sail on, O Union, strong and great.
8. O'Connell asks, "The clause which does away with trial by jury—what, in the name of Heaven, is it, if it is not the establishment of a revolutionary tribunal ?" 9. There are only three departments of

the mind—the intellect, the feelings, and the will. 10. This—trial!
11. American nationality has made the desert to bud and blossom as the rose; it has quickened to life the giant brood of useful arts; it has whitened lake and ocean with the sails of a daring, new, and lawful trade; it has extended to exiles, flying as clouds, the asylum of our better liberty. 12. As I saw him [Webster, the day before his great reply to Col. Hayne of South Carolina] in the evening, (if I may borrow an illustration from his favorite amusement) he was as unconcerned and as free of spirit as some here have seen him, while floating in his fishing-boat along a hazy shore, gently rocking on the tranquil tide, dropping his line here and there with the varying fortune of the sport. The next morning he was like some mighty admiral, dark and terrible, casting the long shadow of his frowning tiers far over the sea, that seemed to sink beneath him; his broad pendant streaming at the main, the stars and stripes at the fore, the mizzen, and the peak; and bearing down like a tempest upon his antagonist, with all his canvas strained to the wind, and all his thunders roaring from his broad sides.

To the Teacher.—If further work in punctuation is needed, require the pupils to justify the punctuation of the sentences beginning page 269.

LESSON 150.

QUALITIES OF STYLE.

Style is the manner in which one expresses himself, and in some respects it must reflect the writer. But there are some cardinal qualities which all good style must possess.

I. Perspicuity.—Perspicuity is opposed to obscurity and ambiguity, and so means *clearness of expression*. This is an indispensable quality; if the thought is not understood or is misunderstood, it might as well have been left unuttered. Perspicuity depends mainly upon these few things:—

1. One's Clear Understanding of what he attempts to say.—You cannot express to others more than you thoroughly know, or make your thought clearer to them than it is to yourself.

2. The Unity of the Sentence.—Many thoughts, or thoughts having no natural and close connection with each other, should not be crowded into one sentence.

3. The Use of the Right Words.—Use such words as convey your thought—each word expressing exactly your idea, no more, no less, no other. Do not omit words when they are needed. Be cautious in the use of *he, she, it,* and *they.* Use simple words, such as others can readily understand, avoiding bookish terms, words that have passed out of use, and those that have no footing in the language—foreign terms, words newly coined, and slang.

4. A Happy Arrangement.—The relations of words to each other should be obvious at a glance. The sentence should not need rearrangement to disclose the meaning, or to unite dislocated parts.

II. Energy.—By energy we mean vigor of expression. In ordinary discourse, it is not always to be sought. We use it when we wish to convince the intellect, arouse the feelings, and take captive the will—lead one to *do* something. When energetic, we select words for strength, and not for beauty; choose specific, and not general, terms; use few words and crowd them dense with thought; place subordinate clauses before the independent, and the strongest clause of the sentence, the strongest sentence of the paragraph, and the strongest point of the discourse, last. Energetic thought is usually charged with intense feeling, and requires an impassioned delivery.

III. Imagery—Figures of Speech.—*Things* stand in many relations to each other, some of which are these: they resemble each other in some particular; they stand one to another as part to a whole, or as whole to a part; they are associated by having been so long together that one suggests the other. Figures of Speech are those expressions in which, *departing from our ordinary style in speaking of things*, we *assert* or *assume* any of these relations. Imagery adds beauty to style. but it also makes the thought clearer and stronger—a diamond brooch may *do duty* as well as *adorn*.

A *Simile* is a figure in which we *assert* a *resemblance* between two things otherwise unlike ; as, The gloom of despondency *hung like a cloud* over the land.

A *Metaphor* is a figure in which, *assuming* the *resemblance* between two things, we bring over and apply to one of them the term which denotes the other ; as, Who *carried* your flag into the very *chops* of the British Channel, and *bearded the lion in his den ?*

A *Synecdoche* is a figure in which the name of a part denotes the whole, or the name of the whole denotes a part ; as, All *hands* to the pumps ! The New *World* is geologically the oldest.

A *Metonymy* is a figure in which the name of one thing long associated with another is taken to denote that other ; as, Please address the *chair*. One needs to listen to the *organ* before reading *Milton*.

IV. Variety.—Variety is a quality of style opposed to uniformity. Nothing in discourse pleases more than light and shade—the same word not appearing with offensive frequency ; long words alternating with short, and long sentences with short ; the natural order now and then yielding to the transposed ; clauses having no rigidly fixed position ; sentences, heavy and moving slowly, elbow to elbow with the light and tripping ; figures sparkling here and there from out the setting of plain language ; the verb in the *assertive* form frequently giving way to the participle and the infinitive, which *assume ;* the full method of statement followed by the contracted ; in a word, no one form or method continuing so long as to weary, but alternating with another, and keeping the reader fresh and fascinated throughout.

To the Teacher.—Question the pupils upon every point taken up in this Lesson, requiring them to give *illustrations* where it is possible.

LESSON 151.

PERSPICUITY—CRITICISM.

General Direction.—*In all your work in Composition attend carefully to the punctuation.*

Direction.—*Point out the faults, and recast these sentences, making them clear.*—

*1. He was locked in and so he sat still till the guard came and let him out, as soon as he stepped out on the ground, he saw the dead and dying laying about everywhere. 2. They used to ring a large bell at six o'clock in the morning for us to get up, then we had half an hour to dress in, after which we would go to Chapel exercises, then breakfast, school would commence at nine o'clock and closed at four in the afternoon allowing an hour for dinner from one until two then we would resume our studies until four in the afternoon. 3. Jewelry was worn in the time of King Pharaoh which is many thousand years before Christ in the time when the Israelites left they borrowed all the jewels of the Egyptians which were made of gold and silver. 4. When it is made of gold they can not of pure gold but has to be mixed with some other metal which is generally copper which turns it a reddish hue in some countries they use silver which gives it a whitish hue but in the United States and England they use both silver and copper but the English coins are the finest.

Direction.—*Point out the faults, and recast these sentences, making them clear:*—

(Some may have each many meanings; give these.)

1. James's son, Charles I., before the breath was out of his body was proclaimed king in his stead. 2. He told the coachman that he would be the death of him, if he did not take care what he was about, and mind what he said. 3. Richelieu said to the king that Mazarin would carry out his policy. 4. He was overjoyed to see him, and he sent for one of his workmen, and told him to consider himself at his service. 5. Blake answered the Spanish priest that if he had sent in

---

* These four sentences and others in these Lessons, given just as we found them have been culled from school compositions.

a complaint, he would have punished the sailors severely ; but he took it ill that he set the Spaniards on to punish them.

Direction.—*Place these subordinate clauses where they will remove the obscurity, and then see in how many ways each sentence can be arranged :—*

1. The moon cast a pale light on the graves that were scattered around, as it peered above the horizon. 2. A large number of seats were occupied by pupils that had no backs. 3. Crusoe was surprised at seeing five canoes on the shore in which there were savages. 4. This tendency will be headed off by approximations which will be made from time to time of the written word to the spoken. 5. People had to travel on horseback and in wagons, which was a very slow way, if they traveled at all. 6. How can brethren partake of their Father's blessing that curse each other ? 7. Two men will be tried for crimes in this town which are punishable with death, if a full court should attend.

Direction.—*Each of these sentences may have two meanings; supply two ellipses, and remove the ambiguity :—*

1. Let us trust no strength less than thine. 2. Study had more attraction for him than his friend. 3. He did not like the new teacher so well as his playmates. 4. He aimed at nothing less than the crown. 5. Lovest thou me more than these ?

LESSON 152.

PERSPICUITY—CRITICISM.

Direction.—*Place these italicized phrases where they will remove the obscurity, and then see in how many ways each sentence can be arranged :—*

1. These designs any man who is a Briton *in any situation* ought to disavow. 2. The chief priests, mocking, said among themselves *with the scribes,* "He saved," etc. 3. Hay is given to horses *as well as corn* to distend the stomach. 4. Boston has forty first class

grammar-schools, *exclusive of Dorchester.* 5. He rode to town, and drove twelve cows *on horseback.* 6. He could not face an enraged father *in spite of his effrontery.* 7. Two owls sat upon a tree which grew near an old wall *out of a heap of rubbish.* 8. I spent most *on the river and in the river* of the time I stayed there. 9. He wanted to go to sea, although it was contrary to the wishes of his parents, *at the age of eighteen.* 10. I have a wife and six children, and I have never seen *one of them.*

Direction.—*Place these italicized words and phrases where they will remove ambiguity, and then see in how many ways each sentence can be arranged :—*

1. In Paris, every lady *in full dress* rides. 2. I saw my friend when I was in Boston *walking down Tremont street.* 3. The transfers made, *as a whole,* strengthen *rather than otherwise* the new administration. 4. What is his coming or going *to you ?* 5. We do those things *frequently* which we repent of afterwards. 6. I rushed out leaving the wretch with his tale half told, *horror-stricken at his crime.* 7. Exclamation points are scattered up and down the page by compositors *without any mercy.* 8. I want to make a present to one who is fond of chickens *for a Christmas gift.*

Direction.—*Make these sentences clear by using simpler words and phrases :—*

1. A *devastating conflagration raged.* 2. He *conducted* her to the *altar of Hymen.* 3. A donkey has an *abnormal elongation of auricular appendages.* 4. Are you *excavating a subterranean canal ?* 5. He had no *capillary substance* on the *summit* of his head. 6. He made a sad *faux pas.* 7. A net-work is anything *reticulated or decussated, with interstices at equal distances between the intersections.* 8. Diligence is the *sine qua non* of success. 9. She has *donned the habiliments of woe.* 10. The *deceased* was to-day *deposited in his last resting-place.* 11. The *inmates proceeded to the sanctuary.* 12. I have *partaken of my morning repast.* 13. He *took the initiative in inaugurating the ceremony.*

LESSON 153.

ENERGY—CRITICISM.

Direction.—*Expand these brief expressions into sentences full of long words, and note the loss of energy :—*

1. To your tents, O Israel! 2. Up, boys, and at them! 3. Indeed! 4. Bah! 5. Don't give up the ship! 6. Murder will out! 7. Oh! 8. Silence there! 9. Hurrah! 10. Death or free speech! 11. Rascal! 12. No matter. 13. Least said, soonest mended. 14. Death to the tyrant! 15. I'll none of it. 16. Help, ho! 17. Shame on you! 18. First come, first served.

Direction.—*Condense each of these italicized expressions into one or two words, and note the gain :—*

1. He *shuffled off this mortal coil* yesterday. 2. The author surpassed all *those who were living at the same time with him*. 3. To say that revelation is *a thing which there is no need of* is to talk wildly. 4. He *departed this life*. 5. Some say that ever *'gainst that season comes wherein our Saviour's birth is celebrated* this *bird of dawning* singeth all night long.

Direction.—*Change these specific words to general terms, and note the loss in energy :—*

1. Don't *fire* till *you see the whites of their eyes*. 2. *Break down* the *dikes*, give Holland back to *ocean*. 3. *Three hundred men* held the hosts of *Xerxes* at bay. 4. I *sat* at her *cradle*, I *followed* her *hearse*. 5. Their *daggers* have *stabbed* Cæsar. 6. When I'm *mad*, I *weigh a ton*. 7. *Burn* Moscow, *starve back* the *invaders*. 8. There's no use in *crying over spilt milk*. 9. In proportion as men delight in *battles* and *bull-fights* will they punish by *hanging, burning*, and the *rack*.

Direction.—*Change these general terms to specific words, and note the gain in energy :—*

1. Anne Boleyn was *executed*. 2. It were better for him that a *heavy weight* were *fastened to him* and that he were *submerged* in *the waste of waters*. 3. *The capital of the chosen people* was *destroyed* by a *Roman general*. 4. Consider the *flowers* how they *increase in size*. 5. Cæsar

was *slain* by *the conspirators*. 6. *The cities of the plain* were annihilated.

Direction.—*Arrange these words, phrases, and clauses in the order of their strength, placing the strongest last, and note the gain in energy:*—

1. The nations of the earth repelled, surrounded, pursued, and resisted him. 2. He was no longer consul nor citizen nor general nor even an emperor, but a prisoner and an exile. 3. I shall die an American; I live an American; I was born an American. 4. All that I am, all that I hope to be, and all that I have in this life, I am now ready here to stake upon it. 5. I shall defend it without this House, in all places, and within this House; at all times, in time of peace and in time of war. 6. We must fight if we wish to be free, if we mean to preserve inviolate our rights, if we do not mean to abandon the struggle.

LESSON 154.

FIGURES OF SPEECH—CRITICISM.

Direction.—*Name these figures of speech, and then recast each sentence, using plain language, and note the loss of beauty and force:*—

1. Lend me your *ears*. 2. The robin knows when your grapes have *cooked* long enough in the sun. 3. A day will come when *bullets* and *bombs* shall be replaced by *ballots*. 4. Cæsar were no *lion* were not Romans *hinds*. 5. The soul of Jonathan was *knit* to that of David. 6. Borrowing *dulls the edge* of husbandry. 7. He will bring down my *gray hairs* with sorrow to the grave. 8. The *pen* is mightier than the *sword*. 9. If I can *catch him once upon the hip*, I will *feed fat* the ancient grudge I bear him. 10. The destinies of mankind were *trembling in the balance*, while death *fell in showers*. 11. O Cassius, you are *yoked with a lamb* that *carries anger as the flint bears fire*. 12. Nations shall *beat their swords into ploughshares*, and *their spears into pruning-hooks*. 13. The Morn in *russet mantle clad walks o'er the dew* of yon high eastern hill. 14. The air *bites* shrewdly. 15. He doth *bestride* the narrow world *like a Colossus*. 16. My *heart* is in the coffin there with Cæsar.

17. The *gray-eyed* Morn *smiles* on the *frowning* Night. 18. The good is often buried with men's *bones*. 19. Beware of the *bottle*. 20. All nations respect our *flag*. 21. I have no *spur to prick the sides* of my intent. 22. I *am as constant as the northern star*. 23. Then *burst* his mighty *heart*. 24. Lentulus returned with *victorious eagles*. 25. Death hath *sucked the honey* of thy breath. 26. Our *chains are forged*. 27. I have *bought golden* opinions. 28. His words *fell softer than snows on the brine*. 29. *Night's candles are burnt out*, and jocund Day *stands tiptoe* on the misty mountain top.

Direction.—*In the first four sentences, use s i m i l e s ; in the second four, m e t a p h o r s ; in the third four, s y n e c d o c h e s ; in the last four, m e t o n y m i e s :*—

1. He *flew with the swiftness of an arrow*. 2. In battle some men *are brave*, others *are cowardly*. 3. His head is as full of plans *as it can hold*. 4. I heard a *loud* noise. 5. Boston is the *place where* American liberty *began*. 6. Our dispositions should grow *mild*, as we grow old. 7. The *stars can no longer be seen*. 8. In battle some men are *brave*, others are *cowardly*. 9. We passed a fleet of ten *ships*. 10. English *vessels* plough the seas of the two *hemispheres*. 11. They sought the king's *life*. 12. I abjure all *dwellings*. 13. *His convivial habits* have been his ruin. 14. Have you read *Lamb's Essays?* 15. The *water* is boiling. 16. We have prostrated ourselves before the *king*.

Direction.—*The parts of a figure should agree, and should unite to form one whole. Correct these errors :*—

1. The *devouring* fire *uprooted* the stubble. 2. The *brittle* thread of life may be *cut* asunder. 3. All the *ripe fruit* of three-score years was *blighted* in a day. 4. *Unravel* the *obscurities* of this *knotty* question. 5. We must apply the *axe* to the *fountain* of this evil. 6. The man *stalks* into court like a *motionless* statue, with the *cloak* of hypocrisy in his *mouth*. 7. The thin *mantle* of snow *dissolved*. 8. I smell a *rat*, I see him *brewing* in the air ; but I shall yet *nip him in the bud*.

LESSON 155.

VARIETY IN EXPRESSION.

Remark.—You learned in Lessons 52, 53, 54, that the natural order may give way to the transposed; in 55, 56, that one kind of simple sentence may be changed to another; in 57, that simple sentences may be contracted; in 61, that adjectives may be expanded into clauses; in 67, that an adverb clause may stand before, between the parts of, and after, the independent clause; in 68, that an adverb clause may be contracted to a participle, a participle phrase, an absolute phrase, a prepositional phrase, may be contracted by the omission of words, and may be changed to an adjective clause or phrase; in 73, that a noun clause as subject may stand last, and as object complement may stand first, that it may be made prominent, and may be contracted; in 74, that direct quotations and questions may be changed to indirect, and indirect to direct; in 77, that compound sentences may be formed out of simple sentences, may be contracted to simple sentences, and may be changed to complex sentences; and, in 79, that participles, absolute phrases, and infinitives may be expanded into different kinds of clauses.

Direction.—*Take sentences and illustrate all these changes.*

Direction.—*Recast these sentences, avoiding offensive repetitions of the same word or the same sounds :—*

1. We have to have money to have a horse. 2. We sailed across a bay and sailed up a creek and sailed back and sailed in all about fourteen miles. 3. It is then put into stacks, or it is put into barns either to use it to feed it to the stock or to sell it. 4. This day we undertake to render an account to the widows and orphans whom our decision will make; to the wretches that will be roasted at the stake. 5. The news of the battle of Bunker Hill, fought on the 17th of June in the year of our Lord 1775, roused the patriotism of the people to a high pitch of enthusiasm.

Direction.—*Using other words wholly or in part, see in how many ways you can express the thoughts contained in these sentences :—*

1. In the profusion and recklessness of her lies, Elizabeth had no

peer in England. 2. Henry IV. said that James I. was the wisest fool in Christendom. 3. Cowper's letters are charming because they are simple and natural. 4. George IV., though he was pronounced the first gentleman in Europe, was, nevertheless, a snob.

LESSON 156.

THE PARAGRAPH.

The Paragraph.—The clauses of complex sentences are so closely united in meaning that frequently they are not to be separated from each other even by the comma. The clauses of compound sentences are less closely united—a comma, a semicolon, or a colon is needed to divide them.

Between *sentences* there exists a wider separation in meaning, marked by a period or other terminal point. But even sentences may be connected—the bond which unites them being their common relation to the thought which jointly they develop. Sentences thus related are grouped together and form what we call a Paragraph, marked by beginning the first word a little to the right of the marginal line.

Direction.—*Notice the facts which this paragraph contains, and the relation to each other of the clauses and the sentences expressing these facts :—*

After a breeze of some sixty hours from the north and north-west, the wind died away about four o'clock yesterday afternoon. The calm continued till about nine in the evening. The mercury in the barometer fell, in the meantime, at an extraordinary rate ; and the captain predicted that we should encounter a gale from the south-east. The gale came on about eleven o'clock ; not violent at first, but increasing every moment.

1. A breeze from the north and north-west. 2. The wind died away.

3. A calm. 4. Barometer fell. 5. The captain predicted a gale. 6. It came on. 7. It increased in violence.

Direction.—*State and number the facts contained in the paragraph below :—*

I awoke with a confused recollection of a good deal of rolling and thumping in the night, occasioned by the dashing of the waves against the ship. Hurrying on my clothes, I found such of the passengers as could stand, at the doors of the hurricane-house, holding on, and looking out in the utmost consternation. It was still quite dark. Four of the sails were already in ribbons : the winds whistling through the cordage ; the rain dashing furiously and in torrents ; the noise and spray scarcely less than I found them under the great sheet at Niagara.

Direction.—*Weave the facts below into a paragraph, supplying all you need to make the narrative smooth :—*

Rip's beard was grizzled. Fowling-piece rusty. Dress uncouth. Women and children at his heels. Attracted attention. Was eyed from head to foot. Was asked on which side he voted. Whether he was Federal or Democrat ? Rip was dazed by the question. Stared in stupidity.

Direction.—*Weave the facts below into two paragraphs, supplying what you need, and tell what each is about :—*

In place of the old tree, there was a pole. This was tall and naked. A flag was fluttering from it. The flag had on it the stars and stripes. This was strange to Rip. But Rip saw something he remembered. The tavern sign. He recognized on it the face of King George. Still the picture was changed. The red coat gone. One of blue and buff in its place. A sword, and not a scepter, in the hand. Wore a cocked hat. Underneath was painted—"General Washington."

LESSON 157.

THE PARAGRAPH.

Direction.—*Weave the facts below into three paragraphs, and write on the margin what each is about:*—

The Nile rises in great lakes. Runs north. Sources two thousand miles from Alexandria. Receives two branches only. Runs through an alluvial valley. Course through the valley is 1,500 miles. Flows into the Mediterranean. Two principal channels. Minor outlets. Nile overflows its banks. Overflow caused by rains at the sources. The melting of the mountain snows. Begins at the end of June. Rises four inches daily. Rises till the close of September. Subsides. Whole valley an inland sea. Only villages above the surface. The valley very fertile. The deposit. The fertile strip is from 5 to 150 miles wide. Renowned for fruitfulness. Egypt long the granary of the world. Three crops from December to June. Productions—grain, cotton, and indigo.

Direction.—*Weave these facts into four paragraphs, writing on the margin of each the main thought:*—

The robin is thought by some to be migratory. But he stays with us all winter. Cheerful. Noisy. Poor soloist. A spice of vulgarity in him. Dash of prose in his song. Appetite extraordinary. Eats his own weight in a short time. Taste for fruit. Eats with a relishing gulp, like Dr. Johnson's. Fond of cherries. Earliest mess of peas. Mulberries. Lion's share of the raspberries. Angle-worms his delight. A few years ago I had a grape vine. A foreigner. Shy of bearing. This summer bore a score of bunches. They secreted sugar from the sunbeams. One morning, went to pick them. The robins beforehand with me. Bustled out from the leaves. Made shrill, unhandsome remarks about me. Had sacked the vine. Remnant of a single bunch. How it looked at the bottom of my basket! A humming-bird's egg in an eagle's nest. Laughed. Robins joined in the merriment.

LESSON 153.

PARAGRAPHS AND THE THEME.

Direction.—*Weave these facts into four paragraphs:*—

Note that the several paragraphs form a *composition*, or **Theme**, the general subject of which is

WOUTER VAN TWILLER (according to Diedrich Knickerbocker).

I. **Who he was.**—Van Twiller was a Dutchman. Born at Rotterdam. Descended from burgomasters. In 1629 appointed governor of Nieuw Nederlandts. Arrived in June at New Amsterdam—New York city.

II. **Person.**—Was five feet six inches high, six feet five in circumference. Head spherical, and too large for any neck. Nature set it on the back-bone. Body capacious. Legs short and sturdy. A beer-barrel on skids. Face a vast, unfurrowed expanse. No lines of thought. Two small, gray eyes. Cheeks had taken toll of all that had entered his mouth. Mottled and streaked with dusky red.

III. **Habits.**—Regular. Four meals daily, each an hour long. Smoked and doubted eight hours. Slept twelve. As self-contained as an oyster. Rarely spoke save in monosyllables. But never said a foolish thing. Never laughed. Perplexed by a joke. Conceived everything on a grand scale. When a question was asked, would put on a mysterious look. Shake his head. Smoke in silence. Observe, at length, he had doubts. Presided at the council, in state. Swayed a Turkish pipe instead of a sceptre. Known to sit with eyes closed two hours. Internal commotion shown by guttural sounds. Noises of contending doubts, admirers said.

IV. **Exploits.**—Settled a dispute about accounts thus: sent for the parties; each produced his account-book; Van T. weighed the books; counted the leaves; equally heavy; equally thick; made each give the other a receipt; and the constable pay the costs. Demanded why Van Rensselaer seized Bear's Island. Battled with doubts regarding the Yankees. Smoked and breathed his last together.

Direction.— *Weave these facts into four paragraphs, write on the margin the special topic of each, and over the whole, what you think is the general subject of the Theme :—*

The prophets of Baal accept Elijah's challenge. They dress a bullock. Call on Baal. Are mocked by Elijah. Leap upon the altar. Cut themselves. Blood. Cry till the time of the evening sacrifice. No answer by fire. Elijah commands the people to come near. Repairs an old altar with twelve stones, one for each tribe. Digs a trench. Sacrifices. Pours water three times upon it. Prays. Fire falls, consumes flesh, wood, stones, dust, licks up water. People see it. Fall on their faces. Cry out twice, "The Lord, he is the God." Take the prophets to the brook Kishon, where they are slain. Elijah ascends Mount Carmel. Bows in prayer. "Go up now, look toward the sea." Servant reports, "There is nothing." "Go again seven times." "Behold there ariseth a little cloud out of the sea, like a man's hand." Orders Ahab to prepare his chariot. Girding up his loins, he runs before Ahab to Jezreel.

LESSON 159.

PARAGRAPHS AND THE THEME.

Direction.— *Weave these facts into as many paragraphs as you think there should be, using the variety of expression insisted on in Lesson* 150, *and write on the margin of each paragraph the special topic, and over the whole, the general subject of the Theme :—*

Fort Ticonderoga on a peninsula. Formed by the outlet of Lake George and by Lake Champlain. Fronts south ; water on three sides. Separated by Lake Champlain from Mount Independence, and by the outlet from Mount Defiance. Fort one hundred feet above the water. May 7, 1775, 270 men meet at Castleton, Vermont. All but 40, Green Mountain boys. Meet to plan and execute an attack upon Fort T. Allen and Arnold there. Each claims the command. Question left to the officers. Allen chosen. On evening of the 9th, they reach the lake. Difficulty in crossing. Send for a scow. Seize a boat at anchor. Search, and find small row boats. Only 83 able to cross. Day is dawning when these reach the shore. Not prudent to wait. Allen orders all who will follow him to poise their firelocks. Every man responds. Nathan Beman, a lad, guides them to the fort. Sentinel snaps his gun at A. Misses fire. Sentinel retreats. They follow. Rush upon the parade ground. Form. Loud cheer. A. climbs the stairs. Orders La Place, it is said, in the name of the great Jehovah and the Continental Congress, to surrender. Capture 48 men. 120 cannon. Used next winter at the siege of Boston. Several swords and howitzers, small arms, and ammunition.

Direction.—*These facts are thrown together promiscuously. Classify them as they seem to you to be related. Determine the number of paragraphs and their order, and then do as directed above:—*

Joseph was Jacob's favorite. Wore fine garments. One day was sent to inquire after the other sons. They were at a distance, tending the flocks. Joseph used to dream. They saw him coming. Plotted to kill him. In one dream his brothers' sheaves bowed to his. In another the sun, moon, and stars bowed to him. Plotted to throw his body into a pit. Agreed to report to their father that some beast had devoured him. Joseph foolishly told these to his brothers. Hated him, because of the dreams and their father's partiality. While eating, Ishmaelites approached. They sat down to eat. Were going down into Egypt. Camels loaded with spices. At the intercession of Reuben they did not kill Joseph. Threw him alive into a pit. Ishmaelites took him down into Egypt. Sold him to Potiphar. Judah advised that he be raised from the pit. Jacob recognized the coat. Refused comfort. Rent his clothes, and put on sackcloth. They took his coat. Killed a kid, and dipped the coat in its blood. Brought it to Jacob. "This have we found; know now whether it be thy son's coat or no."

LESSON 160.

PARAGRAPHS AND THE THEME.

Direction.—*Classify these promiscuous facts, determine carefully the number and the order of the paragraphs, and then do as directed above:—*

Trafalgar a Spanish promontory. Near the Straits of Gibraltar. Off

Trafalgar, fleets of Spain and France, October 21, 1805. Nelson in command of the English fleet. The combined fleets in close line of battle. Collingwood second in command. Had more and larger cannon than the English. English fleet twenty-seven sail of the line and four frigates. Thirty-three sail of the line and seven frigates. He signaled those memorable words: "England expects every man to do his duty." Enemy had four thousand troops. Signal received with a shout. They bore down. The best riflemen in the enemy's boats. C. steered for the center. C. in the *Royal Sovereign* led the lee line of thirteen ships. A raking fire opened upon the *Victory*. N. in the *Victory* led the weather line. C. engaged the *Santa Anna*. Delighted at being the first in the fire. At 1.15 N. shot through the shoulder and back. At 12 the *Victory* opened fire. N.'s secretary the first to fall. Fifty fell before a shot was returned. "They have done for me at last, Hardy," said N. They bore him below. At 2.25 ten of the enemy had struck. The wound was mortal. At 4 fifteen had struck. The victory that cost the British 1,587 men won. These were his last words. At 4.30 he expired. "How goes the day with us?" he asked Hardy. "I hope none of our ships have struck." N.'s death was more than a public calamity. "I am a dead man, Hardy," he said. Englishmen turned pale at the news. Most triumphant death that of a martyr. He shook hands with Hardy. "Kiss me, Hardy." They mourned as for a dear friend. Kissed him on the cheek. Most awful death that of the martyr patriot. The loss seemed a personal one. Knelt down again and kissed his forehead. His articulation difficult. Heard to say, "Thank God, I have done my duty." Seemed as if they had not known how deeply they loved him. Most splendid death that of the hero in the hour of victory. Has left a name which is our pride. An example which is our shield and strength. Buried him in St. Paul's. Thus the spirits of the great and the wise live after them.

To the Teacher.—Continue this work as long as it is needed. Take any book, and read to the class items of facts. Require them to use the imagination and whatever graces of style are at their command, in weaving these together.

LESSON 161.

ANALYSIS OF THE SUBJECT OF THE THEME.

Analysis of the Subject.—A Theme is made up of groups of sentences called Paragraphs. The sentences of each paragraph are related to each other, because they jointly develop a single point, or thought. And the paragraphs are related to each other, because these points which they develop are divisions of the one general subject of the Theme.

After the subject has been chosen, and before writing upon it, it must be resolved into the main thoughts which compose it. Upon the thoroughness of this analysis and the natural arrangement of the thoughts thus derived, depends largely the worth of the Theme. These points form, when arranged, the **Framework** of the Theme.

Suppose you had taken *The Armada* as your subject. Perhaps you could say under these heads all you wished : 1. *What the Armada was.* 2. *When and by whom equipped.* 3. *Its purpose.* 4. *Its sail over the Bay of Biscay and entrance into the English Channel.* 5. *The attack upon it by Admiral Howard and his great Captains—Drake and Hawkins.* 6. *Its dispersion and partial destruction by the storm.* 7. *The return to Spain of the surviving ships and men.* 8. *The consequences to England and to Spain.*

Perhaps the 1st point could include the 2d and the 3d. Be careful not to split your general subject up into very many parts. See, too, that no point is repeated, that no point foreign to the subject is introduced, and that all the points together exhaust the subject as nearly as may be. Look to the arrangement of the points. There is a natural order ; (6) could not precede (5) ; nor (5), (4) ; nor (4), (1).

To the Teacher.—Question the pupils carefully upon every point taken up in this Lesson.

Direction.—*Prepare the framework of a theme on each of these subjects :—*

1. The Arrest of Major André. 2. A Winter in the Arctic Region.

LESSON 162.

ANALYSIS OF SUBJECTS.

Direction.—*Prepare the framework of a theme on each of these subjects:—*

1. Battle of Plattsburg. 2. A Day's Nutting. 3. What does a Proper Care for one's Health demand?

LESSON 163.

ANALYSIS OF SUBJECTS.

Direction.—*Prepare the framework of a theme on each of these subjects:—*

1. A Visit to the Moon. 2. Reasons why one should not Smoke. 3. What does a Proper Observance of Sunday require of one?

LESSON 164.

ANALYSIS OF SUBJECTS.

Direction.—*Prepare the framework of a theme on each of these subjects:—*

1. The Gulf Stream. 2. A Descent into a Whirlpool. 3. What are Books Good for?

LESSON 165.

HOW TO WRITE A THEME.

I. Choose a Subject.—Choose your subject long before you are to write. Avoid a full, round term like *Patriotism* or *Duty;* take a fragment of it; as, *How can a Boy be Patriotic?* or *Duties which we*

Schoolmates o:ce Each Other. The subject should be on your level, should be interesting to you and suggestive, and should instantly start in your mind many trains of thought.

II. Accumulate the Material.—Begin to think about your subject. Turn it over in your mind in your leisure moments, and, as thoughts flash upon you, jot them down in your blank-book. Pay little regard to their order on the page or to their relative importance ; but, if any seem broad enough for the main points, or heads, indicate this. Talk with no one on the subject, and read nothing on it, till you have thought yourself empty ; and even then you should note down what the conversation or reading suggests, rather than what you have heard or read.

III. Construct a Framework.—Before writing hunt through your material for the main points, or heads. See to what general truths or thoughts these jottings and those jottings point. Perhaps this or that thought, as it stands, includes enough to serve as a head. Be sure, at any rate, that by brooding over your material, and by further thinking upon the subject, you get at all the general thoughts into which, as it seems to you, the subject should be analyzed. Study these points carefully. See that no two overlap each other, that no one appears twice, that no one has been raised to the dignity of a head that should stand *under* some head, and that no one is irrelevant. Study now to find the natural order in which these points should stand. Let no point, to the clear understanding of which some other point is necessary, precede that other. If developing all the points would make your Theme too long, study to see what points you can omit without abrupt break or essential loss.

IV. Write.—Give your whole attention to your work as you write, and other thoughts will occur to you, and better ways of putting the thoughts already noted down. In expanding the main points into paragraphs, be sure that everything falls under its appropriate head.

Cast out irrelevant matter. Do not strain after effect, or strive to seem wiser than you are. Use familiar words, and place these, your phrases, and your clauses, where they will make your thought the clearest. As occasion calls, change from the natural order to the transposed, and let sentences, simple, complex, and compound, long and short, stand shoulder to shoulder in the paragraph. Express yourself easily —only now and then putting your thought forcibly and with feeling. Let a fresh image here and there relieve the uniformity of plain language. One sentence should follow another without abrupt break; and, if continuative of it, adversative to it, or an inference from it, and the hearer needs to be advised of this, let it swing into position on the hinge of a fitting connective. Of course, your sentences must pass rigid muster in syntax; and you must look sharply to the spelling, to the use of capital letters, and to punctuation.

V. Attend to the Mechanical Execution.—Keep your pages clean, and let your handwriting be clear. On the left of the page leave a margin of an inch for corrections. Do not write on the fourth page; if you exceed three pages, use another sheet. When the writing is done, double the lower half of the sheet over the upper, and fold through the middle; then bring the top down to the middle and fold again. Bring the right end toward you, and across the top write your name, the date, and the name of the teacher who is to correct the Theme. This superscription will be at the top of the fourth page, at the right-hand corner, and at right angles to the ruled lines.

To the Teacher.—Question the pupils closely upon every point in this Lesson, and insist that they shall practice what is here laid down.

Additional Subjects for Themes.

1. Apples and Nuts.
2. A Pleasant Evening.
3. My Walk to School.
4. Pluck.
5. School Friendships.
6. When my Ship comes in.
7. Ancient and Modern Warfare.
8. The View from my Window.
9. Homes without Hands.
10. I can.
11. My Friend Jack.
12. John Chinaman.

13. Irish Characters.
14. Robin Hood.
15. A Visit to Olympus.
16. Monday Morning.
17. My Native Town.
18. Over the Sea.
19. Up in a Balloon.
20. Queer People.
21. Our Minister.
22. A Plea for Puss.
23. Castles in Spain.
24. Young America.
25. Black Diamonds.
26. Mosquitoes.
27. A Day in the Woods.
28. A Boy's Trials.
29. The Yankee.
30. Robinson Crusoe.
31. Street Arabs.
32. Legerdemain.
33. Our Neighborhood.
34. Examinations.
35. Theater-going.
36. Donkeys.
37. The Southern Negro.
38. A Rainy Saturday.
39. The Early Bird catches the Worm.
40. Spring Sports.
41. How Horatius kept the Bridge.
42. Jack Frost.
43. My First Sea Voyage.
44. Monkeys.
45. Grandmothers.
46. The Boy of the Story Book.
47. Famous Streets.
48. Pigeons.
49. Jack and Gill.
50. Make Haste Slowly.
51. Commerce.
52. The Ship of the Desert.
53. Winter Sports.
54. A Visit to Neptune.
55. Whiskers.
56. Gypsies.
57. Cities of the Dead.
58. Street Cries.
59. The World Owes me a Living.
60. Politeness.
61. Cleanliness akin to Godliness.
62. Fighting Windmills.
63. Along the Docks.
64. Maple Sugar.
65. Umbrellas.
66. A Girl's Trials.
67. A Spider's Web.
68. The Story of Ruth.
69. Clouds.
70. A Country Store.
71. Timepieces.
72. Bulls and Bears.
73. Bores.
74. Our Sunday School.
75. The Making of Beer.
76. Autumn's Colors.
77. The Watched Pot never Boils.
78. The Mission of Birds.
79. Parasites.
80. Well-Begun is Half-Done.
81. The Tides.
82. The Schoolmaster in "The Deserted Village."
83. A Day on a Trout Stream.
84. A Stitch in Time saves Nine.
85. Of What Use are Flowers?
86. A Descent in a Diving Bell.

LESSON 166.

LETTER-WRITING.

Letters need special treatment. In writing a letter there are five things to consider—The Heading, The Introduction, The Body of the Letter, The Conclusion, and The Superscription.

THE HEADING.

Parts.—The Heading consists of the name of the **Place** at which the letter is written, and the **Date**. If you write from a city, give the door-number, the name of the street, the name of the city, and the name of the state. If you are at a Hotel or a School or any other well-known Institution, its name may take the place of the door-number and the name of the street; as may also the number of your post-office box. If you write from a village or other country place, give your post-office address, the name of the county, and that of the state.

The *Date* consists of the month, the day of the month, and the year.

How Written.—Begin the Heading about an inch and a half from the top of the page—on the first ruled line of commercial note. If the letter occupies but a few lines of a single page, you may begin the Heading lower down. Begin the first line of the Heading a little to the left of the middle of the page. If it occupies more than one line, the second line should begin farther to the right than the first, and the third farther to the right than the second.

The door-number, the day of month, and the year are written in figures, the rest in words. Each important word begins with a capital letter, each item is set off by the comma, and the whole closes with a period.

Direction.—*Study what has been said, and write the following headings according to these models :—*

1. Ripton, Addison Co., Vt.,
   July 10, 1875.
2. 250 Broadway, N. Y.,
   June 6, 1860.
3. Saco, Me., Feb. 25, 1877.
4. Polytechnic Institute,
   Brooklyn, N. Y.,
   May 3, 1868.

1. ann arbor 5 july 1820 michigan. 2. champlain co clinton n y jan 14 1800. 3. p o box 2678 1860 oct 19 chicago. 4. philadelphia 670 1858 chestnut st 16 apr. 5. saint nicholas new york 1 hotel nov 1855.

THE INTRODUCTION.

Parts.—The Introduction consists of the **Address**—the Name, the Title, and the Place of Business or Residence of the one addressed—and the **Salutation**. Titles of respect and courtesy should appear in the Address. Prefix *Mr.* to a man's name, *Messrs.* to the names of several gentlemen ; *Master* to that of a young lad ; *Miss* to that of a young lady ; *Mrs.* to that of a married lady ; *Misses* to those of several young ladies ; and *Mesdames* to those of several married or elderly ladies. Prefix *Dr.* to the name of a physician, but never *Mr. Dr.;* *Rev.* to the name of a clergyman, or *Rev. Mr.* if you do not know his Christian name; *Rev. Dr.* if he is a Doctor of Divinity, or write *Rev.* before the name and *D.D.* after it. Prefix *His Excellency* to the name of the President,[*] and to that of a Governor or of an Embassador ; *Hon.* to the name of a Cabinet Officer, a Member of Congress, a State Senator, a Law Judge, or a Mayor. If two literary or professional titles are added to a name, let them stand in the order in which they were conferred—this is the order of a few common ones: *A.M., Ph. D., D.D., LL. D.* Guard against an excessive use of titles—the higher implies the lower.

---

[*] The preferred form of addressing the President is, *To the President, Executive Mansion, Washington, D. C.;* the Salutation is simply, *Mr. President.*

Salutations vary with the station of the one addressed, or the writer's degree of intimacy with him. Strangers may be addressed as *Sir, Rev. Sir, General, Madam*, etc. ; acquaintances as *Dear Sir, Dear Madam*, etc. ; friends as *My dear Sir, My dear Madam, My dear Jones*, etc. ; and near relatives and other dear friends as *My dear Wife, My dear Boy, Dearest Ellen*, etc.

How Written.—The Address may follow the Heading, beginning on the next line, or the next but one, and standing on the left side of the page; or it may stand in corresponding position after the Body of the Letter and the Conclusion. If the letter is of an official character or is written to a very intimate friend, the Address may appropriately be placed at the bottom of the letter ; but in all other letters, especially those on ordinary business, it should be placed at the top and as directed above. Never omit it from the letter except when the letter is written in the third person. There should always be a narrow margin on the left-hand side of the page, and the Address should always begin on the marginal line. If the Address occupies more than one line, the initial words of these lines should slope to the right, as in the Heading.

Begin the Salutation on the marginal line or a little to the right of it when the Address occupies three lines ; on the marginal line or farther to the right than the second line of the Address when this occupies two lines ; a little to the right of the marginal line when the Address occupies one line ; on the marginal line when the Address stands below.

Every important word in the Address should begin with a capital letter. All the items of it should be set off by the comma, and, as it is an abbreviated sentence, it should close with a period. Every important word in the Salutation should begin with a capital letter, and the whole should be followed by a comma, or by a comma and a dash.

Direction.—*Study what has been said, and write the following introductions according to the models:*—

1. Prof. March, Easton, Pa.
    My dear Sir,
2. Messrs. Clark & Maynard,
    771 Broadway,
        New York City.
    Gentlemen,
3. My dear Mother,
        When, etc.
4. Messrs. Vallette & Co.,
    Middlebury, Vt.
        Dear Sirs,

1. mr george platt burlington iowa sir. 2. mass cambridge prof james r lowell my dear friend. 3. messrs ivison blakeman taylor & co gentlemen new york. 4. rev brown dr the arlington washington dear friend d c. 5. col john smith dear colonel n y auburn.

LESSON 167.

LETTER-WRITING—CONTINUED.

THE BODY OF THE LETTER.

The Beginning.—Begin the Body of the Letter at the end of the Salutation, and on the *same* line, if the Introduction is long—in which case the comma after the Salutation should be followed by a dash;—on the line *below*, if the Introduction is short.

Style.—Be perspicuous. Paragraph and punctuate as in other kinds of writing. Spell correctly; write legibly and with care. Avoid blots, erasures, interlineations, cross lines, and all other offenses against epistolary propriety. The letter "bespeaks the man." *Letters of friendship* should be colloquial, chatty, and familiar. Whatever is interesting to you will be interesting to your friends, however trivial it may seem to a stranger. If addressing one of your family, write just as you feel, only *feel right*.

Business letters should be brief, and the sentences short, concise, and to the point. Repeat nothing, and omit nothing needful.

Official letters and *formal notes* should be more stately and ceremonious. In formal notes the third person is generally used instead of the first and the second; there is no Introduction, no Conclusion, no Signature, only the name of the Place and the Date at the bottom, on the left side of the page, thus :—

Mr. & Mrs. A. request the pleasure of Mr. B.'s company at a social gathering, on Tuesday evening, Nov. 15th, at eight o'clock.

32 Fifth Ave., Nov. 5.

Mr. B. accepts with pleasure [or *declines with sincere regret* *] *Mr. & Mrs. A.'s kind invitation for Tuesday evening, Nov. 15th.*

Wednesday morning, Nov. 6th.

THE CONCLUSION.

Parts.—The Conclusion consists of the **Complimentary Close**, and the **Signature**. The forms of the Complimentary Close are many, and are determined by the relations of the writer to the one addressed. In letters of *friendship* you may use, *Your sincere friend; Yours affectionately; Your loving son* or *daughter*, etc. In business letters you may use, *Yours; Yours truly; Truly yours; Yours respectfully; Very respectfully yours*, etc. In official letters you should be more deferential. Use, *I have the honor to be, Sir, your obedient servant; Very respectfully, your most obedient servant;* etc., etc.

The Signature consists of your Christian name and your surname. In addressing a stranger write your Christian name in full. A lady addressing a stranger should prefix, to her signature, her title, *Mrs.* or *Miss* (placing it within marks of parenthesis), unless in the letter she has indicated which of these titles her correspondent is to use in reply.

How Written.—The Conclusion should begin near the middle of the first line below the Body of the Letter, and, if occupying two or

---

* Or regrets that a previous engagement (or illness, or an unfortunate event) prevents the acceptance of ———; or regrets that on account of ——— he is unable to accept ———.

Letter-Writing—Continued.

more lines, should slope to the right like the Heading and the Address. Begin each line of it with a capital letter, and punctuate as in other writing, following the whole with a period. The Signature should be very plain.

Direction.—*Write two formal notes—one inviting a friend to a social party, and one declining the invitation.*

Direction.—*Write the conclusion of a letter of friendship, of a letter of business, and of an official letter, carefully observing all that has been said above.*

Direction.—*Write a letter of two or three lines to your father or your mother, and another to your minister, taking care to give properly the Heading in its two parts, the Introduction in its two parts, and the Conclusion in its two parts. Let the Address in the letter to your father or your mother stand at the bottom.*

LESSON 168.

LETTER-WRITING—CONTINUED.

THE SUPERSCRIPTION.

Parts.—The Superscription is what is written on the outside of the envelope. It is the same as the Address, consisting of the Name, the Title, and the full Directions of the one addressed.

How Written.—The Superscription should begin just below the middle of the envelope and near the left edge—the envelope lying with its closed side toward you—and should occupy three or four lines. These lines should slope to the right as in the Heading and the Address, the spaces between the line should be the same, and the last line should end near the lower right-hand corner. On the first line the Name and the Title should stand. If the one addressed is in a city, the door-number and name of the street should be on the second line, the name of the city on the third, and the name of the state on the fourth. If he is in the country, the name of the post-office should be on the second line, the name of the county on the third, the name of the state on the fourth. The number of the post-office box may take the place of the door-number and the name of the street, or, to avoid crowding, the post-office box or the name of the county may stand at the lower left-hand corner. The titles following the name should be separated from it and from each other by the comma, and every line should end with a comma except the last, which should be followed by a period. The lines should be straight, and every part of the Superscription should be legible. Place the stamp at the upper right-hand corner.

Direction.— *Write six Superscriptions to real or imaginary friends or acquaintances in different cities, carefully observing all that has been said above.*

Direction.— *Write two short letters—one to a friend at the Astor House, New York, and one to a stranger in the country.*

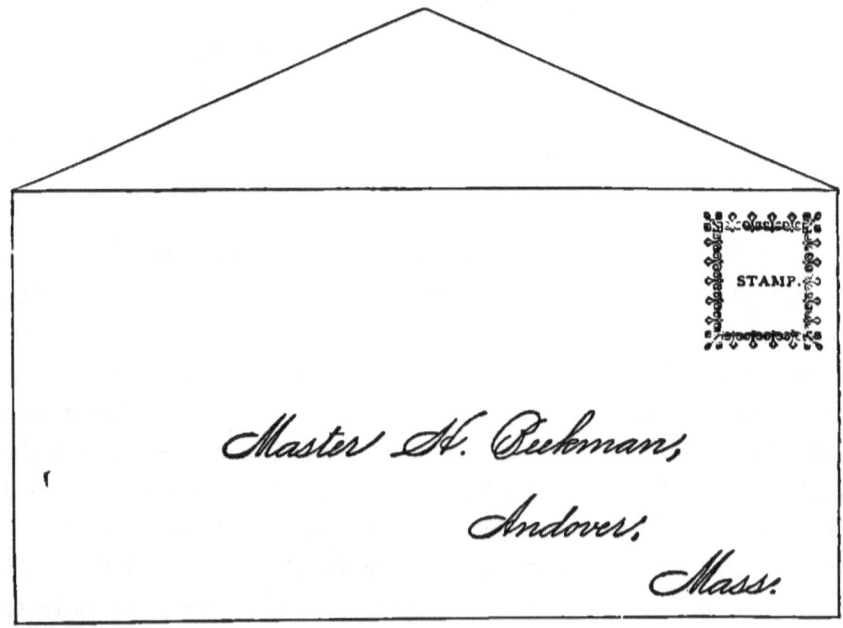

Ithaca, N. Y., June 15, '85.

My dear Friend,

You tell me that you begin the study of English Literature next term. Let me assume the relation of an older brother, and tender you a word of counsel.

Study literature, primarily, for the thoughts it contains. Attend to these thoughts until you understand them and see their connection one with another. Accept only such as seem to you just and true, and accept these at their proper value.

Notice carefully the words each

author uses, see how he arranges them, whether he puts his thought clearly, what imagery he employs, what allusions he makes, what acquaintance with men, with books, and with nature he shows, and in what spirit he writes.

Your study of the author should put you in possession of his thought and his style, and should introduce you to the man himself.

Pardon me these words of unsought advice, and believe me,

              Your true friend,

                    John Schuyler.

Master H. Beekman,
    Andover, Mass.

A SUMMARY OF THE RULES OF SYNTAX.

At the request of many teachers, we here append a Summary of the so-called Rules of Syntax, with references to the Lessons which treat of Construction.

I. A noun or pronoun used as subject or as attribute complement of a predicate verb, or used independently, is in the nominative case.

II. The attribute complement of a participle or an infinitive is in the same case (Nom. or Obj.) as the word to which it relates.

III. A noun or pronoun used as possessive modifier is in the possessive case.

IV. A noun or pronoun used as object complement or as objective complement or as the principal word in a prepositional phrase* is in the objective case.

V. A noun or pronoun used as explanatory modifier is in the same case as the word explained.

For Cautions, Principles, and Examples respecting the cases of nouns and pronouns, see Less. 119, 122, 123, 125. For Cautions and Examples to guide in the use of the different pronouns, see Less 86, 87.

VI. A pronoun agrees with its antecedent in person, number, and gender.

With two or more antecedents connected by *and*, the pronoun is plural.

With two or more singular antecedents connected by *or* or *nor*, the pronoun is singular.

For Cautions, Principles, and Examples, see Less. 118, 142.

VII. A verb agrees with its subject in person and number.

With two or more subjects connected by *and*, the verb is plural.

---

* An "indirect object" or a noun of measure, etc., used adverbially, is treated as the principal word in a prepositional phrase (see Less. 85).

With two or more singular subjects connected by *or* or *nor*, the **verb is singular.**

For Cautions, Examples, and Exceptions, see Less. 142.

VIII. A participle assumes the action or being, and is used like an adjective or a noun.

For Uses of the participle, see Less. 37, 38, 39.

IX. An infinitive is generally introduced by *to*, and with it forms a phrase used as a noun, an adjective, or an adverb.

For Uses of the infinitive, see Less. 40, 41, 42.

X. Adjectives modify nouns or pronouns.

For Cautions and Examples respecting the use of adjectives and of comparative and superlative forms, see Less. 90, 91, 128.

XI. Adverbs modify verbs, adjectives, or adverbs.

For Cautions and Examples, see Less. 93.

XII. A preposition introduces a phrase modifier, and shows the relation, in sense, of its principal word to the word modified.

For Cautions, see Less. 98, 99.

XIII. Conjunctions connect words, phrases, or clauses.

For Cautions and Examples, see Less. 100, 107.

XIV. Interjections are used independently.

www.ingramcontent.com/pod-product-compliance
Lightning Source LLC
Chambersburg PA
CBHW030018240426
43672CB00007B/1006